FARNES

This is the story of a very tall, 6 ft 6 in or so man, a genuine giant, and fed-up bank clerk who loved cricket and hated his job with a loathing that was as intense as his feeling towards the game. He played hookey one day from the hated bank to watch Bill Woodfull's 1930 Australians play in the wind and cold against Essex on their county ground at Leyton and never went back. Instead he became the fastest bowler in England and the fastest amateur in the world, bowling with ferocious speed when roused (and that took some doing) on the field but staying a very handsome amiable giant, who painted and wrote poetry and was often surrounded by pretty girls attracted by his great charm, away from it.

He found true love in a hotel in Torquay in World War Two when, above the age for conscription, he volunteered first to learn to fly and then, on his return from Canada with his wings, volunteered again to be a fighter pilot. But there was no fighter into which he could squeeze his frame, so he learnt to night fly in bombers. The woman he planned to marry was waiting at the RAF station for him to return from a night flying exercise piloting a Wellington bomber when he crashed into a wall on landing while helping a colleague practice taking off and landing in the dark.

KEN FARNES

DIARY OF AN ESSEX MASTER

By David Thurlow

(signature)

WITH A FOREWORD BY BARRY NORMAN

The Parrs Wood Press
MANCHESTER

First Published in 2000

THE PARRS WOOD PRESS
St Wilfrid's Enterprise Centre,
Royce Road, Manchester, M15 5BJ

© David Thurlow

ISBN: 1 903158 06 0

This book was produced by Andrew Searle, Bob Wells and Ruth Heritage of The Parrs Wood Press and was printed in Great Britain by:

Fretwell Print and Design
Healey Works
Golbourne Street
Keighley
West Yorkshire BD21 1PZ

For the seven grandchildren

ABOUT THE AUTHOR

David Thurlow has been a cricket fan since he was a little boy, and first heard of Ken Farnes while listening on the radio to the 1938 final Test against Australia - Hutton's match - aged six. This is his first cricket book, although he has written on athletics (his second love) and crime fact and fiction. He was a journalist on national newspapers for nearly forty years, mainly on the Daily Express and then until retirement with News International. He lives in Southampton and is as keen follower of Hampshire.

CONTENTS:

PHOTOGRAPHS BETWEEN PAGES 48 AND 49

PHOTOGRAPHS BETWEEN PAGES 128 AND 129

ACKNOWLEDGEMENTS

This book could not have been written without the help of many people, particularly Ken Farnes's nephew and niece, David Farnes and Mrs Joan Sharp, who let me have the family photo album and Farnes's diary from his South African tour.

Very many thanks also to Essex County Cricket Club - Tony Debenham and the late Peter J Edwards and staff, CW Murphy, Secretary of the Old Worksopian Society, Ian Watson and the Royal Liberty School, Andrew Jenner and Gidea Park CC, John Wilcox, son of Denys, for the family scrapbooks and photos, Stephen Green and his Library staff at Lord's, David Frith for access to his fine collection of photos, Lionel King for the answers to the questionnaire he sent to Farnes's contemporaries in the mid-1980s and Diana Norman for the letters her mother received and photographs.

Others who gave me great help were: EW Swanton, Trevor Bailey, Henry Barker, Brian Belle, Geoffrey Chapman, John Dennis, Dr Tony Ferguson, George Langdale, Norman Lenton, Dr Robert Naismith, Nicholas Vere-Hodge, Julia Waterman, Peter Checksfield and Justin Willsmore. I ducked and dived into many newspapers and publications (particularly Wisden). Many thanks to them all.

I'd like to give my appreciation to Andy Searle of The Parrs Wood Press for agreeing to publish the book and for his hard work in editing and producing this finished product. Thanks too to Pat Symes who gave me the idea and, of course, Ken Farnes himself for providing such wonderful information about his early days in his book 'Tours and Tests'.

FOREWORD

By Barry Norman

As a small boy I was steeped in cricket lore and legend long before I ever saw a first-class match. My Cockney grandfather, a lifelong devotee of Surrey, would spin me riveting stories of such bygone giants as 'Ayward and 'Itch, 'Obbs and Sandham and then, already enraptured by this most magical and infuriating of games, I would borrow armfuls of books from the public library and read about more recent Titans such as Hammond and Hutton (a public school education made me more familiar than my grandfather with aspirates), Bradman, Compton and Edrich – the small, belligerent Bill, that is, not his angular left-handed nephew John.

The Second World War was not quite over at the time and so among my heroes were its two most notable cricketing victims, Kenneth Farnes and Hedley Verity. I cared little about their counties (Essex and Yorkshire) for I have always been a Middlesex man but in my mind Farnes and Verity were tragic, romantic figures. Verity was the left-arm spinner, the magician, who once took ten wickets for ten runs in a single innings, and Farnes was the fastest English bowler of his generation, the fastest since Larwood and probably the fastest probably until Tyson.

And when I finally saw my first match, a victory Test – England versus Australia at Lord's in August, 1945 – it occurred to me that if Fate had been kinder both of these men might have been playing. Verity would have been 40 – no age the for a spinner – and Farnes only 34, lacking perhaps the raw speed of his youth but making up for it in swing and movement off the seam.

Well, the years went by, new cricketing heroes – Trueman and Statham, Peter May and the peerless Jim Laker among them – came along and I married. I was impressed to learn that my father-in-law, Arthur Narracott, air correspondent – or rather, in those more lordly days, aviation correspondent – of The Times had played minor counties for Devon. And I was delighted that his divorced wife, my mother-in-law Aeron, was as big a cricket nut as myself. Until the end of her life she would give short shrift to any non-cricket lover who turned up at her house while the Test matches were on TV and radio. Good weather at the ground, no interruptions at home, England doing well (though this, of course, was always a rare occurrence) and this was her idea of bliss. If the occasional gin and tonic was to hand – and it usually was – it just made things even more perfect.

My original assumption was that her own interest had stemmed from her ex-husband's participation in the game. It was only gradually – and never in any detail until after her death when her letters, which she had always kept to herself, eventually came to light – that I realised that her involvement with cricket had been at a much higher level than I had imagined and that, with a little luck, my stepfather-in-law would have been Kenneth Farnes (David Thurlow deals with that very nicely in chapter 21.).

However, I married when I was 24, a village leg-spinner and opening bat, and I've often wondered what it would have been like after another duck and nought for plenty to have Ken Farnes on hand to offer advice and coaching. Come to that, I've often wondered what it would have been like to simply know him and this book offers the answer – I reckon we'd have got on well. He appears to have been a thoroughly nice bloke and the combination of that and my hero-worship of outstanding sportsmen should have been enough to create some kind of bond between us.

I've always got on well with cricketers. As a television "celebrity" I was invited to join the Lord's Taverners and was thus priviliged to spend several years playing alongside the kind of men who, in other circumstances, would barely have welcomed me onto the same ground, let alone into the same team, as themselves. Just to drop a few names at random I have, in my time, played with or against the likes of Ian Botham, Colin Cowdrey, Bobby Simpson, Bill and John Edrich, John Snow, Viv Richards, Mike Brearley, Colin Milburn, Eddie Barlow, Mike Denness, Steve Waugh, John Murray, Denniss Lillee and Fred Titmus. And I only stop there because I wouldn't want you to think I was bragging.

From those Tavener's games I retain two outstanding impressions: first, that even in a charity match it was obvious that in their pomp the kind of people I have mentioned were used to playing a game so elevated as to bear only a passing resemblance to the one with which I struggled all my playing days; and, two, that cricket, more than any other game, is character-building. These guys were not just great company, on and off the field, but they were also – whether they knew it or not, or would admit it or not –

deeply philosophical. At whatever level you play, cricket does that to you. You can go into a game knowing you're in the best form of your life and come out of it having been bowled first ball, dropped a sitter and been hammered all over the field by the entire opposition, including the number eleven. And you don't know why. Next time you approach the game with your confidence so shattered that your co-ordination is shot to pieces and you emerge having scored fifty, taken a five-fer and held two blinding catches. And you still don't know why.

It's bad enough coping with that when you merely play at weekends but if the game is your life you can, surely, only survive such unpredictable vagaries of fate if you develop a fairly strong philosophical streak.

As David Thurlow reveals Ken Farnes clearly had such a streak. I only wish I had seen him play, more still that in my Taverners days I had been able to play alongside him. Because of his unfair advantage – namely, that he had a wonderful gift for the game and I had none – he would, no doubt, have been a touch better than me on the field but I reckon I'd have been more than his equal at the pavilion bar. And that's important in cricket, too.

INTRODUCTION

One thing separates Ken Farnes from other England cricketers of his generation: in a short career of ten years he played only 173 first class games, including 15 Test matches.

He was a natural who could break away from his schoolmaster role for four days, bowl like the champion he was, go back to school, be chaired by the boys up the long drive to Worksop College, Nottinghamshire, and then carry on teaching until the summer holidays began. Then he joined his county, Essex, to strengthen the fastest of all county attacks in that decade.

On his day he was the fastest bowler in the world, and for the second half of the 1930s he certainly was the fastest amateur. EW Swanton maintains he was the fastest English bowler he saw in England, once describing his speed as ferocious and *'when he was absolutely flat out he seemed, at the moment of delivery, to be almost shaking the head off his shoulders.'* When he hurled the ball down at over 80 mph from a height of eight feet and was in absolute top form he was unplayable. On a hard pitch he was difficult to play. On a pitch that gave the fast bowler any assistance he was deadly.

When Wisden nominated him in 'Three More Studies in Greatness', it wrote:

'He was an entirely natural talent married to exceptional physical endowment. He could make the ball rise sharply on a hard wicket and to add extra nip to his bowling he perfected a downward flick of the wrist at the point of release. He had the ball in a loose grip with one finger on either side of the seam, and a natural body action enabled him to impart swerve and occasionally make the ball dip late or break back from the off. I once asked Hardstaff (England batsman Joe of Nottinghamshire) what it was like facing up to Farnes. 'He got such a degree of lift off a good length that it was terribly difficult to time him' he said.'

As The Times said when he was tragically killed in a World War Two night flying accident in October 1941:

1

Ken Farnes

'He was a fast bowler in the true sense in which the adjective is applied to Kortright, Lockwood and Richardson and to no other Englishman of his generation except Larwood. He was, perhaps, a bowler of moods - either destructively hostile or complacently amicable - but in his full fighting feathers he was a danger to any batsmen in the world.'

It was something that the Australians in general, and Stan McCabe in particular (Farnes dismissed him seven times), discovered.

Farnes was around 6 ft 6 inches tall, fifteen and a half stone, slim but powerful, a body-building fanatic with a short 11-stride run up, a canter rather than a gallop, but when he reached the crease he used pace and bounce with devastating results. The ball would lift sharply and test the rib cage of any batsman.

When he tried to bowl faster and shorter to a leg side field, at a slower pace than Larwood on the 1932/33 alleged bodyline tour, in the Oxford v Cambridge match at Lord's in 1933 (the year he won an athletics blue for shot putting for Cambridge) it caused some controversy and did not really work.

Larwood was his hero (and in later years Larwood had some very nice things to say about Farnes and his ability, especially *'on his day when his blood was up'*). He admired his pace and his accuracy and although it is difficult to think of two great players so unsimilar in height and build (5 ft 8 to 6 ft 6, 18 pace run up against 11 or 12), making it impossible for Farnes to copy his hero's action, there is no doubt that Farnes tried to copy his thinking, accuracy and the way in which he bowled.

He played against him, indeed capturing the great man's wicket on one occasion, but they were social seas apart, although there is no doubt they talked and that Farnes took the tips given with the appreciation that his own pupils at Worksop took the advice he handed them. Farnes followed Larwood into the England side and improved year upon year and, but for the war, might have been as good and fast as anyone before and most since.

This charming and handsome young man, who took 10 wickets in his first Test match against Australia, played only sporadically from 1930 until 1939 - the decade when Germany began their attempt to control all of Europe With the threat of World War Two growing ever more menacingly year by year, the number of times he played was curtailed by two factors: he was a schoolmaster and therefore could normally only play from the end of the summer term at the end of July, and knee trouble, missing 1935 altogether because of it.

If his headmaster at Worksop College, where he was a very popular teacher and housemaster, had not been so accommodating, Farnes, dark-haired with a slow smile and a sense of humour which made him the darling of the ladies, would have played even less.

As it was this deep-thinking introspective young man only played 79 matches for Essex and a total of 173 first class games altogether at home and on tour, including 15 Test matches (60 wickets at an average of 28.65), in nine years for a lifetime average of 21.45 from 690 wickets. He took 10 wickets in a match seven times including 8 for 43 and 3 for 60 as the Gentlemen beat the Players in 1938 for only the second time since 1914, and took five wickets or more in an innings 41 times. Gubby Allen, his captain in Australia, said some years later: *'I have never seen anyone bowl faster or better'* - and he had seen them all.

1938 was his year of years, taking 14 wickets for Essex against Worcester and then in the next match a life-time best of 15 for 113 against Glamorgan, his 8 for 38 in the second innings his career best. He finished his short but brilliant career in fine style in 1939 with a hat trick, his only one, in his last but one match of only seven. He still captured 33 wickets for Essex in that final season, and eight wickets in his last ever county game against Northants.

Right from the moment he began his county career in 1930, when he was spotted by the leading Essex batsman of the pre-First World War period, Peter 'Percy' Perrin, Farnes was a success. To him to be able to play cricket was Valhalla. Playing county cricket was no drudge, just a marvelous way to spend his time doing what he loved best. He left his boring banking job on a whim to watch Essex play Australia and never went back, deciding to become a schoolmaster instead.

In his second county match he took five Kent wickets, bagging the great wicket-keeper/batsman Les Ames twice and the immortal Frank Woolley once in the match. By 1932, when he was a student at Cambridge University, he was considered good enough for a Test Trial and played in a farcical game at Cardiff when the wind was so strong it nearly blew him backwards and he and Larwood both fell on the soaked pitch before the game was abandoned. When Larwood was not picked for England against Australia in 1934 Farnes was and played in the first two Tests, taking 10 wickets in the first including the great Don Bradman.

After Cambridge he became a schoolmaster but was still able to go on the tour to the West Indies 1934/5, after which a leg injury put him out for a year. On his return in 1936 he showed just how good he was by taking the middle stumps of Gimblett, Hardstaff and Hammond in just a handful of overs in the Gentlemen v Players match at Lord's, his favourite fixture on his favourite ground. He was picked for the 1936/7 tour of Australia and New Zealand and when finally given his chance he took it at great speed, taking 6 for 96 in the Australian innings in the 5th Test including the great Bradman.

Schoolmastering kept him out of international cricket early in 1937 and when he had the chance to play he was injured again. 1938 was his best year, taking over 100 wickets for only the second time and playing in the Tests against Australia in his inevitably shortened season.

A life-long cricket fan, Norman Lenton, was at the Oval for Hutton's 364 and after the Australian's second innings went out to have a look at the pitch. He said: *'Farnes was so exciting to watch. At the end I went out to look at the pavilion end from which he had been bowling. There was a depression in the ground in the shape of his front foot cricket boot which must, I think, be a tribute to the accuracy of his run up.'* For Farnes was always ready to learn, this accuracy being built following the 1932 Varsity match when he bowled 21 no balls because his run-up was completely out of synchronisation.

He went on the tour to South Africa during the winter of 1938/39, which explained only eight games in total in 1939 because of the commitments to his job when he came back. It was still the age of amateurs who worked for a living and played for fun when they had the time.

Typically he wanted to join up even though he was by then 29 and not under any compulsion. He wanted to be a fighter pilot but he was so big that he could not squeeze into any cockpit. So he chose bombers and trained in Canada, returning home as a Pilot Officer in the RAF Volunteer Reserve with his wings, passing out as a navigator as well.

He volunteered for night bomber flying training when there was a desperate shortage of such people, and it was on one of these flights when piloting a Wellington bomber on the eve of becoming part of an operational squadron, that he died at Chipping Warden, on the border of Northamptonshire and Oxfordshire.

He was one of two England cricketers to die in action. The other was Hedley Verity, the successor to Peel and Rhodes as Yorkshire's slow left-handed bowler, who died as an Italian prisoner of war after being wounded in battle. His last words as he lay badly injured to the men he led was 'keep going', his motto in life. He took 15 wickets in Ken's second Test in 1934 when England beat Australia by an innings. In his career he took 1,956 wickets, including 144 in tests, with an average of 18.07.

It is one of the coincidences that fill life that Verity and Farnes were the two who ended the innings of 80 of Australian batsman Ross Gregory in the fifth Test at Melbourne in 1937. The scorecard read:

RG Gregory c Verity b Farnes 80.

Sergeant Observer Gregory of the Royal Australian Air Force, who played for Victoria as a schoolboy, died on active service in June 1942, aged 26. Captain Verity received his fatal wounds leading a company of the Green Howards in the invasion of Sicily and died on 31 July, 1943, aged 38. Kenneth Farnes died on 20 October, 1941, aged 30.

AN APPRECIATION

by Paul Cave

It was a long time ago - and yet none of my admiration for Kenneth Farnes has in any way dimmed. He was not only a great bowler, he was a delightful and charming companion and undoubtedly one of cricket's modest men.

There had been much talk of war during the winter. Few seemed to believe it and the Daily Express comfortably assured its readers that there would not be a second world war. The 1939 cricket season was about to start when a stranger arrived at the office of the recently launched Barnsley Express weekly newspaper. *'We would like you to keep wicket for Doncaster in the Yorkshire League,'* he told me, adding excitedly *'Ken Farnes is going to play for us.'*

This was a sensational announcement, for Ken Farnes was England's main fast bowler, indeed one of the fastest English bowlers ever - certainly in my lifetime. In fact Farnes had only just returned from England's winter tour of South Africa which ended with the timeless last Test abandoned as a draw after 10 days duration to allow the MCC team to catch the boat home. The previous summer Farnes had been playing in Test matches against Donald Bradman's Australians. Indeed he was the most successful bowler when England won the Oval Test by an innings and 579 runs after the young Leonard Hutton had made his record breaking 364 runs.

For six years Farnes had been a schoolmaster at Worksop College, about 20 miles south of Doncaster, when not playing cricket for England. Being on the staff of the College was important to Ken for, although he was only 28 years old in 1939, he was looking to the future. There was no money for him in cricket for he was not a professional player and as an amateur cricketer was only paid comparatively small expenses while playing for England and Essex.

Among the other masters at Worksop was Ronnie Farnfield, a useful club cricketer and seemingly good friend of Farnes. It was Ronnie, I believe, who was the possessor of the car that conveyed the pair of them from Worksop to Doncaster.

6

How the idea of Ken playing for Doncaster Town originated I do not know. Certainly playing in local matches was Ken's approach to keeping fit - virtually akin to net practice. At that time the Yorkshire League was much stronger than the Yorkshire Council competition or any other league in the county. The League included teams from most of the main centres - Leeds (with their home games being played on the Headingley Test venue), Sheffield (playing at Bramall Lane where the playing surface was uniquely shared between the Yorkshire County Cricket Club and Sheffield United football club; it was only in the 1970s that the football club threw out cricket so that they could have spectators on the fourth side of the ground), Barnsley, Rotherham, Hull, King Cross, Halifax, Doncaster and others.

When I went to work as a young reporter at Barnsley in the previous winter, it was to Shaw Lane, home of the Barnsley cricket club, that I went as the coming cricket season approached. After an early net practice, the club asked me if I would play for them in their Wednesday team; they were unable to offer me a regular wicket-keeping place on Saturdays for they had signed up Harry Crick, understudy to Arthur Wood, the Yorkshire and England keeper.

Unknown to me, when Barnsley officials heard that Doncaster was looking for a new wicket-keeper they recommended me to the neighbouring club. To be asked to keep wicket to England's legendary fast bowler! The previous two seasons I had enjoyed keeping wicket for Colwyn Bay (only subsequently did I learn that I had been recommended to Lancashire for the way I stood up to JR Jones, the Bay's tough tearaway fast bowler). Would Farnes be faster than Jones even if he was not bowling in a Test match? Yes, he certainly was - and the Doncaster pitch was not the friendly batting strip in the style of the square at Rhos-on-Sea.

Unlike most of the other Yorkshire League clubs, Doncaster had not previously had a star player. Their professional Joe Burton was an extremely useful left arm slow bowler, but their main source of players appeared to be the Doncaster police force. So it was sensational news when it was announced that Ken Farnes and his friend Farnfield were to play for Doncaster Town in their home matches.

Rightly or wrongly, it was accepted by the rest of the team that the Club could only afford Ken's expenses with the help of the home gate receipts. How much did he receive? The figure was thought to be £5 a match. And £5 was regarded as a good middle-class wage at that time.

Most of the semi-professional batsmen with other League clubs regarded the recruitment of Ken Farnes as an exciting challenge, a case of getting their heads down and concentrating even harder. Most treated the great Test player's bowling with respect, certainly at the start of their innings. However there was an exception....

Playing Rawmarsh in a League match at Town Moor, Doncaster batted first and were all out for 94. Only the Doncaster captain, the Rev PHK Whitaker (30) and S Hubbard (20) reached double figures. It was a disaster and the Rev Whitaker was far from pleased. He was a Warwickshire county second eleven player and a county rugby forward - and he was large and robust with a brand of swear words reserved for batsmen who were out for ducks, bowlers who failed to bowl to their fields and fielders who dropped sitters. For a start Ken had been out for a duck (and so had I).

The Rawmarsh innings was opened by a cheerful individual who enquired of me: *'What's Farnes like?'* *'A bit nippy'* I replied, to which the batsman announced, *'He can't be all that fast. He's not taking much of a run up.'* And he proceeded to pull Ken's first ball viciously - but fortunately to a fielder. He did precisely the same to the next ball. It did seem that any ball now he was going to smash one to the boundary. I could hear Phil Whitaker muttering something along the lines of *'Come on, Ken. Get stuck in.'*

Ken looked hurt. Generally Yorkshire League openers treated his early deliveries with care. Yet here was someone who appeared to be middling the ball and wanted to hit him out of the ground. Ken stared down the wicket, seemingly taking stock of the batsman, and then started marking out his run up afresh. He never appeared to take more than 11 or 12 paces in his approach to the bowling crease. More important, I had not before seen that look on his face. I shouted to the slips, *'I'm off. I'm going further back'* as I ran backwards towards the boundary behind me, keeping an eye on Ken. I wanted to be looking when the next ball arrived. I could see trouble ahead!

Probably Ken Farnes of England may have bowled faster against the Aussies and South Africa than the next ball he bowled at Doncaster that afternoon - but not much. The ball went perilously close to the chin of the previously confident batsman before it slammed into my gloves with such power and pace that I was propelled on to my back as I clung on to it. Then

8

there was PANDEMONIUM! For a start the batsman had fallen or trodden on his wicket and was picking himself up to return to the pavilion. It seemed a long time before the next batsman appeared from the pavilion to face Ken's next ball.

I have gone through the subsequent years with the belief that Rawmarsh were all out for 14 runs or something like that. Not true. It just felt like it. Certainly ten of the batsmen did not reach double figures, including four who made ducks. However the number 8 batsman made 30 runs before Ken had him caught. They were all out for 63. Ken took six wickets for 30 runs and Burton had three for 30. Checking the scorecard recently I was pleased to see that the extras only came to three. The ball was whizzing around that afternoon. Ken was truly terrifying. He gave me a grin as we walked off, saying *'How did you like that?'*

Yorkshire League matches were well advertised, not only on the hoardings but on bus and tramcars and in newspaper advertisements. Often it was not just a case of publicising say Doncaster Town v Sheffield United. For example, their fixture in 1939 was billed:

Cricket at Town Moor
Doncaster Town v Sheffield United
Come and see the battle between....
FARNES v SMURTHWAITE

The week before a young medium paced swing bowler named J Smurthwaite had played for Yorkshire's county team and taken a lot of wickets (5 for 7 against Derbyshire who were out for 20!) and was promptly dropped for the next game (Umpire and Yorkshire bat Dickie Bird suffered the same fate after making a double century post-World War Two). So he found himself playing against Doncaster.

Those were the days when cricket was attempting to forget short bodyline bowling, especially exploited by Harold Larwood with a tight leg-side field. It was also a long time before the introduction of helmets.

Despite the Rawmarsh match, I cannot recall that Farnes ever set out to actually attack a batsman's body. He outwitted them with speed and change of pace. Obviously he did not bowl full out at Doncaster. All the same he concentrated on aiming to dismiss the batsman. In any case the

Doncaster team were soon friendly enough with him to gee him up if an opposition batsman was staying around.

Certainly the Doncaster captain was keen to see his team do well. He was a fine captain - and an extremely kind man whom I am sure was loved by his parishioners. What I found strange was his overuse of swearing on the cricket field. He had a special collection of swear words reserved for those who ran him out - and this happened quite often. Phil never seemed to swear in front of his father who was also a clergyman.

What was it like keeping wicket to Farnes? It was an exciting experience. It was also challenging. For no very fast bowler is straight up and down and Ken, more accurate than most in length, might have a ball that was cutting away towards the slips followed by one that went wide down the leg-side. There was invariably a *'sorry about that'* or *'well taken'* at the end of the over.

We got off to a good start. Of course I had been worrying in advance and it was not until Ken bowled his first over at Doncaster that all nervousness that had built up in me disappeared - and I enjoyed the cricket from then on.

Ken sealed the good relationship from the start with ' well done' at the end of the first over. It was a mater of pride on my part that in the matches that I played with him that I let virtually no byes off his bowling. My big regret was that he did not play in the away games.

We got on well together. Firstly, I knew the Epping Forest area well (Ken came from nearby Gidea Park) as my grandparents lived near the Bell Inn, Epping. My grandfather, AJ Cable, had been a good cricketer and through him at an early age (from 13 to 14) I found myself keeping wicket for the Epping Town team during my summer holidays. The other point in my favour was that he was writing a book on his life story and seemingly was keen to learn about journalism.

In his MCC blazer he was an impressive personality. At 6 ft 5 or more, he always seemed to be the tallest person around the Doncaster ground, and when not out on the field he was often surrounded by boys and girls waiting patiently for his autograph. It did not matter that as the season went on most admitted they already had secured his signature several times before. He appeared sublimely happy. He must have been a fine schoolmaster.

As a bowler how fast was he? Was he as fast as Larwood? To me, no one in my life has been as fast as Larwood. In my schooldays I saw him bowl twice. One occasion was at Horsham for Notts against Sussex on the very day England were playing Australia at Trent Bridge, the first Test match following the bodyline series in Australia. Larwood refused to play in the Test on the grounds that he was not fit - and proceeded to bowl at a devastating pace.

I asked EH Bowley, the Sussex batsman, for his autograph two or three hours after he had been carried off the pitch after being hit by a rising ball from Larwood. The left side of his face was a horrible mess from the blow. He was a very brave man. Indeed all batsmen in those non-helmet days must have been extremely brave to face Larwood.

In the match at Horsham he bounced a ball at tremendous pace over the batsman's head and over wicket-keeper Lilley before hitting the sight screen on the boundary without bouncing. You almost felt sorry for the sight screen.

To me, Frank Tyson appeared the bowler who came nearest Larwood in speed. The England scorer Bill Frindall agrees. He said that Larwood was the most feared and accurate fast bowler of all time. For a handful of English seasons and one Australian summer Tyson was the fastest bowler in world cricket.

This certainly did not mean that Farnes was not extremely fast. The amazing thing about him is that he achieved so much when in fact he played comparatively little county cricket.

I was not to see him again as a week or so later I had a week's holiday and his school had broken up and he had begun his Essex duties. So after Saturday's game with Doncaster I went to north Wales to see my parents and play for Colwyn Bay through their annual cricket week. In the middle of a match there I received an unexpected telegram inviting me to play for the Lancashire Club and Ground eleven at Old Trafford that Saturday.

Lancashire were suddenly short of wicket-keepers because two of the county players had been caught by the county coach, Harry Makepeace, smoking pipes after they had been warned not to do so. They were sacked on the spot!

So off I went to Old Trafford to play with Cyril Washbrook, Albert

Nutter and other established professionals. Right at the start I missed a catch off Nutter and then luckily managed to dismiss five of the batsmen. It seemed a wonderful cricket world.

A week later Germany invaded Poland. Suddenly cricket no longer mattered. Sadly it was not too long before I heard that Ken Farnes had died in a flying accident.

CAST

Some of those with whom he played:

ESSEX PLAYERS

Denys Wilcox: great friend and Captain of both Cambridge University and then, from 1933 to 1939, one of the captains of Essex during Farnes's short career. Denys ran the family Alleyn Court prep school at Westcliff which produced six Essex players, including his son John and two Essex captains, Denys and Trevor Bailey. Ken was usher at his wedding. Wilcox, who made a century in the Varsity match and many more, including two in a match in 1937, was tipped as a possible England captain in 1937/8 but his hopes were dashed when Wally Hammond became an amateur and was appointed instead. He died sadly from leukaemia at the age of 42. He scored 5,482 runs, averaging 30.70 and made eight centuries for Essex.. He was also a friend of PG Wodehouse, later Sir PG, who was an old boy of Dulwich College (for whom Wilcox played brilliant cricket) and wrote fan letters to Wilcox when Captain of Cambridge.

Tom Pearce: batsman (11,139, hs 211 no and avge 33.96), captain, chairman and then President. Joint captain with Wilcox 1933 until 1938. Last year before the war TA duties kept him out of cricket. Sole captain in 1946. Once made a century while his wife was undergoing a serious appendicitis operation at the hospital overlooking the Chelmsford ground. He batted throughout most of the day and during his innings bulletins were regularly sent from the hospital giving him an update of his wife's progress, and in return the staff were able to tell Mrs Pearce as she came out of her anaesthetic that her husband had made a hundred. The operation was a great success.

Peter 'Percy' Perrin: discovered Farnes. Chairman of Test selectors from 1931 to 1939. His poor fielding kept him out of the England side although he scored 29,172 runs, hs 343 no, avge 36.19 with 65 hundreds. He was a Wisden Cricketer of the Year in 1905 when he was at the height of his batting powers.

Morris (known as Stan) Nichols: 15,736 runs including 20 centuries, avge 26.31, hs 205, 279 ct, 1608 wickets for 21.16, best 9 for 32, 10 in an innings 22 times. Did double eight times, five in succession to start of World War Two. With Read he destroyed Yorkshire, then the county champions, in 1935 when they bowled them out for 31 and 93, Essex winning by an innings and over 200 hundred runs, Read taking 6 for 111 and 3 for 51 and Nichols 4 for 17 and 7 for 37 and Nichols beating Yorkshire on his own with 146.

Holcombe Douglas 'Hopper' Read: qualified to play for Essex by birth and Surrey by residence. Surrey did not want him so it was Essex's gain. He was one of the great quartet of fast bowlers - Farnes, Nichols, Stephenson - and arguably the quickest at the top of his form. Probably played less cricket than any other fast bowler who played for England and that says something with Farnes's short career! In 1934 in his first game he knocked Jack Hobbs's cap off and bowled him with his sixth ball on a day when the great man was looking for a comfortable century. The next year it was he and Nichols who bowled out Yorkshire for 99 and he won a cap against South Africa in the final Test, but after a mainly amateur tour of Australia and New Zealand to heal the bodyline wounds in 1935/6 the senior partner of the firm where he was a chartered accountant congratulated him on his bowling but gave him the choice: profession or cricket and he never played county cricket again. He took 131 wickets with an average of 21.19. Forget his batting because he was worse than Farnes once having 15 ducks in a season, eight in succession!

CAG 'Jack' Russell scored 23,610 runs with 62 100s, hs 273 and an avge of 40.91. He also took 276 wickets at a cost of 27.10 each. He was the first English batsman to score a hundred in each innings of a Test match - v South Africa in Durban in 1922.

Jack O'Connor 27,819 hs 248 avge 35.21 71 hundreds 537 for 17,523.

Top professional batsmen between wars scoring a hundred against all 16 counties and both Universities and reaching 1000 runs 16 times. Scored nine centuries in a season. Played in nine Tests in England and three v WI in 1929-30.

Ray Smith. Umpire Frank Chester said he was *'the torch bearer of the true spirit of cricket.'* Great all rounder, medium pace seam (1,317 wickets, avge 30.23), ferocious hitter (11,125 including 6 hundreds and hs 147), 179 catches and took 335 wickets in one-day war time charity matches when he captained the British Empire X1.

His cousin Peter Smith. film extra as well as excellent cricketer (1,610 wickets with his leg breaks) and victim of a cruel hoax when, while in a Chelmsford cinema on the eve of the third Test v West Indies in 1933, his name flashed up on the screen and he was told to leave immediately because he had been picked, but on arrival at the Oval discovered it wasn't true and had to wait until 1946 against the Indians.

Lt Col JWA Stephenson: one of the great quartet of fast bowlers and a joint captain in 1939. Had wonderful match in Gents v Players 1936 when he took 9 for 46 but never quite gained a cap, injury and army duties sometimes stopping selection: In 61 matches scored 1,050 runs and took 174 wickets at 23.88 and he was renowned for his enthusiasm, even though a trifle eccentric, in playing the game.

Tommy Wade: wicket-keeper who was partner in the great stand with Farnes when he made his top score of 97 no. Wade scored 4,972 runs with hs 96 and ct 413 and stumped 177.

Nigel Wykes: another from Alleyn Court who was also a schoolmaster - at Eton - who could only play during school holidays.

Leonard Crawley: another schoolmaster, later journalist (golf for The Daily Telegraph), who was restricted in his playing. Only played 56 times between 1926 and 1936 but a wonderful bat once scoring 176 no in 185 mins in 1927. Sometimes fielded in a trilby. He was English Amateur golf champion and was in four Walker Cup sides, including the winning one in 1932. Had a cricket avge of 33 with hs 222.

Lawrence Charles Eastman: 12,965 runs, avge 20.57, seven hundreds and 975 wickets with medium paced bowling at 26.77. Killed after bomb exploded close to him.

Paul Gibb: one of the game's eccentrics. Started with Scotland, then Cambridge University where he became a fine bat and wicket-keeper, picked for England as keeper for washed-out Old Trafford Test, went to South Africa 1938/39 and played in all Tests as a batsman, played for Yorkshire and after World War Two flying Sunderland flying boats, returned to Yorkshire, was England keeper v India in 1946, went on 1946/7 Australia tour where he was dropped after two Tests as keeper, dropped out of cricket until 1951 when he joined Essex as a professional and set a wicket-keeping record before retiring to become an umpire from 1957 to 1966 before ending life as a bus driver. He had a Test average of 44.69.

Dicky Vere Hodge: played 23 matches between 1936 and 1939 while studying to be a doctor (later an orthopaedic surgeon). Hit two centuries.

ENGLAND PLAYERS

Gubby Allen (Middlesex): his whole life was steeped in cricket which he played exceedingly well and was unlucky not to regain the Ashes when he led the MCC to Australia in 1936/7. He was a fast bowler on the Bodyline tour (and disagreed with some of Douglas Jardine's tactics) and was one of a group of fast bowlers up to World War Two who vied for the opening slots for England. He took 81 Test wickets for 29.37, 788 wickets in his career and scored one Test century and 11 others in his career which ended with him as Sir George, Chairman of the Test Selectors, President of the MCC and Middlesex.

Les Ames (Kent): one of the greatest wicket-keepers (and forerunner of Evans and Knott in Kent) he took Larwood, Voce and Farnes fast and Tich Freeman (3,776 wickets for 18.42 but only 66 in Tests for 25.86) and

Wright (slow) without trouble. He was also a fine batsman scoring 37,248 runs at 43.51 with 102 centuries and had a Test average from 72 innings of 40.56 with eight tons.

Bill Bowes (Yorkshire): Bodyline hero with Larwood and Voce (but not as fast). Was England's no 1 until Farnes reached his prime and his scholarly, bespectacled appearance belied an unemotional approach of going for the batsman hammer and tong. He took 68 Test wickets for 22.33 and 1,639 in his career for 16.76, a wonderful performance. After retirement became a cricket journalist.

Edward 'Nobby' Clark (Northants): Another contender for an England fast bowling place, often spoilt by injury. Played in eight Tests and took 1,208 wickets for 21.49 during his career.

Denis Compton (Middlesex): not only one of the all-time best batsmen, he was a cavalier, highly entertaining cricketer who seemed more of a playboy than a serious sportsman although he was in fact both. With his 'twin', Bill Edrich, they both scored over 3,000 runs in a season in 1947 - Denis 3,816 with 18 centuries and Bill 3,539. He was also a fine left arm spin bowler and an England footballer and for good measure won an FA Cup winners' medal for Arsenal. His playboy image was strengthened by his love of the social life and there are tales (which may or may not be true) that he and Bill arrived at Lord's for the day's play in dinner jackets. He scored 38,942 runs with 123 hundreds and an average of 51.85, had a Test average of 50.06, hs 278, from 5,807 runs and took 622 wickets in his career, avge 32.27. His only weakness came when calling for a run! He died a household name, one of few cricketers who have become and remained one.

Bill Copson (Derbyshire). rival for fast bowler's place in England side for several seasons. Not as fast as Farnes but deadly, once taking four wickets in four balls in 1937 against Warwickshire. Took 100 wickets in a season three times and in his career took 1,896 and 15 in Tests for 19.80. Became an umpire.

Bill Edrich (Middlesex): Not the most beautiful batsman to watch but a

17

Ken Farnes

high scorer both for Middlesex (whom he captained) and England after his move from Norfolk where the Edrich family put out most of the regular Norfolk team for several years. When he and Compton spent almost the whole of the summer of 1947 at the crease Middlesex won the County Championship. He was known for his guts in the game and his love of life. He scored 36,965 runs with an average of 42.39 with 86 100s and had an average of 40 in Tests.

Harold Gimblett (Somerset): 23,007 runs avge 36.17, highest score 310, 50 centuries and three Tests.

SC Griffiths (Sussex): kept wicket for England twice, a good bat and Secretary and later President of the MCC.

Walter Hammond (Gloucestershire): became Captain of England when he became an amateur (v Australians 1938, then on the South African and post-war tour of Australia). Before Bradman the best batsman in the world and certainly the best English batsman until World War Two. Wonderful slip fielder, England class and above bowler with lifetime figures of 50,551 runs, 167 centuries, average 56.11, 723 wickets for 30.59, 819 catches and 7,249 runs in 85 Test appearances with 22 centuries (average 58.45), 83 wickets and 110 catches.

Joe Hardstaff (Notts): immaculately dressed and stylish middle order batsman who scored 2,000 runs in a season three times and 1,000 13 times. In his long career he scored 31,847 with 83 centuries with an average of 44.35. He played in 23 Tests, scoring 1,636 with an average of 46.74.

Len Hutton (Yorks): second professional England captain who won back the Ashes in 1953. Prolific opener who made 3,429 runs in 1949 with an average of 68.58. He also made 2,000 runs plus eight times in a season. His most famous innings was his 364 against the Australians at the Oval in 1938 which took 13 hours 20 minutes. He made a total of 40,140 runs with 129 centuries at an average of 55.51 and played in 79 Tests, scoring 6,971 at an average of 56.67 including 19 centuries.

Harold Larwood (Notts): considered by many as the fastest bowler of all time. He was at the centre of the Bodyline row and without him any form of severe leg theory attack would have been impossible because he was able to combine his speed with a deadly accuracy outside the leg-stump. Jardine used him to spearhead the attack to contain Bradman and managed to keep the Don's average down to a little over 50. He played for England for the first time in his third season of first-class cricket and this former coal miner's action and accuracy and length was a model for many bowlers who followed him, including Farnes. He was hated in Australia but eventually retired there and lived out his long life happily amongst them. In Tests he took 78 wickets at an average of 28.35 and 1,427 in his career for an astonishingly low average of 17.51.

HDG Leveson-Gower (Surrey): former England batsman who went on tours to West Indies, North America and South Africa early in the 20th century and then ran teams to play tourists and Universities. His highest score was 155 out of 7,638, which included three Tests and four centuries.

Maurice Leyland (Yorks): battling left-hander and wit who scored 2,764 runs in Tests (nine hundreds, 46.06 average) and 33,659 for 40.50 with 80 hundreds in his career.

Eddie Paynter (Lancs): better left handed Test batsman than a county one who incredibly was left out of the 1934 and 1936/7 series against Australia. He had a Test average of 81 in South Africa and in all Tests 59.23 with a career 42.26 with 45 hundreds and 20,075 runs. He once left his sick bed in hospital to bat for England in the 1932/33 season.

Bryan Valentine (Kent): great company and wit who captained Kent after World War Two, played in several Tests and scored 18,306 runs with an average of 30.15.

Hedley Verity (Yorks): a leading left-arm spinner in the history of the game, he followed in the Yorkshire tradition of Wilfred Rhodes (and even opened for England like Wilfred did). Almost medium pace he could tie batsmen up on good wickets but on sticky ones he was impossible and his greatest feat was to take 14 for 80 (including Bradman) between noon and late afternoon at Lord's in 1934 and win the match. He took 200 wickets in seasons 1935-37. He took 1,956 wickets in all for 14.90 and in Tests 144 for 24.37. He scored one century in his short life which ended in Italy in World War Two.

Bill Voce (Notts): with Larwood he provided a terrifying opening attack for his county and also for England, particularly in the Bodyline series. He was a strong left armer who came back into the England side for the 1936/7 tour and was the main fast bowler until injury when Farnes took over and kept the job - when he could play - until the end of his short career. Voce took 1,558 wickets in his career at a cost of 23.08 and in 27 Tests took 98 for 27.88. He was no mean bat scoring four centuries for Notts and a 66 as highest score with a Test average of 13.39.

Arthur Wellard (Somerset): another fast bowler (right arm) of the era who played for England in three Tests on the 1936/7 tour and took 1,614 wickets for 24.35 in his long career.

Doug Wright (Kent): his figures never did him justice nor his Test performances. On his day no batsman felt safe against this leg-break bowler who was faster than his contemporaries. He took 2,056 wickets for 23.98 and in Tests 108 for 39.11.

RES Bob Wyatt: England (several times), Warwickshire and Worcestershire captain, England player from 1927 to 1936, played before and after World War Two, later Chairman of the Selectors, a good all-rounder who scored 39,403 runs at 40.05 and 85 centuries, took 901 wickets at 32.85 and in 84 Test innings amassed 1,839 runs with two hundreds at 31.70 and took 18 wickets. Should have captained the first England side in which Farnes was to play but the Essex man broke his thumb in the Test trial.

1.

THE BOY

KEN FARNES was born a bowler, a natural. His great height even as a boy turned him into a fast bowler. His father Sidney, company secretary and accountant to Truman's brewery in London's east end, was a good club cricketer with Gidea Park in Metropolitan Essex, and it was into that team that Farnes followed him when a boy at the Royal Liberty School in Romford.

He was born, the second son, on 11th July 1911 in Leytonstone, Essex, and the family, father, mother Florence, older brother Norman (later a dentist) and Ken moved to nearby Gidea Park when Ken was five. To him it was moving to a foreign country and he longed to return to 'England' until he discovered The Green.

The best way to recreate the magic of The Green and everything to do with it is to quote Ken Farnes himself in his autobiography, published a year before he died. It was called 'Tours and Tests' and is about as self-effacing as it is possible for an autobiography to be. Pages are spent describing the countryside on his many tours but his game is left hidden under big, great bushels. In the early pages he actually writes about himself and it is a rare record of his youth:

'Once the horror of its vastness had left me I came to love the Green. For here was high grass with snug thicket, hollow walnut tree and huge spreading elm. Here too was a level space of low grass which became in the course of time virtually our own cricket pitch.

'For some while however, before cricket became the main occupation of the spacious leisure hours, the Green offered numerous possibilities for spending the summer days. Tree climbing became a high art and every tree was known for the ease or difficulty with which it might be scaled. You graduated from the smaller trees in the hedgerow down towards Parkway to one of the walnut trees,

then on to its neighbour which had a difficult twist before the main branch and so on to the elms to whose huge limbs you had to jump and cling and then swing a leg up and over. Once astride, dizzy heights were attainable.

'Leafy caves could be made in the brushwood hedge and there was ammunition in plenty for warfare in the clay bank higher up the Green. Except in very dry weather bombs from this store could be hand-pressed and pushed on to the end of a firm stick from which they could be sent whirling with satisfactory velocity and no great degree of accuracy. In haymaking time, too, the rough sheaves were a source of much joy for bruiseless tumbling and acrobatics, for shelters built of high grass walls and for strategic hiding places. The glades among the scattered trees were ideal ground for dueling with laths from buildings under construction in nearby roads or for wrestling contests.

'Denis, Harold and I were the chief possessors of the Green and all its significance. They lived on opposite sides of it while my home was higher up towards the golf links. We three formed the main gang which was occasionally added to by more distantly acknowledged recruits.

'When cricket became our chief preoccupation we took turns as batsman, bowler and wicket-keeper.'

What a joyful start for a boy. William The Outlaw and his gang, in reality in Essex (the first stories came out about the same time, 1919), not imitating anyone because they did not know the characters existed for they were first! They roamed and played and fought with all the energy of a boy in his prime with no thought of anything but the great adventures available in their spot of heaven. It is little wonder that from the beginning Ken Farnes was to become such a happy, content and brilliant young man. And so to cricket. He wrote:

'The ground of course needed some tending and in early summer a few hasty attempts at cutting the grass on our knobbly pitch in a strip about a yard wide, and then at rolling it, were made when we were not too impatient to get on with the game itself. The stiff stalks of grass that would not succumb to the mower and would spring up after the roller had passed over them, mattered but little. The boundary was on the road that curved round from close short leg to deep long on beyond the dry bed of the former Reed Pond. A thick hedge was long stop close in and elsewhere the outfield was somewhat rough. Six or seven might easily be run if the ball went no farther than an average cover point's distance from the wicket.

'But there was always an element of risk in running too many in case the ball was found while the batsman was halfway between wicket and wicket. Crafty pretence of not find the ball on the part of the fieldsman had also to be suspected always. The clay bank already referred to ran parallel to the pitch at a distance of some eight or nine yards and so onside play along the ground was not very productive of runs there but a lofted hit might go across the road into somebody's front garden - an acknowledged four. The bushes at wide mid-on sometimes hindered play for long periods, especially as a forbidding neighbour frowned upon us if we trampled down searching for the ball. A hit into his garden, of course, made him loom, like a positive ogre in our imagination of the consequences.'

The rules of play being set there was the problem of the kit:

'Our kit was pretty comprehensive. From home I was able to supply a set of brass-bound stumps, a huge pair of pads, a dark brown bat, an enormous pair of wicket-keeping gloves, batting gloves and a 'compo' (ball) which was quite indestructible. Most of these had been used by my father whose green carpet cricketing bag we used for carrying the gear to the Green. Denis supplied a pair of skeleton pads. He also provided at one time a first-class leather ball, the gold lettering of which (or perhaps its donor) conveyed that it was the sort used in Test matches. For a while this was so carefully used that it was only brought out for catches of not more than three yards.

'But the compo, seamless and brown, lasted for season after season. Lost in the hedge a hundred times it always seemed to turn up. Our first leather was actually one that my father had saved from his playing days.. Occasionally I had seen it and even held in my fingers with great awe and at last, one birthday, it was given to me. My pride in being the possessor of it was unbounded and ecstatic.   .

'Harold provided a bat too and also a supplementary set of stumps without the brass. Denis was a given a Phil Mead (the great Hampshire batsman who scored over 55,000 runs and 153 centuries) bat one summer but as it weighed nearly three pounds none of us could wield it. Another bat, and one which we much coveted, belonged to John Smith, the elder brother of Jimmy, who was sometimes allowed to join us. It was an Autograph - name of wonder! True, a few cracks were prevented from spreading by a nail or two but it was a very fine weapon. I once made a swap with Jimmy of ten cigarette cards (not knowing then that he was to be in two sets himself when a Test player) *and a water pistol for it. When John heard about the transaction however the deal was rescinded.*

What an idyllic picture he paints. His memory of those days is wonderful, a picture of sheer happiness when days never seemed to end and when the game would last forever. And in the natural progression of such things when boys were not sat in front of PCs, playing games on the computer, but were outside in the fresh air, whether learning the game in rural Essex or back streets in cities, north and south, they needed a club and that was how the Reed Pond Cricket Club came to be formed, a club without captain, fixture list nor annual meeting. Farnes remembered it equally clearly:

'There were three mutually acknowledged members, augmented occasionally by more distant friends whose prowess we didn't consider to be on a par with our own. Jimmy Smith sometimes came, usually without the Autograph, Ray with his Wisden, Harold's brother Alan, younger and an inferior player, Geoffrey Chapman and his friend Ivan and even Eric Fleet, who insisted on gripping the bat with the hands in reverse order. Visiting cousins were given the privilege of playing and on rare days a parent or two and my elder brother might join us.

'However, as a rule, the game was a game for three and our average number of innings each evening probably about four or five. Byes were not allowed nor could a run be scored behind the wicket. A square leg hit into the Malcolms' garden was sometimes firmly ruled as out by the bowler and wicket-keeper and a bowler's appeal and decision for lbw produced many arguments. As I owned most of the kit I was out in this way more seldom than the others. The bowler had to do most of the fielding in front of the wicket, the wicket-keeper most of that behind. The ball, frequently lost in the hedge or long grass, was searched for by everyone as soon as the batsman had run six.'

And it was on the Green during those lovely long evenings after school or at the weekends when everyday was for cricket that Farnes began to bowl:

'It was here that we first began to try to bowl overarm, and for a while the batting triumphed over the bowling because direction, let alone length, was vague in the extreme. Denis bowled slow, Harold medium with rather a stiff sideways action and I began to develop a bit of pace being loose and lanky.'

And so the road to Lord's and Tests began:

'Being a fast bowler was fun but it had its disadvantages. If the other two were not smart enough in stepping away to leg and received the ball on the thigh or ribs too many times, my membership might be in a precarious way. There was one time I remember when for several evenings I was not allowed to play as I bowled too fast. Moodily I watched the game from the region of mid off as Denis and Harold batted and bowled silently together.

'On one occasion Geoffrey was batting and Denis keeping wicket, his most successful accomplishment. I bowled a fast, high full toss which missed Geoffrey and hit the unsighted Denis on the head. With a considerable effusion of blood and maternal anxiety he left the field to sadness and me. The batsman, if I remember rightly, retired, giving as his reason that he had to get home to supper. Harold said that it was not worth just two of us playing so we packed up the kit in the green cricket bag and carried it home.

'There were other crises. Behind the hedge and across the road lived Beryl Young. (Shades of Violet Elizabeth Bott, eh?) She and her friend Rene Butcher came on to the Green one day and stood watching us play. Naturally we supposed they were admiring our skill. It was therefore a stunning shock when Beryl suddenly pounced on the ball which had eluded the wicket-keeper and ran with it into her house followed by the Butcher girl. The whole thing was so sudden that we had hardly began to chase after the robbers when the front door closed behind them. Our one and only indestructible compo had suddenly been taken from us. Astounded and desperate we walked into the robbers' garden and knocked on the door. It was opened by a wicked maid who listened to our demands and then told us to be off as no cricket ball had been brought into the house. Cricket was over for the day.

'Our feats are unrecorded in any score book but one or two stand out in my mind. Denis made the biggest hit, pulling the ball right into a cul-de-sac across the road wide of mid on. As the stroke was off my bowling, my praise of the stroke was somewhat grudging. But the greatest feat of all was performed by a non-member. My brother, Norman, came down one day and hit the ball clean over the grass-grown pond-bed, over the road and straight into the Drapers' garden where it smashed a flower pot. The crash formed a fitting climax to the ball's flight which we watched with open-mouthed amazement.

'During the period of the Club's whole activities only two matches were arranged. The first was to be against a team gathered by a boy named Roper but it never took place because the opponents never turned up. The second was *against the Romford High School for Girls and took place at Raphael Park. I had nothing to do with the arranging of the match and when the time came for it to be played I was unable to turn out owing to a bilious attack.'*

Thus he missed romance overcoming an umpire's impartiality:

'I don't even know the result of the contest but one very sorry incident occurred which was not quite cricket. Bob Vining, slightly older than ourselves and a very infrequent player, was umpiring when Denis went into bat. Bob was all out to impress one of the fair opponents and it so happened that she was bowling at the time of Denis's arrival at the crease. He played the first ball firmly to mid off. There was no appeal but Bob gave him out lbw as a sort of bouquet to his fair charmer.

'The standard of our cricket could not have been very high but we were certainly keen. I remember one conversation with Denis which is amusing to recall. He wondered if we would ever be good enough to play for the county and he didn't see why we shouldn't be. I have a feeling that I felt pretty confident about it inside but didn't dare to utter a word lest I should ruin my chances by doing so.

'County cricket seemed the province of the gods.'

Geoff Chapman, now a retired schoolmaster in his late 80s and living in Devon, remained a very good friend until Farnes was killed. Geoff was at the funeral with Farnes's brother Norman and his wife, and other members of the family in the RAF part of the military cemetery at Brookwood. It was a bright sunny day with robins flitting

Geoff was not an active part of the Reed Pond club because he and his brother, another Ken, enjoyed natural history more. But Geoff said: *'I was a year older and Ken was far and away the better cricketer. I loved cricket and I would play for anyone who would give me a game but I was just one of the AN OTHER variety.'*

The two Kens and Geoff were all together at Royal Liberty School, Romford, where Geoff's father was a master until he became a headmaster in Matlock, Derbyshire. They lived close together in Gidea Park, a pleasant place to live in those days with little traffic, respectability and no street violence.

Geoff has one abiding memory of those days:

'I can see him now when he was not much more than 12. He was a perfect natural bowler. I have just got this glimpse of him, not a particularly tall

boy, a stride from the wicket, his right arm arrow straight and he seemed to take a little leap with his arm so taut and right up before release.'

He had a perfect action at 12.

'He dropped the little skip later on but he had one characteristic when he got a wicket, something he never lost from his schooldays - he always gave a little hitch to his trousers at the back, a little self-conscious indication of satisfaction.

'Another thing he never lost was his modesty - typically low key was his inscription when sending his book to his friend; it read simply 'Whacko, my old fruit!' - his easy going friendliness, his sense of humour, his interest in other people because he came from a very nice family who were always doing things together and always had the latest developments about the house like a home movie camera.

'I remember they made a film of the two boys walking upstairs eating a banana but when they showed it they reversed the film so they were coming down regurgitating the fruit and ending up with the whole banana again! They were that kind of family, very happy together and very happy and kind when entertaining their sons' friends. Kindness was the dominant theme of that household.

'So Ken, who did not laugh a lot but smiled a great deal in a way that told you a great deal about him, was what he was. But behind his easy going modesty and occasional moodiness there was a streak of great determination. When he made up his mind to do something this streak showed itself. Nothing could dissuade him. It showed when he was on tour in New Zealand and there was a mountain to climb and he was the only one of the team to do it. Nothing was going to stop him when his mind was made up even though he could see it was no picnic and he did it.

'It also showed in the way he walked out of the bank and never went back and how he behaved when the war began and it ultimately led to his death. He wrote to me - I was in the Army from the start because I was in the territorials before the war - and said he was going to join the RAF and qualify as a pilot because he did not want to be a penguin, the RAF phrase for non-flying personnel. He wanted to win his wings and be a pilot.'

2.

THE SCHOLAR AND WORKER

THROUGHOUT his schooldays at Romford Liberty School Farnes and his friends kept the Reed Pond Cricket Club. Occasionally they tried their luck in the local park where there was more space and a much better wicket. But using the park also meant a loss of freedom because the gates closed at dusk and instead of finishing the game in the gloom of the early dusk they had to leave. There was also the bye laws which did not allow cricket in the park until the first of May so that they could not play in the Easter holidays.

When the trio first went to school they were all roughly the same standard. Farnes's brother Norman was in the first eleven and the school played on a lovely ground with a splendid chestnut tree for a pavilion.

Farnes was in the first intake of boys when the school opened in 1921, set in the grounds of a lovely Georgian house built in 1769 and still there. Before the school opened the park had been used as an Army camp for the Artist's Rifles, amongst whom were World War One poets Wilfred Owen (a cadet officer) and Edward Thomas, a sergeant instructor in map reading. Their poetry may have been among those which attracted the new boy to his lifelong passion.

It is a desperately sad fact that up until World War Two around 2000 boys attended the school and of those 103 were killed in the war, around five per cent. Their names are recorded on a Roll of Honour in a Memorial Window in the school hall.

Once again I quote from 'Tours and Tests' because Farnes is the one who remembers most:

Denis and I got into the second Xl but I remember only one match against a school from some far part of the country beyond the station. My chief memory is of their fast bowler whose speed scared me considerably. Denis's chief recollection is of the clouds of dust that I churned up when I bowled. In 1921 we all separated and played together only on the Green in the evenings.

'In my first summer at the new school (1923, aged 12) *I was amazed to find that I was chosen to play in the First game one Saturday morning. I well remember the incredulous look on the faces of the other members of my form when my name was read out. It was an embarrassing moment for me and I covered my blushes as well as I could. I was on the verge of the first eleven and augmented the staff in their match against the school team that year.'*

The school team photograph shows him as a very small boy amongst much bigger boys. By the time of the 1925 photo he had grown greatly and even more and more mature in his last year as captain, 1928.

'The following season I became a regular member of the school side and took a few wickets. I even bowled out the school cricket captain in a practice match which then seemed an incredible feat. We were fortunate in having in our headmaster (Mr SB Hartley), an extremely keen and very able cricketer. Every Monday evening he coached us in all departments of the game. We swung straight bats, got our left legs to the ball - sometimes - and cupped the hands for high catches.'

It was then that Farnes learnt how to use his natural talent to be a fast bowler and discovered that bowlers are born not bred, certainly the best of them. He says:

'His chief counsel to me in bowling was to keep the action high and so make full use of my numerous inches - for I was always on the lanky side. Bowling is more of a natural art than batting and the essentials of it seem to me to be instinctive rather than acquirable. If there is no 'life' in a bowler's action advice will not put it there. My looseness and a certain degree of strength - brute force, if you will - presumably gave me a good start and so I tried to get the high action, tried to bowl a length and highly enjoyed being considered a fast bowler.

'No idol, no model, just a fast growing boy who could use that to bowl extremely fast as one lunchtime when I was having a net before afternoon school the chief games master, rather excited, said ' do you know you have a natural leg break action!' Really I think it was just my loose wrist which may have made me appear to cut the ball. At any rate I've not seen much evidence of fast leg breaks in my bowling, I'm sorry to say. I could spin the ball and turn it from leg and did actually take five wickets in this way bowling slow against a school at Grays on a matting wicket. And sometimes when tired I did revert to this type of bowling but I was naturally cut out for bowling the fast seam stuff.'

Ken Farnes

One school match was against Romford Rotary Club. One year they had the vicar, a tall man with a large bald pate, playing for them and a short ball from Farnes struck him *'resoundingly on his shiny dome as he stooped to make a cut. At first, hearing a sound just like bat against ball and seeing the ball speeding towards third man I thought the vicar had made an excellent stroke. No head byes were run however and the batsman merely waved cheerfully and carried on.'*

The school had a good side and the happiest time was at Whitsun when the school had matches on the Saturday, Monday and Tuesday. During this time he joined Gidea Park cricket club and it was with them that Farnes was to make the stepping stone from school to county cricket.

With the school matches Farnes began a practice he was to keep up - recording his every performance and as a schoolboy carefully working out his averages. In his last seasons at school he took over fifty wickets at about ten each and averaged about forty with the bat, considering himself an all-rounder.

The school magazine said of him: *'An excellent all round player. As a bowler uses his height to advantage and keeps a good length. A most graceful and promising bat with strokes all round the wicket. Has been a splendid captain.'*

It was not just at cricket that he shined. In his final year he set new school records in the long and high jumps - 18'11 and 5'3 and went on to shine in the Essex inter-school sports. The school finished a close third with Farnes winning both jumps again and running an excellent anchor leg in the relay as the team was second.

It was then that county cricket took over and obsessed him. He wrote:

'County cricket scores in the paper absorbed my attention every morning throughout the summer. Every player's name became familiar to me and I knew pretty well where he stood in the averages. My visits to the county ground were few and far between but they were great days indeed. The first great day was when my brother took me to Leyton to see Essex play against Leicestershire. Captain Nicholas (batsman and wicket-keeper and grandfather of Mark Nicholas, former captain of Hampshire and, in recent years, a television presenter) *had his hand split at cover point trying to catch a swerving drive. I can see the ball now as it came for I was near the boundary in that direction.'*

30

And then he declared his true faith: *'The perfection and precision of the game amazed me and I felt as if I had been on the threshold of Valhalla.'*

He also went to Lord's for the first time, a breathtaking occasion being the first day of the Test against the South Africans in 1924. He saw Arthur Gilligan and Maurice Tate slice through the South African batting until Catterall and Susskind, who made a hundred and 69, stopped the rot. When England went in for the last 20 minutes of play he thought Bissett and Blanckenberg appeared to bowl thunderbolts, *'but Hobbs and Sutcliffe wafted them away easily. I could not see how they could fail to make centuries and said so. They did too. On the lawn at home afterwards - really a forbidden pitch - we tried to play in the first class manner and did seem to have been inspired by the day's play.'*

He went to Lord's another time for one of Patsy Hendren's benefit matches. He hoped he would make a century but he only made 11 and Jack Hearne was the hero with a double century. As they turned to leave the ground the last sight of the day was Arthur Gilligan sending a stump spinning out of the ground to the wicket keeper's feet - *'a wonderful, unforgettable, inspiring sight.'*

The boy did not know that as the man 12 years later he would do the same, not once but three times in the space of 20 minutes on the same wicket against three of the best batsmen in the world.

And there was Essex too, for the headmaster organised an annual day out for the boys to see the county play, and they drooled over JWHT Douglas, the England and Essex captain known by his initials as Johnny Won't Hit Today, Morris (Stan) Nichols, the great bowler, and Jack O'Connor belting the ball round the ground.

In the school holidays Farnes played for Gidea Park second eleven and had one sensational match amongst many good ones, scoring his only century - 101 not out - and taking 5 for 6.

'If the cricket which I played in those days was of a low grade - as it undoubtedly was - yet it was the theme of life for me and from this humble game I extracted an amazing wealth of pleasure.'

It was to continue when he left school in the summer of 1928. But before the real joy of cricket there was a large hurdle to clear and that was what he was going to do with his life. He wrote:

'I had no set ambition to make a living in a particular way. I certainly

31

wanted to play cricket and I had a vague desire to travel - especially in my melancholy moments when Robinson Crusoe adventures and Treasure Island memories filled me with wish-thoughts. If I had thoughts of professional cricket I doubted my ability to become good enough though I mentioned it tentatively to my harassed father. Vague dreams not being a paying proposition, I entered an insurance office which was, at any rate, an occupation.'

It was a boring one. He lasted five weeks, this lanky unhappy youth spending his lunchtimes studying the scores of the MCC tour in the Evening Standard and noting that Larwood seemed to be in grand form. He left insurance for banking and for eighteen depressing months remained a clerk, each day rather like Oscar Wilde's in Reading jail - *'each hour is like a year, a year whose days are long'* - carrying out meaningless tasks in never ending days of drudgery.

He said: *'I conceived a bitter hatred of a London that was a virtual prison for me.'* He travelled daily up and down to the City with his old friend Denis, both tall young men sitting with knees touching in a packed compartment and facing accusations from their elders of trying to cramp the strap hangers. Sometimes the rows nearly came to blows.

When the day's work was over Farnes was gone in a flash, particularly on Saturdays, cricket days, when he just managed to catch the 1.33 pm train from Liverpool Street, usually by leaping into the guard's van as it pulled out. Then to paradise at Gidea Park.

'To arrive late for a cricket match made me so furious that I should have loved to bomb the bank building,' he wrote bitterly ten years on. *'After six months in Leadenhall Street I was given sentence of nearly a year in Lombard Street where I performed the necessary drudgery conscientiously but with despair in my heart. My meagre wages accumulated, the bank was hateful and I didn't want to touch its dirty money. Such were my feelings, altered subsequently when in a new life money could be spent.'*

During his first May with the bank he was given a fortnight's holiday and this coincided with his club's cricket week. One of the matches was against the Essex Club and Ground which was captained by the great Peter 'Percy' Perrin, one of the finest batsmen not to have played for England, but in his day the opposition was more than formidable and he was not the nimblest of men in the field. Farnes wrote:

'It was to be a great day for me, full of significance. I took a few wickets

and made about 17 runs. After the game when I had started on my way home, I was called back to the pavilion and interviewed by Perrin whose easy off driving of my bowling had seemed to me to show up the ineffectiveness of my attempts to get him out He asked me if I could play for the Young Amateurs of Essex (Olympic 1500 metres silver medalist in the 1932 Games, Jerry Cornes, opened for them in those days) *later in the season in a two day match against the Young Amateurs of Surrey. The bank gave me permission to play but in the end I was not selected as only those still at school were eligible. Instead I managed to play for the Club and Ground against Romford on one of those days…*

'Later on I was invited to play for the county - an invitation that amazed me. When the bank refused to give me three days leave I was not so bitterly disappointed as I might have been because I thought that I might fail completely which would be worse than not playing. Yet at the same time I was very disappointed and my love for the bank did not increase.'

His hatred of the bank grew during the winter of 1929 and into 1930. In the spring he was given a roving commission to act as a locum at branches where they were short-staffed through illness or the like. It had no effect on Farnes who said, *'if the job seemed more important it was no more welcome. I had decided that if I were to become the supreme chief of all banks in the world I would still loathe the job.'*

One branch was at Wanstead, just down the road from home, but all the chief clerk would talk about to customers was his new house, delaying work and the bitter young clerk who cursed him.

'And spring was in the air and not only was spring in the air but the Australian team was in England. On the very morrow Australia was due to play Essex at Leyton and on the very morrow I was due for another change, in Baker Street, near the horrible Marylebone branch in the West End which brought back insurance days memories. This was pure persecution.'

It was the final straw:

'When I got home in the evening I said 'I'm not going to Baker Street tomorrow.' 'Where are you going then?' asked my parents. 'I'm going to watch the Australians at Leyton', their tall, ever growing son replied. And to my considerable surprise I did.'

And he never went back.

3.

THE CLUB CRICKETER

THE YOUNG Farnes, just 15 years old, began his cricket career with Gidea Park where his father Sydney was a member in 1926. Gidea Park, with their ground by Gallows Corner on the main road from London to Southend on the sea, was founded in 1863 and is still going strongly.

The first time Farnes represented his club against Essex County and Ground was in 1929 when he was 18. He took two for 65 and scored 19 runs as one of the openers. The next year he did much better and it was because of his 6 for 36 he was spotted by Percy Perrin, a grandee of Essex, a fine batsman who took a few runs off the young bowler but liked his dash and pace. He spoke to him at length after the game and then hurried off to spread the good news to the Essex committee.

That year, as he waited for his chance to come, he took 4 for 12 for the County and Ground against Shenfield, 2 for 44 against Witham and a sparkling 6 for 30 against Loughton in between his debut match for the county and his second game against Kent.

He also had a day off from the county side in 1931, taking 2 for 24 against Romford and opened the innings, scoring 28. By then he was fulfilling the prediction of his headmaster, SB Hartley, a regular batsman for the club, that he would be one of the leading fast bowlers and play for England.

At the start of his club career the schoolboy had a couple of games in 1926, taking six wickets in his first game for the second team and making a duck in a charity match in which Joe Hardstaff's father played.

He played his first school cricket when he was 16, but the next year, 1928, he mixed the two. In Gidea Park's cricket week he took a wicket against Eastern Nomads and then, for the second team, made his only 100, 103 in two hours, and in other games for the second team took 5 for 6 against a South Essex XI, 6 for 14 against Brentwood, 5 for 41 against

South Woodford, adding 56 with the bat, and had 3 for 37 and 25 in the last game of the season. For the school, where he was captain, he took 4 for 17, 6 for 45, 3 for 13, 5 for 14 and 3 for 32 as well as scoring around 450 runs in 12 innings.

1929 was his best year yet, now an unhappy bank clerk who used all the time he could to play the game he loved above all else. The area around Romford was cricket crazy with many teams and some fiercely contested and great matches. He took 60 wickets for 11.51 but was beaten in the averages by another Gidea Park bowler, Jefcoate, who took 80 for 11.37. Farnes, incredibly, headed the batting averages with 463 runs and an average of 22.1. He had some good stands with his old headmaster and scored two half centuries as well as being among the wickets and vying with Jefcoate and another fine bowler Falcon for the biggest haul. In one match against Higham Park he took 3 for 5, 5 for 19 against Chingford, four for 23 against Wickford, two in successive balls, and 5 for 31 in the last game of the season.

He played a lot during 1930 until the county snapped him up. He had six wickets for a handful of runs against University College when the local paper said he was virtually unplayable, taking the last four in six balls. In the return game he managed six more for 76. In the local derby against Romford he had 6 for 36 and then 4 for 30 in the return match, and ended his club career with 63 against Leigh-on-Sea and 2 for 44 before going on to fulfil his destiny.

He never forgot the club and was a regular visitor when he was at home. After his death and the war his old headmaster chaired a committee to raise money to erect a memorial. They wanted something more than a plaque and decided on a memorial scoreboard. It was unveiled in Cricket Festival week in June 1954 by his old skipper, Gubby Allen, who said: *'I am happy to have the opportunity to express my affection and admiration of him. He lost his life in the greatest of all Test matches in giving his life for his country. On that day England lost a great gentleman and a very great fast bowler. There was a touch of hostility in his bowling when stirred but he was gentle and of a kindly nature.'* He said of his 8 for 43 for the Gentlemen v Players in 1938: *'I have never seen anyone bowl faster or better.'*

The plaque that was on the outside of the scoreboard under the trees in a corner of the ground simply stated Farnes's cricket career, said that it was erected by public subscription and ended, *'His Spirit shall Endure.'*

His old headmaster said: *'It is not a lifeless monolith but a machine which is activated with life and if properly worked should give useful information to thousands of cricket lovers for many years.'*

It was not to be. Vandals burnt it down in 1973 and the plaque stands in Farnes' Corner in the pavilion alongside photos of him at school and as an England bowler, and the bat he used in the Melbourne Test of 1937 when he took six wickets in an innings, signed by the players of both sides.

Long after he had left his Essex cricket nursery, Farnes went back to club cricket, first with Worksop Cricket Club in the town by his school and then just up the road at Doncaster, where he played a couple of games in the Yorkshire League.

He had several games for Worksop in 1936 and 1937, but not in 1938, probably because of his Test match commitments, three of which took him away from school in the very busy summer term. Worksop CC was helped greatly by Sir Julian Cahn, a local rich businessman and cricket lover, who collected around him (in the manner of the headmaster of Worksop College) with club captain John Hall, one of his employees, a collection of top cricketers. Among them was South African fast bowler DBP Morkel, GFH Hearne, TD Hounsfield of Derbyshire, GV Gunn of Notts, Australians H Mudge and J Walsh, all registered for the club but not necessarily playing.

Morkel certainly did, he and Farnes being the opening bowlers against pit side Warsop Main in May 1937 (the season where injury kept Farnes out of the England side against the New Zealanders when he was due to play during the holidays. He could not get time off before because he had been away all winter in Australia with the MCC side). Farnes took 5 for 48 in his 13 overs and the South African 1 for 7 off seven overs. When they batted Morkel made 17 and Farnes 1.

In a later match that season, against business side Rose Brothers, Farnes did not get a wicket in 20 overs, five of which were maidens, and gave away 68 runs as the opponents batted for 58 overs for 184 for three declared, but when it came to batting he excelled himself with a fine 85, including four sixes.

A week later, the last of term, his bowling was coming good and he took 5 for 36 against Retford, a neighbouring town, in 13 overs with three maidens, a great tune up for the county games that followed almost immediately. In that year for the club he took 22 wickets for 285 runs, an average of 12.95, and scored 107 runs. The year before he took 17 wickets for them at an average of 10.17 off 64.4 overs, details dug out by George Langdale, historian of the club and a man who played for four counties, Derbyshire, Somerset, Norfolk and Berkshire.

He is not forgotten in the town. When Harold Larwood returned to England for a visit from his home in Australia some years ago, he was given a civic welcome by Worksop where the council had decided to name an estate after him. The other great fast bowler was remembered too because some people there still have the address Farnes Court, Larwood Estate.

The first appearance of Farnes for Doncaster, a railway and mining town in South Yorkshire, was at the end of the 1939 summer term. In a low scoring match against a neighbouring village, Rawmarsh, he and the club's professional J Burton produced some dramatic figures after Doncaster were bowled out for 94 with Farnes getting his usual duck while batting at number five. He and Burton then swept through the mining side and had them all out for 63, Farnes taking six for 30 and Burton 3 for 30.

In his only other game Farnes, just before his blitz of wickets for Essex, had no luck at all, taking just one wicket with some aggressive bowling against Sheffield United.

4.

1930

THE BANK CLERK who played hookey and never went back made his county debut for Essex against Gloucestershire at Chelmsford on June 28, 1930. He had been picked the year before - to his amazement - but the bank refused to give him leave and we know he was not that disappointed because of his fear of failure through inexperience.

But earlier this season he had seen Woodfull and McCabe, Ponsford and Jackson, Oldfield and Grimmett and sat there entranced for three days in the biting cold, sitting at the feet of the Gods, waiting for crumbs to fall his way.

It took courage and a lot of faith in yourself to walk away from a job in the days of the Depression, and it was only the young bank clerk's overwhelming hatred for his job and his over-riding love for the game of cricket, and his ambition to succeed, that made him unemployed and in love with the game.

He was in Minehead on holiday when the telegram arrived inviting him to play against Surrey and then Gloucestershire. He knew he would not be back in time for the Surrey game and was doubtful about the other because he had not played cricket for a fortnight and would be out of practice. The adrenalin flowed, however, and kept him awake the night before the game, but he was there ready for battle.

Imagine the thrill of arriving at the ground, meeting the others in the team, no doubt tongue-tied because Farnes was a shy man all his life, even standing in awe of Nichols, Jack Russell and Eastman and then going out onto the pitch, a young man whose dream had come true, a hackneyed phrase, a cliche but in this case absolutely true. And it was a thrill that never left him during his short career. He loved county cricket with an intensity that sometimes seemed overwhelming.

His first game was not a success, not the stuff of stories in which the novice overcomes everything and turns in a match-winning performance which has the crowd on its feet. He took 0 for 60 off 11 overs in the west country side's first innings and 0 for 16 in the second.

Ken himself described the match with all the awkwardness of the new boy joining the hardened professionals and regular amateurs. He said:

'I met most of the Essex team for the first time in the dressing room - Jack Russell, O'Connor, Eastman, Nichols, Joe Hipkin and the rest and our captain HM Morris usually known as 'Whizz'. Arthur Dader too was playing and Pope, Smith and Sheffield. Gloucestershire were led by BH Lyon.

'Whizz won the toss and we batted - to no very good purpose for Charlie Parker and Tom Goddard were soon among us. Being an unknown quantity I was put in at No. 7, a considerably higher position than I have usually achieved since. When I faced Parker, the slips and wicket-keeper, who seemed to cluster right to my bat, gave gasps of amazement that were half genuine, half barracking, as the ball went on beating bat and wicket. I scraped eight runs, which was more than most of those above me had made, before Tom Goddard bowled me. I had walked out to bat as if on air in an unreal world, surprised that I was not extremely nervous as I had expected to be. Essex secretary Brian Castor said 'well tried' as I got back to the pavilion and I did not feel too displeased. But they had found me out and I went further down the order in the next innings.

'Roy Sheffield, who I had left behind in the middle, now set about the bowling and made 65 in quick time. But we were in the field by the middle of the afternoon.

'When I was on I bowled poorly and Dacre drove and hooked me all over the place (Hammond was not playing) so that I finished up with 0 for 60. Nichols finished off their innings on the second morning. Whizz said to me as we went off the field 'I was just going to put you on too - lucky, wasn't it?' I'm afraid that really I was a little disappointed at not getting another bowl. I did have an over and two in the second innings but failed to take a wicket. They beat us by four wickets.

'I had taken no wickets, made eight runs and fielded badly in my first county match. On leaving I said to the skipper hopefully 'I'm going to bowl and bowl until I can bowl a length.' At any rate my pride at having played for the county outweighed any disappointment I may have felt at my failure.

'After a few weeks I was invited to play again - this time against Kent at Southend.'

The Kent match was the second of the six in which he played that first summer. It was the making of him. For the first time - and in only his second ever first-class game - he took five wickets in an innings, finishing up with 5 for 36. This was more than he had hoped for or dreamt of. It was reality and showed that there was a future ahead in the game.

His first wicket was Aidan Crawley, who edged one to wicket-keeper Sheffield; the second the great Frank Woolley, caught in the slips by Jack Russell, and what a scalp for the rookie; then the equally great Les Ames with a magnificent ball that clean bowled him (and Farnes did the same to the soon-to-be England wicket-keeper in the second innings), followed by Knott and Tich Freeman.

His performance would have been given much greater prominence but for one thing - Tich Freeman took all 10 Essex wickets for 53 in 30 overs (in a season's haul of 275 wickets from nearly 2000 overs) and then went on to take another six in the second innings, giving him figures of 16 for 94 in Kent's victory by 277 runs.

The Essex fast bowler only managed a total of 6 for 118 in the two innings, with 1 for 82 off 29 overs in the second. He scored only one run, being bowled by Freeman for one in the first innings and by Wright for nought in the second. But Woolley in the first innings, and Ames twice!

This is how the new boy saw it:

'In August the Essex team usually alters its composition and there is some competition to get into the side...In 1930 HWF Franklin came in and took over the captaincy from Morris who had played as long as his business affairs permitted. As far as I remember I was only invited to play because Arthur Daer was unavailable for this match. Kent also had an August side with Aidan Crawley and CJ Knott in it.'

It was a time when the county was growing in strength and were, throughout the decade, to become a side to contend with, with an attack to frighten anyone and with batting that grew better year by year. They were no longer the poor relations to neighbours Kent, Surrey and Middlesex, but a side that could produce surprises, whether it was beating the best (like Yorkshire and Surrey), but then throwing it all away at the last moment. They were entertaining and enjoyed their cricket and pleased the spectators.

Essex lost the toss and Farnes came on as first change:

'I bowled calmly with an aim for length which I was allowed to achieve. The Southend air and probably some green in the wicket did the rest. Crawley edged one to Sheffield at the wicket and I had taken my first wicket in first-class cricket - a rather difficult feat to believe at the time.

'But better still was to follow. Frank Woolley moved with genteel dignity to the crease and very soon snicked one that left him a bit. Jack Russell (bless him) made a grand catch at second slip, almost brushing aside first slip less he should fumble it in his eagerness to secure the important wicket and, I am convinced, to see that I should not be discouraged by a dropped chance off my bowling.

'I took Ames's wicket in this spell and went into lunch feeling pretty pleased. Afterwards I had Knott caught in the gully and Freeman was bowled and I finished up with 5 for 36.'

Farnes was happy. He had his first mention in Wisden because of it – *'Farnes, a Romford amateur, bowled effectively on Wednesday.'* Farnes wrote his thoughts after the game:

'It was this match against Kent and those that followed as a result of it that gave me the entry into first-class cricket. It never occurred to me that there were other things I might do; to play as much as possible seemed the natural and unquestionable thing. Why had I this ardent desire to play could be answered easily, I suppose, by the psychologists but the real significance is that I had a passion - or even a mania - for cricket and first-class cricket was the abstract chief deity.'

Imagine one of our superstars of today spouting such words! He would be considered mad. He went on:

'It is all very well to question my aims and motives now that I can look back; then I was an unquestioning fanatic and this complete faith in the rightness of my ambition was undoubtedly the driving force that kept me on endeavouring to improve. I was shocked and incredulous when Aidan Crawley, after making 175 against us in Kent's second innings, told me he was not going to play much more first-class cricket as he was going to be too busy and didn't like the game anyhow.'

'Not that I have any regrets at having devoted so much time to what is after all merely a game. For it has enabled me to meet many grand people and to see much of the world that had seemed beyond my reach. And besides, did it

not save me from continuing to be the saddest of disgruntled bank clerks? Peter Perrin had taken on the role of fairy godmother.'

His next match was against Glamorgan at Swansea and the Welsh rain came down. It poured all Wednesday morning and finally stopped for play to start at 3.30 with the wicket scarcely fit for any game. After an hour, with Glamorgan batting and Farnes opening the bowling with Morris Nichols, play was abandoned. The next day the gale was so strong in one of the worst storms that Swansea had seen for years that marquees were blown away, the covers were damaged and the pitch practically ruined. Play did start late on Friday but no one was greatly interested and it petered out with only a total of three hours play being possible.

Farnes in his first away game for the county bowled three overs for 6 runs. He commented: *'Itching to play I could only walk impatiently up some of Swansea's quieter but disconsolate streets or take a bus to the Mumbles to be blown about by the blustering sea air.'*

It was a long train trip to Derby for the next match starting the next day but when it did Farnes took two wickets, bowling GM Lee and having Stan Worthington (who played for England against India, scored a century and once made 100 in an hour against Notts) lbw, but he was completely overshadowed by colleague Peter Smith who took four wickets in sixteen balls.

Farnes described what it was like to spend a wet August Sunday in a provincial county town: *'Sunday in a provincial town is likely to prove dull. In itself it was an interruption in the game. It was a long, irritating day. In the evening, we went for a walk by the canal and it seemed somehow fitting that the distended corpses of two or three dogs floating in the canal should destroy a large part of the pleasure of our attempt to pass the time pleasantly.'*

His views on his opponents, views seen through the fresh eyes of a young intelligent cricketer in only his third game, are interesting:

'Worthington (opening bowler) had a rather curious run, his legs seeming to move in such a way as to suggest that they were only remotely connected with his body. The most successful bowler was Tommy Mitchell. He owed his presence in the county team in the first place to his ability to spin a billiard bowl. It was this at any rate that made the impression and brought about the investigation as to whether he could spin a cricket ball equally well. Derbyshire have strange ways of unearthing their bowlers. Copson I regard as one of the phenomena of cricket for

he did not play the game until he was eighteen, an age where nearly all players have settled down sufficiently to show whether they will be first- class or not.

'By this time I had been found out and my place in the batting order next to the roller seemed assured. That day I performed in the true manner of a No. 11. Somehow I scraped four runs and remember vividly my extraordinary shot at the first ball I received from Mitchell. Nigel Wykes called it a Chinese cut in delighted derision when I returned to the pavilion. I began to realise more fully that I was not quite in the class of Jack Hobbs. I don't remember being bowled but I do remember the Chinese cut.'

So keen was I to bowl again after all the interruptions of the past week that I almost tired myself out in the nets. However I took a couple of wickets.'

So on to Blackpool on the late season tour, his first visit to the north west. Lancashire needed to win the match to clinch the championship and the weather had changed to the beginning of a heatwave, but the town's ground was in a hollow which cut out any breeze that might affect the game.

There was a good crowd because Blackpool in those days was even more the playground of the northern holidaymaker. It was a massive resort that contained everything a family seeking seaside and fun (to use Stanley Holloway's immortal phrase) and those not wanting to take their young Alberts to see the lions at the Tower, or go on the sands or to the Pleasure Beach, made their way to Stanley Park.

As Essex walked onto the field Jack Russell took one look at the wicket and told Farnes, *'This'll just suit you.'* It did. In his first over, bowling to that wonderful batsman Eddie Paynter (he who came from his hospital bed to help win the Ashes three years later), he shaved the off stump so delicately that there was scarcely the sound of a snick but the off bail fell to the ground. That was in strong contrast to his speed a few years later when his trick was to send a stump cartwheeeling a dozen yards or so to the feet of the wicket-keeper. He also bowled Iddon and Hopwood and had Tyldesley caught as he took 4 for 51 in a 29-over spell. He commented:

'Having bowled 29 overs during the day I was too tired to sleep and only dropped off when it was almost time to be getting up. When I arrived downstairs I was amazed to see the tables had been laid for lunch. Fortunately Essex had already gone into bat the night before and my disturbed state of mind at being late at the ground was needless.'

Ken Farnes

His batting made no difference. He did not receive a ball in the first innings and in the second he had one from the majestic Australian fast bowler Ted McDonald, a player from whom Farnes was to learn a lot. Farnes said of McDonald, he of the immaculate gleaming black hair and bronzed hawk-like feature:

'He was then thirty-eight years old yet he was still fast and still preserved that beautiful action - the most nearly perfect possible. He took quite a long run, working up easily to a maximum speed at the moment of delivery. After he reached the crease his left arm straightened sharply and pointed straight above him. The whole thing, with the follow-through, was extremely graceful and rhythmic, a grooved action seemingly effortless, yet the ball became a thing of vivid life as it left his hand.

'George Duckworth (then the England wicket-keeper) *told me that he had very long arms and amazingly supple shoulders. He could put both arms over his head and clasp his hands under his chin. He could use the full width of the crease and so was able to avoid any holes caused by the bowling which inconvenience most bowlers. And in spite of his speed he was so light that he could have bowled in dancing pumps.'*

Lancashire duly won by 174 runs, Farnes bowling Duckworth in the second innings, and took the championship, a feat toasted in champagne at lunch.

The last match of the season was against Warwickshire at the county ground at Leyton. One could never say it was picturesque but it had history, with a large pavilion full of memories of famous Essex players such as Charlie McGahey, Kortright, Peter Perrin and the recently retired former England captain and 1908 Olympic middleweight boxing champion JWHT Douglas, who was soon after drowned at sea with his father off the Finnish coast when the ship they were travelling on collided with another in thick fog.

It was also in the metropolitan part of the county and when the ground was bought in 1886 for £12,000 this pearl (as it was known) was reported locally as a place that *'gave unwonted loveliness to a district which but for a short while since, presented an appearance of the abomination of desolation.'* By buying the ground the county ensured that they would soon become first-class and in 1894 they were invited to join the championship for the following season.

It was a far cry from the start of Essex cricket. In 1776 the match between Essex and Kent at Tilbury was a very tough encounter, making bodyline and hostile bowling milksop stuff indeed. Essex took exception to Kent including a player who should not have been there. They refused to play and a fight broke out. According to GB Buckley in his 'Fresh Light on Pre-Victorian Cricket':

'The Kentish men being likely to be worsted, one of them ran into the guardhouse and getting a gun from one of the invalids fired and killed one of the opposing party. On seeing this they all began running to the guardhouse and there being but four soldiers there, they took away the guns and fell to it doing a great deal of mischief. An old invalid (a soldier disabled by injury or ill-health) was run through the body with a bayonet and a sergeant was shot dead. At last the Essex men took to flight and running over the drawbridge made their escape. The Kentish men then made off in their boats and search is making after them!'

Leyton remained the county ground until 1933, the last great occasion there being the world record 555 partnership for the first wicket by Herbert Sutcliffe and Percy Holmes for Yorkshire in 1932.

All was peaceful however the day that Farnes first played at home and Essex beat the Midlands club by an innings, putting them into sixth in the championship, which was ten places higher than they had been two years earlier. The Warwickshire wickets were shared between five Essex bowlers, Farnes taking two of them, cartwheeling the stumps of Hill and Davies - *'wickets that stand out in my mind because they occurred rather unexpectedly and the sight of a stump seen hurtling out of the ground has always struck me as being one of the finest in cricket. It sends a shock through the spectators and from the middle you can hear a gasp from all round.'*

The gasp was something that was to be repeated more and more in his career. In the second innings he took four wickets, the initial exciting spell being 4 for 23 but ending the innings with 4 for 50. He wrote:

'I forget who was umpiring and I hope he will forgive me if I mention what was a very forgivable mistake if what I believe is true did occur. He gave Tiger Smith out caught at the wicket off me. There was certainly a click and the ball was probably deflected. As Tiger passed me on his way to the pavilion he muttered that he didn't play the ball at all. Actually it must have just touched the off stump but failed to dislodge the bail from the grooves. My conscience was pretty easy as the ball seemed worthy of a wicket but it is the only incident I know of a similar nature.'

45

It was during this match that Farnes came across one of cricket's eccentrics, Derek Foster, a fastish Warwickshire bowler who was famed as a contortionist. His trick was to balance a glass of beer on his forehead and then drink it without it touching his hands. He was also renowned for his accuracy with air pistol and catapult, so no one bent over when near him. He was also renowned for his climbing ability, which included entering the pavilion via the balcony. But on his first meeting with Farnes the only unusual behaviour shown was when he tried to overtake one of the Essex players in his car - driving backwards in his MG.

Thus ended the baptism. Six matches, 19 wickets, a reasonable average of 22.15 and a batting average that is best left unrecorded! Farnes wrote:

'I was not in the least satiated but now that I had begun was keener than ever, having had sufficient success for encouragement. My eyes were fixed on the following season at Cambridge.'

5.

1931

FARNES went up to Cambridge in the autumn of 1930 and when the spring came in 1931 he quickly headed for Fenner's, the home of the University cricket club and - in those days - the Athletic Club. In both sports it bred champions of the highest order, turning out England cricketers by the score (England captains Percy Chapman, Arthur Gilligan and Gubby Allen, batsman Duleepsinhji and all rounder RWV Robins in the decade before Farnes), and Olympic gold medalists in number, amongst them Harold Abrahams, Lord Burghley, Bob Tisdall, Guy Butler and Douglas Lowe, who learnt their trade on the strange three laps to a mile cinder track which went the wrong way round - clockwise - to all normal running tracks.

When the freshman from the Royal Liberty School, Romford and now at Pembroke College first stepped onto the ground it was with a sense of awe. It is a feeling shared by many of us when first going into a revered place, whether it be Lord's, or the Oval or a county ground, a football stadium like Old Trafford or Arsenal, or any ground where a favourite sport is played by those at the very top. It is similar to those reaching their goal at the end of a pilgrimage, whether it be Rome or Canterbury or Mecca. The feeling is the same whether spiritual or secular; one of awe, admiration, being with the Gods, whoever they are.

Farnes, because he was articulate and could write well, summed it up:

I have considerable diffidence about writing on cricket at Fenner's and the inter-Varsity match (and for that matter writing a book of cricket reminisces at all) for inside the pavilion one is surrounded by panels bearing in gold letters the names of the players who have represented Cambridge in the Varsity match since the first of these contests (1827) and an atmosphere of tradition is always solemn.

Ken Farnes

With time sorting the wheat from the chaff the names of the eminent players are conspicuous. One lunches or awaits one's turn to bat in the company of the great.

'There is too, at first at any rate, a feeling of insecurity in the very fact that one is not so much playing a game of cricket as battling for a blue. The game itself is as academic as it is practical. Spectators are usually few in number and a large percentage is composed of clergy and dons.

'The ground is large and sufficiently open for there to be a good light yet enclosed by wall and fence and with enough trees dotted around to give it the right air for the game. The pavilion, tall and not prepossessing was looked after by Dan Hayward (brother of Tom, like Jack Hobbs, a Cambridge and England man, discovered playing on nearby Parker's Piece and snapped up by Surrey), who had been there for a very long time and was once himself a cricketer of no mean ability.'

For a freshman the best way to catch the Captain's eye is by showing great promise in the nets. That year it was George Kemp-Welch, a useful opening bat, who watched the tall young man hurl the ball down with great enthusiasm and marked him as a possible. He already had another fast bowler earmarked for the season, Giles Baring, who took 10 wickets for 57 in the two innings of the Seniors' match.

But it was Farnes who was the success of the Freshman's game. He was on the captain's side against the team of the vice Captain, AG Hazlerigg, a fine spin bowler. His team won the toss and batted in this twelve-a-side trial and top scorer was Jack Davies with 68. He was unlucky that he sprained his ankle early in the season, thereby depriving him of his blue but letting in AT Ratcliffe, who celebrated his selection with a record 201 in the Varsity match, only to see it go the next day when the Nawab of Pataudi, later an England batsman, score 238 for Oxford. Davies also had the distinction three years later of being the first English bowler to get Bradman for a duck in England, bowling at Fenner's (much to the annoyance of the crowd who had come to see the Don bat, not an undergraduate bowl!) in a game where Australia made 481 for 5 declared.

Back on that May day three years before and Farnes came on after tea and on the orders of his captain - *'come on, three wickets this over'* - did the hat trick bowling Ronnie Farnfield, later a colleague at Worksop College, EG Titley and TP Partington to finish with 5 for 29, enough to make him a certainty for the games leading up to and including the match against Oxford.

48

Ready for action - aged about six

I

The Pavilion

With parents, Sydney and Florence, and
older brother Norman

The Reed Pond Cricket Club

Possession is nine points of the law

<table>
<tr><td>The
Serious Cricketer</td><td>The
Champion Athlete</td></tr>
</table>

IV

His lifelong friend Geoff Chapman
with younger brother Chris Chapman

Hello, Mr Farnes

VI

With Head of the School, Hugh Barker

Don Bradman and Douglas Jardine
- the two central figures of the Bodyline controversy

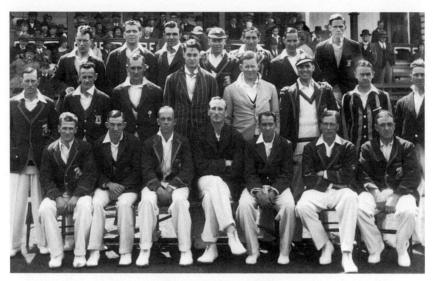

Test Trial, 1932 Cardiff
Back: Tony Mitchell, Arthur Staples, Les Ames, George Duckworth, Nawab of Pataudi,
Herbert Sutcliffe, Robert Scott
Middle: Ernest Tyldesley, Walter Keeton, Hedley Verity, Ken Farnes, Freddie Brown, Bill
Voce, Gubby Allen, Maurice Leyland
Seated: Harold Larwood, Eddie Paynter, Bob Wyatt, Douglas Jardine, K.S. Duleepsinhji,
Frank Woolley, Herbert Sutcliffe

Essex 1933
Standing: Dudley Pope, Jim Cutmore, Peter Smith,
Jim Sheffield, Morris Nichols, Reginald Taylor
Seated: Laurie Eastman, Ken Farnes, Denys Wilcox,
Leonard Crawley, Jack O'Connor

VIII

Denys Wilcox

Walking onto the field at Trent Bridge for his first Test
match in 1934 behind C.F. Walters
and with Hedley Verity

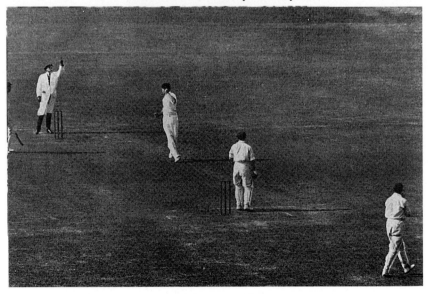

Bradman caught Ames bowled Farnes
in first Test match

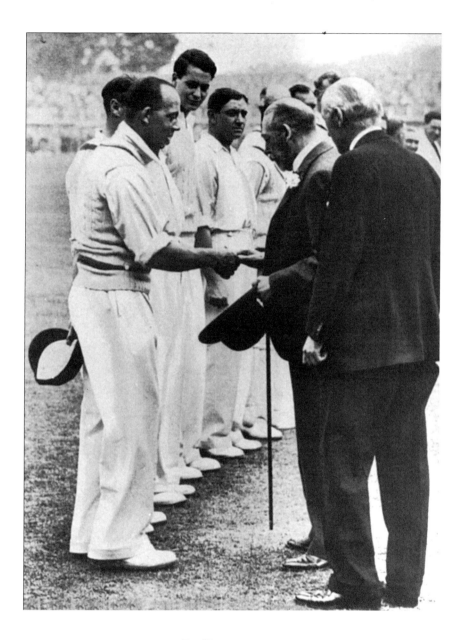

In line to meet
King George V at Lord's

England Bowler

The Approach

England Bowler

The Delivery Stride

England Bowler

The Delivery

England Bowler

The Follow-Through

A man at peace with the world

XVI

When his team batted - and another colleague-to-be DF Surfleet opened and scored 53 - Farnes managed a great 24 not out, one of the highest scores in his long and undistinguished batting career with just a handful of exceptions.

In the second innings he had Titley again and E Cawston, both bowled, but Farnfield ran up 70 good runs. It was not enough. Only Farnes and wicket-keeper JTH Comber eventually got their blues and Farnes only just before the match itself.

Farnes, however, played in nearly all the games. The first was against Yorkshire when Sutcliffe rattled up 173 not out and Farnes toiled for 24 overs for just 1 for 68. The game marked the beginning of a long friendship with Denys Wilcox, who was back in the Cambridge side after a dreadful 1930 season, mainly due he believed to going to an indoor coaching school before the start of the season and not being able to adapt to the slower turf wickets at Fenner's in early May. It shattered his confidence for the rest of the season. But he was back with a vengeance now.

Next was Middlesex, without several of their top men. Rain affected the game and Farnes took no wickets in his 13 overs. Things were not much better against Warwickshire, where he bowled 33 overs and took a total of 3 for 59.

Notts were no easier when he got four wickets for 85 off 41 overs, which was a lot for a fast bowler. The interesting thing about the game is that he met Larwood for the first time and had the nerve to clean bowl him in the second innings. It would be a great bonus if we knew what the two said to each other, the undergraduate talking to the fastest man in the world whom he regarded as his hero, but Farnes, ever modest and hiding his real feelings, just does not say. There is no doubt that Larwood had a great influence on the younger man, who tried to find the speed and accuracy that was the hallmark of the former Nottinghamshire miner. When he wrote his autobiography Larwood named Farnes as number four English fast bowler in his era and none of the Australians in the 1930s.

Against Leicestershire at Grace Road he managed 3 for 88 off 40 overs and a much better 4 for 52 in the first innings against the Free Foresters, although three of the victims were tail enders.

In the run up to the big match he got better. Against Sussex at Brighton he claimed the wickets of Duleepsinhji and the two Langridge brothers in his excellent 5 for 51, and took 5 for 58 against HDG Leveson-Gower's XI (in which three Cambridge batsmen all scored centuries - Wilcox, Kemp-Welch and Brown for the first time in a match since 1890), and against the MCC 1 for 33 in the first innings and 3 for 29 in the second.

The Varsity match contained some very high class cricketers and the experts of the day considered it the best since the end of World War One. It had everything - lots of runs, with the two sides scoring over 1,000 in three days, two double centuries, 201 by last minute choice Ratcliffe, who put on 149 with his captain for the first wicket and then kept going, and by the Nawab of Pataudi for Oxford, who beat the record with his not out 238, good fielding and some aggressive bowling, notably by Farnes, who did not have much luck, finishing with 1 for 79 and 0 for 18, and a good win by Oxford after Cambridge's second innings batting let them down badly and allowed Oxford home by eight wickets.

Wisden said: *'Oxford not only recorded their first win against the Light Blue for eight years but considering the circumstances in which the win was gained, accomplished by far the finest performance credited to either University since the war.'* It also said that because of Farnes's pace and (England captain to be) Freddie Brown's ability to bowl both leg break and fairly speedy googly made Oxford go very warily for some time before Pataudi took over and punished all the Cambridge bowlers severely in a masterly innings.

Farnes finished his first year at Cambridge with the creditable figures of 31 wickets for 724, an average of 23.35, behind Freddie Brown's 22.13 with 66 wickets. His batting, not surprisingly, was bottom of the table - 2.50 average from 10 innings. Wisden said: *'K. Farnes, a freshman with some experience of county cricket in the Essex side, was happily in residence and became the regular fast bowler.'*

At end of term Farnes (and Wilcox who averaged 27.50) began what was to become his regular mode of cricket - the last week or so of July and August and a bit of September playing for Essex. It was to happen this way for the next nine years.

Cambridge was not all cricket. One important joy was being reunited with his Reed Pond friend Geoff Chapman. They had kept in touch but Geoff did not know that his friend was coming up to Cambridge until he read it in The Cricketer. Geoff was at Downing College and Farnes at Pembroke, but they contacted each other and spent a lot of time together, particularly when they were both studying for their Part 1 of the geography Tripos exam (which both passed).

Geoff can remember him as an ordinary undergraduate, full of fun but not easy to get to know, rather remote in that way, but a very good friend when you broke through the reserve. Geoff said:

'We had some good times. We once went on a yachting holiday on the Norfolk Broads with another friend, Henry Moore, and had a great time sailing around. And another time we were all punting on the Cam and had our food with us. Ken was at one end of the boat and the fellow with the butter at the other and in a typical undergraduate act picked up the dish and threw it over. The dish fell off the butter and with a cricketer's typical reaction he caught the butter not the dish.

'We were all paralysed with laughter at the natural reaction and Ken was laughing helplessly with the butter stuck to one hand and amazingly the dish was not broken.'

The two stayed great friends during their University days. Farnes's fame did not alter him, nor did his membership of the Hawks Club, the club for top sportsmen. Geoff found him as natural as ever. He also found that Farnes was very well read and it was he who introduced him to the turn-of-the-century English poet James Elroy Flecker and Masefield's novels. *'I think he had a romantic fibre in him that made this source of travel and far off places so attractive to him.'*

Geoff noticed another change in his friend - in his bowling action:

'He seemed to be throwing the whole of his torso back, almost leaning back when he reached the wicket, giving him an extra impact in the final thrust. He had a very long strong back almost behind vertical at full speed.

'I often counted the number of strides he took to the wicket, it was 11. I have often thought that no fast bowler need take more. He never took too long a run like many fast bowlers, not like the village blacksmith thundering up from the other side of the hill.'

When Farnes rejoined Essex, against Sussex at Brighton, the first of nine matches in which he played that year, his county were struggling (they were to finish 10th). He was already becoming a popular member of the team with his affable personality, a man who could not be roused, although

51

some thought a good kick would motivate him and make him more aggressive. His attitude was one of love of the game and much aggression when it came to bowling, but not in any other way. His arrival meant that Morris Nichols, the best of the Essex bowlers, had support in the attack, strengthening it immensely, well as others had played before.

In the Sussex game he bowled both the Langridge brothers and Parks as well for his 3 for 124 before Duleepsinjhi started hitting out to make 133. Farnes managed some kind of minor record with his batting, being two not out in both innings!

His first ever game at Headingley lost a day through rain and Yorkshire were without Sutcliffe, Bowes and Verity, who were all at Lord's for the Gentlemen v Players. His only victim was Maurice Leyland, whom he bowled for one, but it made little difference, Yorkshire winning by 10 wickets.

His best performance of the season came at the first match Essex played at Clacton (often to be his happy hunting ground) against Lancashire at the end of July. He did not do much in the first innings, but in the second he let rip. Wisden acknowledged that his and Nichols's bowling played a big part in an Essex win by an innings and 64 runs.

On the final day Lancashire, who had followed on needing 204 to save an innings defeat, had reached 46 with all wickets standing when play ended. The next day Farnes changed all that with such a formidable performance on a slightly worn pitch that the game was over in 100 minutes. He took the first five wickets and then got another to finish with 6 for 57. Tyldesley and Paynter were among his victims and a large part of the 12,000 crowd who watched the game over its three days was there to see the triumph.

July ended with 2 for 45 against Somerset at Leyton and 0 for a total of 26 in a rain affected game at Northampton. On to Worcester where the home team scored a formidable 389, with Farnes taking two wickets for 107 in 32 overs, a large number of overs about which he did not complain because he was a super fit and strong young man, always ready to hurl the ball down from his great height so that it came off the pitch fast and high, digging up into the batsman's ribs and making him play a shot. All the time he was learning.

Next was Middlesex on the dead pitch at Leyton, where he

managed just one wicket and only had one more against Glamorgan in the rain at Cowbridge. His last match was at Southend against Notts and once again he had Larwood, caught in the second innings for 30, his only wicket. In the first innings, in a bitterly cold wind which ruined the game, he bowled George Gunn and Keeton and ended with 2 for 19 as Notts were skittled out for 58.

At the season's end he had taken 20 wickets for 567 runs with an average of 28.35, which left him disappointed but, because of his temperament, with the determination to become very much better next year. His batting again was abysmal - average 5.66 - but his fielding was improving, his very long arms able to reach balls that smaller mortals could not. Larwood topped the averages that year. Farnes was way down with 51 wickets for 1291 runs, an average of 25.31. It was back to the nets.

6.

1932

IN THE LAST game of the 1932 season Farnes achieved a state of mind that everyone seeks: pure contentment. It came, not at a moment of triumph, but at the end of a day when his bowling had been knocked around the field at Leyton by a good friend, Bryan Valentine (180), and the other Kent batsmen.

Leyton, you will recall, was not the most beautiful ground in the world. One Essex captain summed it up when he told one of his players to go and field amongst the dirt and broken bottles on the far side. But for Farnes it held great memories before it was closed at the end of the next season and Essex spread their games around various grounds in the county with Chelmsford as headquarters (as it still is).

Farnes wrote: *'I have one or two pleasant memories of the place. It was there that I saw my first county match; it made a tremendous impression on me'*, which was only natural for a dreamer, a romantic, a poet and painter who saw far past the ordinary picture that mere mortals saw.

And it was so that on that lovely August evening in that scruffy, grubby and unlikely setting that he had a feeling that fits into what CS 'Jack' Lewis called Joy. He wrote:

'It was there too that a day's fielding in the late summer heat brought about in me an amazing evening's contentment. I cannot explain the reason - just positive physical well-being probably. I had not done well myself for Kent had thumped our bowling but it was just the end of the season and I still remember the glow of pure contentment that I felt that evening.'

If he found true happiness that evening, he certainly did not when he was picked to play in a Test trial for the 1932/33 tour of Australia (which turned out to be a total triumph with the Ashes regained even at the expense of considerable hostility by the Australians over what they termed unsportsmanlike bodyline bowling).

The trial was played on the fast bowler's graveyard at Cardiff and the lack of pace in the wicket was not helped by the fact that it rained and rained and rained as the wind howled. It was the worst gale in a game of cricket that Farnes ever encountered and only two hours of play were possible before it was washed out.

In those two hours Larwood (who headed the season's averages with 162 wickets at 12.86, ahead of Verity, also with 162 wickets at 13.88), played for the Rest against the best players to see what they made of him, and Farnes struggled in the appalling conditions. Larwood naturally had the best end. Farnes wrote:

'I had a tremendous struggle to get up to the crease, let alone bowl, against the wind which was blowing directly down the wicket. Duleepsinhji (nephew of Ranji and an England batsman) was in the nineties when the rain came and rejoiced the hearts of those who did not want any more play to spoil their chances of going on the tour. One or two of the players had agitated for my inclusion in the touring side but I certainly was not ripe for it and was not in the least disappointed nor surprised when I was not included. What a tour it was - and would have been for a greenhorn - shaking the foundations of the Empire as it did.'

As it was Farnes had his best season so far even though he missed two games through injury, straining his side and damaging his knee slightly. It was probably the start of his cartilage trouble which was to plague him until 1935, the season he missed to have an operation which cured him.

It started at Fenner's in May with five wickets in an innings for the University and making it six against the Free Foresters the next month. For good measure he took five wickets in an innings twice for Essex, who did not have a good season, finishing 14th in the championship.

He had spent the winter practicing, building up his strength, which included Mr Universe-style body building (and more of that later), increasing his pace, working on his direction and trying to learn how to be better than just a straightforward paceman, but one who could move the ball off the seam. His height was becoming more and more important as he understood that a ball coming from eight feet and pitching just right, particularly on a drying pitch, could be lethal. His speed was not yet anything as fast as Larwood, Voce, Bowes and Allen but he was catching up fast, having age on his side.

His first match came in mid-May, in the sunshine of an East Anglian day, was against his own county and he took a total of five wickets for 88 off 43 overs. In the next match he took five wickets in an innings against Middlesex, where he clean bowled Lee, Hearne and Nelson and had Carris and his old friend Surfleet caught. The Morning Post reported: *'The old superstition that bowlers of any pace could not bowl on a soft pitch was brushed aside by Farnes with his fastish medium.'*

This followed his first half century, a sparkling 56 with two sixes and 52 of them in an hour with Wilcox scoring a century in the University's 301. In the second innings he claimed three more of the Middlesex men, including Carris and Surfleet a second time. Wisden recorded: *'After his batting success Farnes proved so deadly with his fast bowling that he quickly gave his side a big advantage.'* - they won by an innings and 10 runs - *'In two short spells he dismissed five of the Middlesex batsmen for 10 runs.'*

One commentator reported: *'In the early part of last season he showed promise as a bowler and as he succeeded in getting over 50 wickets in first class cricket he was by no means a failure. But as a batsman he certainly did not shine and in some 19 first class matches he did he did not get as many runs as wickets. In the practice match, the first of the term, he showed that his batting had vastly improved but that is a mild phrase to use to cover the display which he gave on this ground when in 70 minutes he scored 56 after giving nothing approaching a chance until he had made 42.'*

He followed this with 2 for 73 against Notts - CB Harris and George Gunn - and against the touring All India (England won the only Test), he bowled with speed but few wickets, three in the first innings and one in the second as India easily disposed of the University side by nine wickets.

He was back to five wickets in an innings, making it the round half dozen, against the Free Foresters for 71 runs (three bowled) and in bowling 54 overs he had twelve maidens and seven wickets. And a further five in a match against Sussex at Hove where he had John Langridge twice.

In the run up to the Varsity match he showed increasing speed against HDG Leveson Gower's X1, but only two wickets, and aggression against the MCC where he caught and bowled the Nawab of Pataudi for 112, held a fine catch in the slips but was extremely expensive in his first spell, including a wide and two no balls in a first over which cost 12, and 24 runs in the first three as he struggled to find his length, something that

was to bother him on the big day. In the second innings he bowled his
county captain Tom Pearce as well as RT Stanyforth, who led England's tour
of South Africa in 1927/8. His match figures were not good - 1 for 90 and
a slightly better 2 for 46 in the second.

The Varsity match, watched by over 40,000 people, was as tight as
ever, a tremendous game which swung both ways, and although Oxford
were 63 behind after the first innings they managed a draw as the rain came.
Cambridge won the toss for the seventh year in succession and put together
their third highest total in the history of the match. Wilcox and Ratcliffe
both made centuries (Farnes taking part in a ninth wicket stand of 54, of
which he made 11, with Ratcliffe) in 415 for eight (and Australian BW
Hone added a third with 167 for Oxford). But Wisden rebuked:

*'While producing in the course of three days a considerable amount of
high class batting the match will by many people be chiefly remembered for the
general poverty of the cricket prior to lunch on the opening day. Oxford neither
bowled nor fielded really well and the batting of Cambridge never rose above a
mediocre level. Far too many balls of poor length and direction were sent down
and a high proportion of these escaped fitting punishment. Matters improved as
the game progressed but early visitors to Lord's on Monday will not easily forget
the indifferent quality of the cricket displayed in the initial stages of the contest.'*

Farnes came under the lash too - and justifiably - because he
bowled 21 no balls. He tried to rectify this by starting his run further back
and taking the same number of paces but it did not work. He took 5 for 98,
his third five in an innings in his short season, and it would have been six
if Cambridge captain Hazlerigg had not dropped the great South African
Tuppy Owen-Smith at first slip in Farnes's first over. Oxford would then
have been 142 for 5 instead of 200 and the South African out for 31 instead
of 67 when he was eventually caught by Wilcox off Farnes.

EW Swanton remembers the match for one reason: *'I can still hear
the ball thudding round Peter van der Bijl's ribs and Peter giving great groans.
You could hear him in The Tavern. He was hit several times in the ribs and
Farnes certainly bowled pretty quick, not like Larwood and Voce. He was
certainly quicker than anything else after 1932, the next chap to him being
Gubby Allen. Larwood did not bowl fast after bodyline.'* Wisden said: *'Farnes
accomplished a capital bowling perfor-mance but proved a great sinner of no
balls being called on no fewer than 21 occasions.'*

He had had a brilliant season with Cambridge, ending with an average of 20.85 with 41 wickets for 855. His batting improved too - 11.20 in nine matches.

Once he had finished for the University and his form duly noted by the selectors (which resulted in him being picked for the Test trial in July), he moved slightly south back to Essex, for whom he played 11 matches during which he took five wickets in an innings against Hampshire at Southampton and Gloucestershire at Southend. This was a game that turned on the arrival of Hammond, who was unwell and did not want to play. But to any county Hammond was a star draw and at holiday time an even bigger one. He was the Bradman in this country at the time and until after World War Two. He pulled in the crowds like no one else in English cricket and Gloucestershire without Hammond on the August seaside fixture at Southend was bad news indeed.

When Essex heard that he was not coming they sent an urgent telegram to Bristol asking if someone could persuade the great man to change his mind. They followed that with a phone call emphasising what Gloucestershire already knew, that his presence was worth a fortune on the gate.

Hammond was persuaded and walked out at no. 10 after his train was late to face a sequence of bouncers from Farnes, who had already taken five wickets including three in four maiden overs. Farnes was not just bowling fast, he was digging them in too. Luckily Nichols bowled the no. 11 for a duck (he finished with 4 for 54) and bowled Hammond for four in the second innings, Essex getting revenge for their defeat a week previously at Cheltenham.

In his 11 games for Essex in 1932 Farnes took a total of 31 wickets. Two of these were in the match against Nottinghamshire. It was an interesting game for two reasons. Firstly, Wilcox did very well against Larwood, who was trying out leg theory prior to the 1932/33 bodyline tour of Australia, and caused one evening paper commentator to write of his 68 before he was run out: *'He played one of the best all-round innings of the season. It often happens that a boy who shows many strokes at school drops some of them when he plays in first-class cricket. Wilcox, happily, has reversed the procedure. He has more strokes now and he drove Larwood at times as if he were a slow bowler. He also demonstrated that leg theory, if properly approached, is so much fodder for the batsman.'*

58

Clearly Bradman and his men had not read this before the tour started! The writer added: '*All his strokes were perfectly controlled but he put his bat so hard against the ball that Voce's familiar collection of short legs were changed into long legs.*'

The other involved George Rainy Reynolds Brown, a slow left arm bowler who only played a few matches for Essex but announced that day that as he could never see the ball bowled by anyone of Larwood's pace he would stand upright with his head out of the way of the bounce. He did so and Farnes wrote: '*He then committed the blunder of strolling up the wicket while Larwood was walking back to the starting point of his run up, to tap down the pitch at a place that would have been a good length from the other end, thus exaggerating the shortness of Larwood's bowling. However fine a gesture this may have been, demonstrating George's toughness and his fearlessness of the consequences, it was not judicial - rather it was lunacy, suicide. Fortunately the wicket was dead.*

'*But the next morning when we were changing at Southampton to play Hampshire we saw his thigh. It would have made Turner sigh for no sunset of his could have equalled the vividness of pigment such a range of hues and Brown only made five.*'

In the match against Yorkshire at Scarborough Farnes took 2 for 135, Nichols catching both Verity and Fisher off his bowling, but Sutcliffe went his happy way, feasting off the Essex bowlers for the second time that season - Farnes was not there for the world record 555 first wicket stand game - and adding 194 to his 313 to give him 507 from the two games. He made up for the young man's absence from the earlier game by giving him the worst thrashing he received during his playing career. He took 75 off four of his overs as spectators ducked as the ball went whistling over their heads. The extremely smart and groomed Yorkshire and England opener was, on his day, as good as anyone in the world. He simply took the Essex bowlers apart and with Maurice Leyland, who was no slouch in the world class batting stakes (33,659 with 80 centuries and an England career from 1928 to 1938) put on 149 in 55 minutes. In six overs from Farnes, Nichols and O'Connor they scored 102 runs.

Farnes wrote: '*The worst hammering I ever had was at Scarborough when Sutcliffe and Leyland took 75 off four or five overs of mine*' - (it was actually only Sutcliffe) - '*Sutcliffe was actually dropped about thirteen times*

Ken Farnes

but his innings was still magnificent and very drastically he taught me not to bowl short to him. Then of course everything looked pretty black to me but the game has a spell and these disasters have to be taken.'

He finished the season rather heavily, his Cambridge exertions finally catching up on him, with a single wicket against Sussex and his evening of perfect contentment at Leyton against Kent. His overall aggregate for the season of 72 wickets at 24.30 each was eminently respectable.

The Cricketer, in its summary of the season, said: *'Some judges think that a really great bowler may have been found. He makes every use of his height with a very high delivery and he undoubtedly displays both variation and length. More than one of the best batsmen found that he baffled their concentration and his immediate future may be of considerable importance.'*

7.

1933

THE HIGHLIGHT of 1933, the year in which he amassed his highest wicket aggregate, was his third and last appearance for Cambridge in the Varsity match under the captaincy of his friend Denys Wilcox, and between them they hatched a plan to bowl leg theory at the Oxford batsmen. The fact that he had Farnes as the spearhead of the fast part of the plan was acknowledged in the press in the day preceding the game. One writer said: *'Farnes is one of the few definitely fast bowlers in England; he can make the ball fly, is very strong and does not tire easily. On a dusty Lord's wicket he would be most unpleasant to play; on any he is a menace to batsmen before they have got a sight of the ball.'*

The season followed the Ashes winning MCC Bodyline tour of Australia, 1932/3, which had almost caused a severance of relations between the two countries so angry did the Australians become at what they considered unfair tactics.

On the team's return the MCC issued an edict which banned this form of bowling, although the West Indies in 1933 tried it out on England through Constantine and Martindale, but the English wickets were not up to that form of attack and Jardine stood up manfully for over five hours to the kind of cricket he had given the Australians.

Almost seventy years on the arguments over bodyline and whether it was bodyline or just an advanced form of leg theory which dated thirty years, aided by the skill and sheer pace and accuracy of Larwood, still goes on. On a trip to Australia in 1999 I discovered in the Melbourne Cricket Ground Museum exhibits referring to it that are still as strongly against the way the English played in suggesting that the ball was bowled at the batsman. And I read in one of the many books around that a Queensland fast bowler, Hugh Pud Thurlow (possibly a distant relation), was going to spearhead the Australian bodyline retaliation if the Board had allowed it, which they did not. Pud was an unlucky fellow. His best bowling performance was in his first match, 6 for 59, and he never did better. In his only appearance for Australia, against South Africa, he managed 0 for 86 on a dead wicket and when joining Bradman, who was 299 not out, managed to run himself out, leaving the Don stranded one short of yet another 300. Pud was also the bowler off whom the Don scored his last runs to take him to his highest score (and then world record) of 452 not out.

However, when Farnes (referred to in the pre-match publicity as one *'who has only to bowl a length to reap a harvest of wickets'*), Jahingar Khan and RS Grant tried it on a dead pitch in the rain affected match at Lord's against Oxford in July it was nothing like the sun-soaked hard pitches in Australia, and in those early days of his career Farnes was nothing like as accurate as he was to become later.

At the end of the first rain-affected day, Cambridge, the favourites, had Oxford at 126 for 7. But, as The Times recorded, what a dreary day it was. Their man wrote:

'This they did after a prolonged period of leg theory bowling with an array of short-legs first at one end and then at the other until the spectator unaccustomed to this new technique was nearly driven mad for any of the glory and fun of it for which he may have travelled far to see this one great game of the year.

'And in this respect it must be made quite clear that the Cambridge bowlers who may be subjected to an accusation of having terrified their opponents by what is now loosely referred to as bodyline bowling did no more than any University captain would be expected to ask of them. Farnes alone bowled fast enough to warrant any blame and if the truth must be told he was so inaccurate that his short-legs might as well have been quietly sitting in the mound stand!

'Jahingar Khan and Grant bowled the normal off break round the wicket at medium pace to their shoals of sharks behind the batsman's body.

'Dull, deadly dull with never a ball that could hit the stump with never a stroke that could be attempted until the short pitched ball came to be swept to leg for four and the barren space on the offside which on such a day should surely be busy with young men sprinting to save four runs. Such was the play yesterday. Wonderful tactics no doubt, quite in order and with no suggestion of ill-feeling but utterly unsuited to what had gone before.

'To relieve this dismal story which was in fact felt by everyone at Lord's we

can rejoice in the beauty of the Cambridge fielding which without straining the point of what has been said before gained them wickets and equally so we can thank Walker for his batting (he made 46).

'The very first over suggested there was something strange in the air for Farnes who is admittedly a good and fast bowler, bowling from the Pavilion end, had three short-legs supplemented in the middle of the over by another who was brought over from second slip. One had expected him to start from the Nursery end so making some use of the new ball to go down the hill and his first three overs were in fact an arrant waste of time. The pitch must have been after some rain overnight at least fairly soft on top and hard underneath, an ideal opportunity for so good a bowler. Instead he chose to bowl rather short and most indeterminedly on the leg stump and sometimes well wide of it. That could not offer any wickets and certainly had no intimidating effect on Walker although he was once hit hard on the ribs.

'Farnes bowling almost to the return crease, was clearly not satisfied either by his foothold or the pace of the wicket and was relieved when 13 runs had trickled onto the board.'

The writer, who said that he hated the word leg theory, reported that Farnes came back on ten minutes before lunch with only two short legs and that later, when Oxford had scored 71, was brought back on again but by that time he had lost some of his pace and was quickly taken off. At the end of the day Farnes had not taken a wicket at all. He made amends the next morning, taking the last three wickets and ending up with 3 for 44 with Oxford all out for 164

Farnes saw it differently. He wrote:

'In 1933 we had a very exciting Varsity match. It began dismally enough for the first day was interfered with by rain. I have never seen such a quantity of sawdust strewn over the ground as it was that day at Lord's at the start of the match. Our attack this season was strengthened by the advent of that unique personality Jahangir Kahn who had been a member of the Indian touring team the previous year. Denys Wilcox had insisted on the side being first-rate in the field for it seemed to him only right that a University side should not permit any sloppiness in that direction.

'Until our match with Yorkshire at the beginning of the season Jahangir had not tried to bowl off-spinners around the wicket but was immediately successful with that form of attack.

'When Jahangir and Rolph Grant bowled to the leg-side field there was a *great outcry from the traditionalists who wanted to see the flashing cover drives that beautified the game in their younger days. There was also considerable confusion in their minds for many appeared to see no difference between this authentic attack and mine that had been inspired by Larwood's success in Australia. Their bowling relied on spin, mine with a similar field close in on the leg side relied to a certain extent on intimidation and on the difficulty of having to play rising bowls on the leg stump.*

'Perhaps the grousers then were somewhat justified in their criticism of my sort of bowling though there seemed little reason then not to try to use a method that had proved successful on an MCC tour.'

One reason why Farnes was not too keen on a plan to have lunch with the Oxford team was that Wilcox had been inciting him in the nets at Fenner's to try and bounce the ball over the wall at the back, and cracking his sides and rubbing his hands with enthusiastic merriment *'whenever I nearly succeeded in doing so, as he thought of what the Oxford boys would be in for. This was in the bad old days when bumping the ball was in vogue as a technique. Bill Bowes (Yorkshire and England) had it all wrapped up. I remember walking to Lord's with him from St John's Wood tube station one day when he was playing for the MCC against us. As we walked he produced a newspaper and drew a diagram on it of the way to set a field for that type of bowling. I felt that to bowl it really required a little hate. But not so Bill; he made himself thoroughly unpleasant to the batsmen without passion.'* Hence the old antagonistic spirit during the game - but not after!

Back to the match - *'The infuriating thing was that many of the critics did not distinguish between this mild form of bodyline and the off spin attack that the condition of the wicket fully justified.'*

He added: *'If no cover drives were seen that first day, and if the drizzle and interruptions made the day miserable, it was still a memorable one and the magnificent fielding should have dowsed the grumbles of the worst of the diehards. Sir Pelham Warner said it was one of the finest combined displays of fielding he had seen. The ground fielding was crisp and sure; no runs were given away. But the catching was superb and demonstrated the often but much unheeded remark about fielding being the most important part of the game. Grant made the most astonishing catch. He was fielding at short square leg, four or five yards from the bat. Jahangir bowled a full toss to FGH Chalk who hit it fair and square. Grant threw up his left hand and held the catch. It was all so rapid that there appeared to be a pause of a second or two before he looked up to find the ball in his hand. John*

Human and Basil Allen made some very snappy catches at short leg. Another memorable catch was taken by Jack Davies who sprinted round the square leg boundary and judged the flight of a hit by Owen-Smith off Jahangir perfectly.

'The result of all this was that Oxford who were undoubtedly a really good batting side were 126 for 7 at the close of play.'

Although there were plenty of moans and groans and shouts of protest when any of the Oxford batsmen were hit (their own fault because they missed their shot or did not play at the ball) Plum Warner had no objections. Under headlines of 'Superb Fielding by the Cambridge Team' and 'Leg Theory Brilliantly Exploited' he wrote of the placing of the field by Grant, and Khan bowling with only two men, the other with only one at mid-off, on the off side: *'This setting of the field, with the bowlers keeping an accurate length, to all intents and purposes reduced batting to practically a one stroke game but it was very successful in its results. It has in the past been exploited over and over again by the Australian Trumble and many another slow to medium paced right handed bowler.*

'There was some comment on the lines that this leg theory bowling made the batting dull. But the leg theory as exploited by Khan and Grant, was bowled to me and others by H Trumble on the Melbourne ground as far back as 1904. I have always maintained that it is the course of the ball, that is, its length and not so much its speed, to which those who object to leg theory, or bodyline bowling as the Australians call it, take exception. The tactics employed by Khan and Grant are nothing new and quite fair and legitimate. There is no parallel between them and the leg theory which was the cause of the controversy in Australia.'

Farnes later wrote: *'The next day Jenkins made his first contribution to saving his side by making 26 very valuable runs and Oxford were all out for 164.*

'Rain came again and ended cricket for the day. There seemed little prospect of a result with so little of the game played by the beginning of the third and last day's play.

'Cambridge made 209 and Oxford went in again at 4.15, 45 behind. Hone, the Oxford captain, suggested we should stop a little early to avoid some of the tedium of a tame draw but Wilcox rightly did not agree.

'In an hour they had lost six wickets for 32. An hour and ten minutes were left for play. Jahangir bowled the South African, Melville and Owen-Smith, and I took four wickets (for 27). Just before he bowled Owen-Smith Jahangir said to me "I will bowl Tuppy and then you finish them off."'

Ken Farnes

But, Farnes who was described in one paper as *'bowling like a lion'*, honestly confessed, *'I wasn't able to do my part. Chalk came in and though he had a narrow escape or two batted with splendid courage and defence. Jenkins joined him and refused to be shifted. We had shot our bolt and they held the fort.*

'Jenkins, without a doubt their last line of defence, had thwarted us a second time.'

'It was a great finish' says Wisden *'to what for over two days had threatened to be, owing to rain, a completely ruined fixture.'*

Warner also commented: *'He often dropped the ball short and with his great pace more than one Oxford batsman received a nasty blow, Oldfield the wicket-keeper being bowled off his jaw and Townsend hit his wicket after being struck by a rising ball'*

In an after-match note one Times report said: *'The Cambridge bowling tactics have produced much controversy and a deal of muddled thinking. There were a number of people at Lord's - and they were not by any means all Oxonians - who resented this 'damned leg theory nonsense' because it marred the attractiveness of the play and consequently their enjoyment. Surely spectators who assemble on this occasion should be the last in the world who need to be reminded that when Oxford play Cambridge it is, first and last, a match and not a spectacle.'*

Another commentator said: *'Farnes was clearly the best bowler of the match. He has all the attributes of a first-class bowler, height, strength and a good action. His chief fault at the moment is that he is inclined to bowl too short.'*

He had a great last season at the University. He and Jahingar vied to be top bowler and although Farnes with his extra pace and leg theory disposed of the chief opposition batsmen, Jahingar took more wickets - 44 against 41 - but at greater cost. Farnes took his at 17.39 apiece, great bowling.

He started with four wickets against Sussex (both Langridges again) at Fenner's, had poor matches in the context of wicket-taking against Yorkshire and the touring West Indies, but managed five wickets against Middlesex.

This game had an unusual ending for those days and subsequent attempts at the same kind of tactics have found people in serious trouble. Middlesex were in difficulty, trying to stave off defeat. Seven wickets were down and they needed 100 and more but were determined to stop Cambridge taking the new ball at 200, 20 runs away. For 50 minutes the batsmen, Durston and Ian Peebles (England leg spinner and later Middlesex captain), did not score a run. They ignored donkey drops, did not run for byes and just stood their place without any intention of scoring a run. It was some time before the crowd realised what was going on, particularly as Wilcox, the Cambridge captain, refused to allow his bowlers to deliberately make extras to take the score up to the point where Farnes could come on. Eventually the exasperated Wilcox called on his tall Essex colleague, who, with just five minutes of play left, bowled a ball at which Durston had to play, and even though the ball ran towards the boundary he still did not bother to run. But it broke the deadlock and then Wilcox himself caught and bowled Peebles and the match was unsatisfactorily drawn.

Farnes took four wickets against Notts and the Free Foresters and then had five in an innings twice in succession with ever increasing pace - against Sussex at Hove and his own county at Chelmsford.

The Times man commented on this match: *'With Cook in Farnes was at once put on again. The manner in which Farnes bowled to Cook in each innings* (he had him caught and bowled and caught for 38 and 20) *was rather unfavourably commented on but the most careful observation yesterday could not suggest that he bowled many extravagantly short balls and in truth to those of a normal length Cook played no kind of stroke at all. He slashed wildly at Farnes as soon as he had gone in and might have been caught first on the offside and then on the legside. After a period of tranquility to the slow bowler at the other end from whom he gathered as many runs as possible he was out to a magnificent catch at wide third slip off a perfectly normal ball from farnes which had moved away.'*

Farnes had no victims in the match against the MCC at Lord's and against Leveson Gower's XI when he bowled only three overs to save his ankle for the Varsity match.

At the end of his last year with Cambridge, as well as topping the averages, other games beckoned as well as playing for Essex, who managed fourth in the championship, their best since 1897 when they were third. In his first Gents v Players he took two wickets (Barnett and Watson), and then, to everyone's astonishment, made 22 not out in a stand of 78 with Douglas Jardine, the conquering hero of Australia. At the end of the season he played twice at the Scarborough Festival for Leveson Gower, tired and leg weary with his 1 for 202 in two innings against the MCC Australian XI and slightly better - 2 for 23 - in the match against the West Indies.

But for Essex it was quite different. He came down from Cambridge with a degree in history and geography and his tail well up. Essex were delighted and reported in Wisden: *'When he came into the XI at the end of July the attack was strengthened enormously, in his 10 matches taking 67 wickets at the cost of roughly 16 apiece. By general consent the best amateur fast bowler of the season he was just the man needed to back up Nichols. Ability to make the ball lift and swerve it combined with cleverness in disguising a change of pace and made him difficult to play even on good wickets. He had flashes of greatness and bowled particularly well against Somerset at Taunton when he dismissed 13 for 98 and especially at Southend when in Surrey's second innings his figures were 7 for 21.'*

In fact, he took five wickets or more in an innings five times, starting with his first game against Glamorgan where he bagged six of the Welshmen on his favourite Clacton wicket. He followed that on the same ground with five Gloucestershire wickets in the game - his pace was mainly responsible for their defeat - and four from Middlesex in the same seaside air.

In the Gloucestershire match Hammond was in imperious form. He began in his best style, driving with that thrilling stroke of his and generally giving the large crowd the anticipation that another masterly innings was coming. But when Farnes came on he tended to pitch the ball short and Hammond replied with violent and vicious tactics and hit a rising ball with a cross bat to the boundary over cover point, but when he tried to repeat this Pope caught him on the boundary and he was out for 44 after only 8 in the first innings.

Against Surrey Farnes was inspired and it was largely due to him that Essex had their first win over them since 1914. Essex made 420 and Surrey replied with 271 with Farnes taking four wickets for 116. Essex added 253 for seven (Gover taking 6 for 101) and then Farnes went through the Surrey side like a dose of salts. Four were bowled and he finished with 7 for 21, bowling unchanged and showing great skill in varying his pace. He was much more difficult to play than the day before and his pace off the pitch took a great toll of the Surrey batsmen who found him almost impossible to play.

He had a rest against Northamptonshire only managing four

wickets, but against Lancashire at Liverpool in a different kind of sea air he had 6 for 72 in their first innings, bowling two including Paynter, and making the ball rise disconcertingly on occasions due to varying his length rather than anything in the wicket. He had now passed 100 wickets for the season for the first time.

Farnes did even better against Somerset at Taunton - 7 for 72 and then 6 for 26, including three wickets in 15 balls. His great pace worried all the batsmen and his short pitched deliveries added to the agony with which none could cope on a wicked pitch that greatly favoured speed and an awkward bounce that made the ball get up to rib height.

He had five more in an innings against Worcestershire at Worcester and four and three in the two innings against Hampshire at Bournemouth. And then his Essex triumph ended on a quiet note (although the county did have a record breaking 13 wins), his speed spent for the season and only two wickets against Sussex at the Leyton ground.

His figures for Essex were outstanding - 67 wickets at 16.07 and his final seasonal analysis of 113 wickets for 2078 runs took him high up in the national averages.

There was an end of term report in The Cricketer. It said: '*When bowling normally he showed how good he is, one of the best in the country. It is therefore all the more regrettable that he should adopt methods that arouse profound antagonism. It was not only at Scarborough and Hove that he must have learnt how strongly other cricketers resent the policy with the ball that he chose to adopt. That some of the Essex side were of an opinion decidely unflattering about this no one denies, the effective result of his fast attack when conventional. It has been asserted that he has taken more wickets in the normal way than by the other. That is quite conceivable and certainly commendable.*' It is also true that Farnes may have been bowling to orders (he certainly was in the Varsity match), did not do anyone any damage and received very little criticism from other quarters, including some of the Establishment. By the next year he was a more mature, faster and more accurate bowler.

And the Australians were in England and he was shaping up to be the number one bowler to replace Larwood.

8.

THE ATHLETE

IN HIS THIRD year at Cambridge Farnes took up shot putting. At that time the standard of shot putting in Britain was abysmal (and still is in world terms). The world record in 1933 was 53 ft 1 3/4, amazingly held by a Czech, Frantisek Douda, because it was very much dominated by the Americans then as it is now. His record was shattered by the American Jack Torrance, who hurled the 16 pound shot to 55 ft 1 1/2 in 1934, a record that was to stand for 14 years. It is now 23.12m (75 ft 10 1/2 inches).

The British in comparison were almost pathetic. When Farnes went down to Fenner's for athletics as opposed to cricket, which was also played there within the boundary of its three laps to the mile cinder track (and the wrong way round too as normal four laps to the mile track were anti-clockwise, the University track clockwise), he did not have much to beat.

The British record was 47 ft 8 1/2 ins held by Dr Robert 'Bonzo' Howland, a Cambridge don, who had in his early days won the Oxford v Cambridge event three years in succession and was later to appear almost every time Britain had an international up to World War Two because he was unbeatable by any home grown talent. He won 20 international caps but never the Amateur Athletic Association championships, which then was - and still is - the most important event for British athletes, a major annual championship, attracting the best of Europe. In the AAA championships he came second eight times.

Bonzo increased his record to 48 ft 9 inches in 1935, and that stood like the world record for 14 years before John Savidge, a former Marine and almost as big as Farnes, became the first Briton to reach 50 ft. It was not until 1959 that Arthur Rowe, a northern blacksmith, reached 60 ft and then Geoff Capes, a giant of a policeman, reached 70 ft in 1974.

Britain (or England) have won titles in the European and Commonwealth championships but never in the Olympics.

When Farnes decided to try his enormous hand at shot putting it was because of his great interest in body-building and to help his College, Pembroke.

Shot putting in those days involved tucking the shot, which looked like a small cannonball, into the neck and then shooting across a small circle and thrusting the shot out of your hand and heaving it as far as possible. Nowadays, the technique is to pivot in the circle, which gives greater leverage and speed and extra power.

Farnes's first attempt at the shot went further than anyone else competing on a raw October day in his College trials. It resulted in a highly respectable throw of 40 ft 3 ins. He improved that by four inches three days later in The Seniors' sports, but finished second. He was never to be defeated by a Cambridge University athlete again in his very short career.

As Larwood and Jardine were doing their successful best to regain the Ashes 12,000 miles away in the sunshine, Farnes was out in the cold of Cambridge where the wind from the Ural mountains and Siberia has no break until it reaches the puny Gog Magog Hills past the City on the way to London and is therefore always cold.

In the biting January wind Farnes managed 42 ft 5 in a handicap event, which brought the headline *'Cricketer's great putt'* in the local evening paper. It was a feat he repeated against Trinity Hall before setting his personal best of 42 ft 10 1/2 against Emmanuel College.

In March he won his Blue by sending the shot out 42 ft 1 1/2 and winning the University sports, the championship from which the team to meet Oxford at the White City was chosen. His performances should have been good enough to ensure a win, but on the day he somehow lost two feet, and instead of winning finished a disappointing second to the American J Byles.

And that was that. His novice putting in the raw spring was good enough to place him in the top ten shot putters in the country, but he left athletics for good and concentrated on cricket in what turned out to be one of his best years.

9.

THE TEACHER

WHEN FARNES left Cambridge University in 1933 he played his usual August games for Essex before going to Worksop College in Nottinghamshire as a teacher, a job he kept until he joined up in 1940. He was made a housemaster and taught geography and history, as well as helping coach the cricket team and young athletes, particularly with the shot putt.

He was lucky that his headmaster, Dr FJ Shirley, liked to surround himself with teachers who had prowess in sport and could help establish the reputation of the school in wider fields (later as headmaster of King's, Canterbury, he was thrown out of the public schools' ruling body, the Headmasters' Conference, for alleged poaching of staff and pupils!). He allowed Farnes time off once he became a Test cricketer so that he was able to go on three long winter tours and, occasionally, when he became the spearhead of the England attack in the late 1930s, to play during the summer term in 1934 and in 1938 against Australia.

Otherwise, he was only able to play his games for Essex in the holidays, something other schoolmaster-amateur cricketers had to do in those days. His Essex Captain, Denys Wilcox, was in the same situation.

At Worksop Farnes was more than popular. He was someone who was very well liked and also very much admired. He was one of a crowd of young sportsmen that the headmaster Dr FJ Shirley appointed to his staff, such as cricketers RAS Farnfield, known as Ras (he played in the Freshman's match at Cambridge with Farnes), and DF Surfleet (who played for Cambridge University and 10 matches for Middlesex). And astonishingly the head made the new 24 year old master a housemaster in 1935, an almost unheard of age for such a post in those days.

The young teacher was interested in the arts; he painted and sketched with more than ordinary talent, his knowledge and appreciation of Art were sound and keen, his reading was wide and his literary interests unusual, his chief love being the stylists, among whom he revered above all George Moore.

He could even play the piano, although his range was limited to one song only, 'Smoke Gets in Your Eyes', which he could play fluently and which his mother loved. He would always play it to her when he was at home and she learnt to play it too, his nephew David told me.

Colleagues noted that despite his success and popularity, he never became swollen-headed; they thought that his innate modesty - almost shyness - prevented him from acquiring the usual faults of the outstanding athlete of becoming cocky and self-satisfied.

He was introverted a little, trying to find his real self and not quite sure what he wanted to do with his life. He was happy to be a schoolmaster, not aspiring to greater heights in the teaching profession, but very keen to earn and have a lot of money, although he never seemed to push this, being quite happy where he was. He probably would have climbed the teaching ranks but for World War Two because he had the talent to lead and had quite a large amount of administrative experience by the time he was 30. Where he would have found large sums of money is quite a different matter and he never really gave an answer to that.

School restricted his appearances in first-class cricket, but when time allowed he was able to play for Worksop in the Bassetlaw and District League in 1937 and 1938 (with colleague Surfleet) and for Doncaster Town in 1939 (with colleague Farnsfield), once opening the bowling for Worksop with South African fast bowler DPB Morkel, a rare occurrence indeed that a mid-England club side should have such a pair together in one match.

But nearly all Farnes's teaching time was spent exclusively at school. One ex-pupil, Dr Tony Ferguson, remembers Farnes like this:

He joined the staff at Worksop in the autumn term of 1933. At that time I was a 12 year old in the prep school which was then accommodated within the senior school, although run independently. This tall athletic figure was held in awe by all of us and tales of his prowess as a fast bowler spread more speedily than the ever-recurring rumours of the extra half day holiday that never came.

'I did not come into contact with him personally until I entered the senior school in September 1935 where for a year he taught me geography in the fourth

Ken Farnes

form.

'I have to say that his lessons are memorable chiefly because of his amiable manner and his un-erring accuracy with the blackboard cleaner, a cloth wrapped wooden object measuring about 6 inches by 2 inches by 1 1/2 which he threw, dart-like, at the leading edge of some inattentive or troublesome boy's desk, the effect of which was to concentrate the mind wonderfully. All good natured stuff I assure you but not likely to be tolerated in this day and age!

'I lost sight of him as a teacher after this, much to my chagrin, being taught up to School Certificate level by another master, nothing like as prestigious as being taught by Mr Farnes!

'However life has its compensations and being a keen but not very good cricketer I scraped into the Colt's XI of 1937 and although we had our own master in charge we saw a lot of Kenneth Farnes on or around the first XI field where we were permitted to practice in the nets and play our school fixtures.

'At Worksop at the same time were two other masters who were very talented cricketers - RAS Farnfield (known inevitably as Ras) and DR Surfleet, both of whom had been up at Cambridge with Mr Farnes. Ras Farnfield came from a well known cricketing and footballing family (all Corinthians I think) and Desmond Surfleet played for Middlesex 2nd XI and occasionally their firsts during the summer holidays.

'I got the impression they both narrowly missed their Blues at Cambridge the season Farnes was awarded his.

'To watch these three in the nets and occasionally playing in a match, the School v the Masters for example, was an education in itself - and far more interesting than geography!

'He was appointed housemaster of Pelham in 1935, the house being named after the family name of the Dukes of Newcastle on whose land the school had been built. I was in another house and so did not get to know him as well as those fortunate enough to have him as their housemaster.

'Nevertheless I know of a few anecdotes which do not appear from his cricket statistics. In addition to his cricket he got his Blue for putting the shot. Also not well known was that after his triumph in the first (and his first) Test match against Australia when he took five wickets in each innings one of the newspapers described how he had been met at Worksop railway station by some of the boys and carried shoulder high back to the school.

'In 1937 Plum Warner (Pelham Warner, later Sir Pelham, England

74

cricket captain in the early 1900s and doyen of the game towards the end of his long life) *came to the school - it must have been for some special reason -and spoke in praise of Mr Farnes's bowling in the final match in the Ashes series in Australia, 1936/7, which Gubby Allen's side so nearly won. He took 6 for 90-something, quite a feat on those wickets and in those temperatures.*

'*My abiding memory of him is of a very tall, very modest, very handsome man. My! how many sisters' hearts and I dare say mothers' hearts, fluttered at the sight of him on High Days and Speech Days. He was one of the best, if not the best, fast bowler in England from the demise of Harold Larwood to the outbreak of war and although there were many fine cricketers killed in that conflict none saddened me as much as his loss unless it was Hedley Verity who I knew not but felt I did. Such was the veneration in which we held our schoolboy cricketing heroes.*'

Another former pupil, ex-Head Boy Henry Barker, also remembers him vividly:

'*He was my hero and idol. He was a very tall, extremely handsome man with a really fine physique. He was appointed to his post at Worksop by the late, famous and infamous, Fred Shirley who gathered together the best sportsmen with some kind of teaching experience and of course a degree - however minimal.*

'*Many unkind things have been said and written about Fred but he was a really brilliant headmaster with tremendous ambition for the school but, more especially, for himself. I believe he always wanted to be a Bishop and his move to King's Canterbury had the added attraction of becoming a Canon of Canterbury Cathedral; probably it was part and parcel of the job. He blotted his copybook by taking several boys and masters with him and this resulted in his being slung out of the Headmasters' Conference.*

'*Fred Shirley helped all those under his wing who had ability. Ken was given so much time off that we saw little of him in the classrooms when Test matches and other important fixtures were taking place.*

'*This was all good publicity for the school as was Ken's image and the press were always seeking him out. But he was really a very modest man and certainly not a show-off.*

'*I must have known him for about four years and I left school in the summer of 1938. He had a wonderful sense of humour and was the life and soul of the Staff Common Room.*

'*Ken had a most direct approach to most things and he would administer punishment on the spot. I recall one occasion when he was taking the Shell, the*

75

Ken Farnes

lowest standard of academic life in the senior school, for geography. A friend of mine, JD Bamforth, committed some misdemeanour. Ken, spying a rickety old chair in the corner of the room, pulled it to pieces and armed with one of the legs, said 'come forth Bamforth, put your bum forth Bamforth.' He administered six of the best there and then. There was no nonsense such as sending the boy for the Drill Book and making him wait for two or three weeks for this fearful and degrading punishment.

'Ken was, I honestly believe, the best fast bowler of our time and certainly to watch in action. His run-up and delivery was sheer poetry in motion and his follow through magic. When he returned from the Ashes tour of Australia he was on top form. This bronzed and perfect specimen of manhood with enormous hands, feet and boots, put a single stump on the cricket pitch and knocked it flying five times out of six.

'He taught me how to putt the shot and his coaching led me to getting school colours for athletics, only I think by beating the field with one putt against Achilles, the joint Oxford and Cambridge team in their annual fixture against the school.

'Surfleet was the only person at the school - and he a master - who could really cope to some degree with Ken at the top of his form. The school's opening bat, Walker, could also stand up to him but although I fancied myself as a batsman, I would have turned and run if I saw Ken in full flight.

'His death was a dreadful tragedy and a terrible loss of a wonderful athlete.'

Another of his pupils, Dr Robert Naismith, recalls:

'I used to watch fascinated as he practised bowling in the nets, sometimes into an empty net with just one stump and sometimes to fellow staff members, Surfleet and Farnfield, both of whom were very able batsmen. A cricket ball in his hand looked the size of a pingpong ball.

'The wicket at Worksop College was very true. The groundsman, Jack Wigmore, was from the staff at Trent Bridge and consequently Ken Farnes was able to bowl to us schoolboys at I suppose one half or two thirds pace.

'I was a reasonably good cricketer and one of my lasting memories is of hooking him for four. I kept the ball low and it was one bounce and over the boundary. I don't think I have ever hit a ball with such speed even later in University and club cricket. I think that he bowled a shortish bowl on the leg side deliberately to give me confidence; that was his way but he would never say so.

'He was a man whom I really liked and respected and I think that was an *opinion shared by my friends at school. His athletic walk sticks out in my mind whether on a sports field or striding up the dining hall to the Top table to say Grace.*

'I remember asking him what it was like bowling to Bradman and he said that once Bradman had been in for a couple of overs the best thing to do was to try and send him a ball from which he could only get a single and then have a go at the other batsman.

'Socially he was good fun. He and Farnfield on two occasions took two or three of the senior boys out to dinner at Firbeck Country Club where we were treated as younger equals rather than masters and boys. The story was told that one evening four staff members were returning from the Firbeck and decided to stop as it was too foggy to drive. After sitting for a while hoping the fog would lift one of them had to get out to empty his bladder and discovered that it was a beautiful clear and starry night and the fog was all on the windshield and windows.

'As a housemaster he was, I think, well liked by most boys. I remember being caned by him on one occasion for smuggling bread out of the dining hall and toasting it in my study. The rules stated that I must be caned and caned I was, but I felt that he thought it was all a bit stupid.'

In the matches against the boys, even bowling at half speed, Farnes was still formidable. In his last game before World War Two he managed 85 not out in a total of 217 for 5 declared (Surfleet made 37 and Farnfield 66) and took seven wickets as the boys were dismissed for 118. The school magazine reported:

'The Masters were fortunate to win the toss and batted first on an easy paced wicket. Rhodes and Royle bowled well in the opening overs but Surfleet was in good form and when Farnfield and Farnes came together the bowling received some very rough treatment.

'Farnes bowled at considerable pace and very accurately when the School opened their innings and none of the early batsmen faced him with much confidence. Six wickets were down for 55 and then came a lighter interlude when the fast bowler damaged his own wicket-keeper and he had to be removed!'

Farnes was a dedicated master and when away from the school he did not forget and kept up a regular correspondence with the Headmaster (and to the Headmaster of his old school at Romford too), telling him not much about the cricket, as was his self-effacing way, but about where he was and what he saw so that it could be passed on to the boys. From South Africa during that long timeless tour he wrote:

Ken Farnes

'Our fortnight in Rhodesia has been quite one of the most pleasant parts of the tour. It has been largely holiday and we had a day and a half at the Falls, after spending three nights on the train up from Johannesburg.

'As the train approaches you see what appears to be a dense smoke-screen rising from the bush and the native name for the Falls is Mosi-Oa-Tunya, the Smoke that Thunders. They were very full and magnificent and the spray drenched us in the Rain Forest and at various other places from which we watched the mile width of cataracts - but no hippos as the river is too full. It was one of the very few opportunities we'd had of seeing much wild life.

'We have seen native dances at the Crown Mine Compound in Johannesburg, been down the West Rand Consolidated Mine there and been shown the processes of extracting diamonds from the Blue Ground at Kimberley. We have seen the Union Buildings in Pretoria. attended a Dingaan's Day Service in the Cathedral at Johannesburg and civic luncheons everywhere, spent nights and nights in slow-moving trains, sweltered in the Karroo and already seen De Aar Junction several more times than we should have liked. We've surfed and fished at Durban, driven over the Four Passes at the Cape, seen the Snake Park at Port Elizabeth and, in addition, there has been quite a lot of cricket.'

10.

1934

ON 8TH JUNE, 1934 England, led by CF Walters, walked on to the field at Trent Bridge and Ken Farnes was with them, winning his first cap. The appointed captain, Bob Wyatt, was not there because Farnes, fresh from two terms as a school master, had broken his thumb in the Test trial at Lord's a week earlier.

The early morning mist had lifted and when Woodfull and Bill Ponsford came out to open for Australia, the young Essex man opened the bowling from the pavilion end with the wind blowing over his right shoulder. He had already had a go at them at Chelmsford a month before. In an inspired spell he bowled Woodfull and McCabe and had Bromley caught in his 3 for 111. It was a game spoilt by rain and also - for the crowd - by the fact that neither Bradman nor Oldfield were playing. So Farnes knew the way the opening pair and most of the other Australians batted and was ready for them.

His first over was a maiden and by the second and third over he had warmed up and was making the ball swing in to leg and lift, and had moved his field to have two short-legs. The batsmen left deliveries down the leg side and when Farnes sent down an over of good length balls outside the leg stump Ponsford took three balls on his thigh rather than apply the full face of the bat, although he then edged one through gully for four. He went on like this for eight overs, four of which were maidens, for only 11 runs.

When Australia were 75 without loss the experts in the pavilion were looking for Farnes to return because he was the only bowler looking as though he would get a wicket. And when he did return he dismissed Ponsford first ball, caught at the wicket for 26.

The legendary Jack Hobbs, by then retired after 61,237 first class runs and 197 centuries, was now a journalist and he reported:

Ken Farnes

'Here was the wicket for which we hoped and the crowd was delighted. The next man in was Brown, a youngster having his baptism in England v Australia tests. He had to take the remaining five balls of what proved to be a very fine over. Farnes was faster than his action suggested. His great asset is his height for it enables him to make the ball come up at an acute angle.

'Five minutes from the break Farnes got his second victim. Woodfull made a half cock shot at a ball outside the off stump and played inside it. The ball flew to the left hand side of Verity in the gully. It went so low and quickly that the Yorkshireman appeared to be taken by surprise but as the ball was passing him he dived and got it one handed inches above the ground, a wonderful catch with perhaps just an element of luck.'

Woodfull made 26. It brought in Bradman who crashed two fours off Farnes, one by lying back and cutting him through the covers to bring up the 100, but before the fours he made a wild shot at a ball which went just over his leg stump. Farnes recalled:

'I well remember him coming in to bat that day, the first time I had ever bowled to him, and seeing his expansive smile as he passed me on the way to the crease. He had begun the season with his usual double century at Worcester and had shown a tendency to go hammer and tongs for the bowling at the very start. And here in the Test he tried the same dashing tactics. He swung at my first ball with all his might and missed it; it missed the leg stump by the merest fraction of an inch. Nor did he settle down then but played a scrappy innings of 29.'

What a difference an inch makes! If he had bowled Bradman his name would have been up in lights forever more and he would have played on and on for England no doubt. Those were the days when a newspaper billboard only had to say 'He's out' for most of the nation to understand what it meant. Farnes had the Don caught behind by Ames in the second innings but by then it was not the same. First ball in your first Test is one thing, second innings quite another, even though a considerable feat in your first Test.

However, it did not happen so speculation is useless. What did happen was that Farnes dismissed McCabe again - the second time he had had both Woodfull and McCabe in a match - and he made it a hat trick in the second innings!

On the second day McCabe, who was 50 not out overnight, was

using his favourite hook shot to great advantage when Farnes dropped one short, but he soon fell, attempting an onside shot off a ball that popped and Leyland held an easy catch. Hobbs recalled:

'On this day Farnes started rather more slowly than he did on the first day and, as was the case then, appeared to take some time to warm up. Perhaps the pace reduction was not so real as it looked as he has such an easy action and he bowled well.'

He certainly spoilt Chipperfield's day. The 27-year old all-rounder from New South Wales was playing in his first Test and went into lunch 99 not out. His stomach must have been churning as he waited to go back out again and face Farnes. After the long 40 minutes he played the first two balls, but the third got up sharply and, playing forward, he was caught behind by Ames. Farnes remembered:

'Chipperfield, who had played very little first class cricket all, pulled the game round and by lunch time he had made 99 in his first Test. The interval, during which he ate nothing in order not to affect his form, unsettled him. In the first over afterwards he might have tickled one from me round to leg and probably would have done at any other time but he missed it. Then, having lost confidence, he played an undetermined stroke and edged one to Ames to take the catch behind the wicket. It was most unfortunate for him not to join the select few who had made a century in their first Test.'

His final wicket was that of Bill O'Reilly, when he knocked his stumps everywhere, finishing his first Test innings with the magnificent figures of 5 for 102. Farnes wrote of the lead up to this first Test triumph:

'I got into the trial match early in the season and bowled fast enough to break Wyatt's thumb, an injury that kept him out of the first Test and affected his batting throughout the season. He used to wear an aluminium shield over it later on, and occasionally when making a forcing stroke, ball and thumb piece would flash away together so that you didn't know quite which to watch.

'The comparative lack of competition amongst fast bowlers that year helped me get into the England side for the first time. For Larwood had damaged his foot beyond adequate repair on the rock hard wickets of Australia, Clark had strained himself in the trial match, Gubby Allen was not by then available and I have an idea that Bill Bowes was not fit. Morris Nichols became twelfth man.

'With something of that dreamlike lightness that I had felt at Chelmsford in my first county match I opened the bowling with a maiden and George Geary

*opened from the other end. Woodfull and Ponsford began very circumspectly, the
wicket being a trifle green. Earlier in the season I had played for Essex against
Nottingham at Trent Bridge and had got nothing out of the wicket at all. The
wicket however must have been better for in my second spell I had both their
wickets.*

'*During the afternoon an incident occurred that distracted all attention
from the match for a time. In order to prevent pirate firms from taking
photographs of the match, the people who had the right to do so from inside the
ground rigged up lines of gas-filled balloons to obscure the view from their rivals
perched on rooftops outside the Trent Bridge enclosure. Precarious scaffolding was
erected by the pirates to raise their cameras above the lines of obstructions and a
war of manoeuvres went on. One large balloon, a little smaller than a barrage
balloon, dominated the scene and completely spoilt the chances of the cameramen
on a house top near the main gates of the ground.*

'*In desperation they sent a man along on top of a taxi to cut the moorings
of the monster. Soon after England had begun her innings the balloon went up. It
soared into the heavens, holding up the game but descended some safe distance
from the scene of the conflict.*'

Australia were all out for 374 with Chipperfield top scoring and
England replied with 268 with Hendren 79, Sutcliffe 62 and Geary an
unexpected 53. Farnes says: '*As we were over a hundred behind it seemed safer
for us to play for a draw and I was told that we did not particularly want
Woodfull's wicket to fall on that, the third night of the match. Perversely I
knocked his leg stump out of the ground in my first or second over. Hammond
bowled Ponsford early on too.*'

In came Bradman. Jack Hobbs said: '*It is worth setting on record that
Bradman began his innings much as he did in Australia on the last tour against
Larwood. When Farnes was bowling he made one or two weird shots.*' Farnes
dismissed him for 25 making a defensive stroke from a ball that got up just
above ordinary height and he got a touch and Ames took the catch.

McCabe was going very well into the fourth day, but when he was
88 he had a wild slash at a ball from Farnes and was caught at first slip by
Hammond. This came when the Australians were going flat out for runs
and soon after Hammond caught Darling off Farnes for his ninth wicket
and the pair combined again to take the wicket of Chipperfield. Farnes
finished with 10 for 179 in the match, a wonderful achievement for anyone

in their first Test, but typically (and irritatingly!) modest he does not mention it in his autobiography.

All he had to say to end such a momentous occasion was about his batting in the second innings. Woodfull declared at lunchtime with the score at 283 for 8, leaving England 380 to get in four and three quarter hours. England batted poorly (Walters top scoring with 46) but it always seemed that time would run out before all the wickets had fallen. It was not to be. Tiger O'Reilly was in the mood and took 7 for 54. Farnes wrote: *'I remember walking gloomily in to bat with the clock showing less than quarter of an hour to go and walking back still more gloomily with the hands very little altered.'* Oldfield caught him at the wicket and Australia were home with 15 minutes to go.

For Farnes his triumph (which the boys at College loved so much they met him at the gates on his return and chaired him up the drive) was spoilt by injury. He damaged his heel in the pits dug by the bowlers in the crumbling soil at Trent Bridge and he should not have played in the second Test at Lord's, not knowing the injury was as bad as it proved to be. It kept him out of the last three Tests, the final one giving Australia back the Ashes with a victory by a ridiculous 562 runs in what was dubbed as the great timeless Test (later to be usurped in South Africa in 1939). Ames could not bat and England needing over 700 to win managed just 145. Nothing changes.

The second Test was a big disappointment for the Essex giant. Although he did not bowl badly, hampered as he was by his damaged foot, he took no wickets, although he came very close on several occasions with chances not taken as Verity went through the Australians on a sticky, worn wicket. It was the first time England had beaten the old enemy at Lord's in 38 years and Verity's 7 for 67 and 8 for 43 (including 5 for 1 at one stage) were exceptional performances.

Bowes, Clark and Allen made up the England pace attack for the rest of the series, while Farnes bowled as often as possible for Essex, who dropped four places in the table. He had managed a couple of games for them in May to try and win his place in the England side. They were the 1 for 119 on a dead pitch at Trent Bridge and his three wickets against the Aussies, the team he had played hookey to watch as a disgruntled bank clerk four years earlier.

Ken Farnes

He was back with the county at the end of his first summer term. His captains - as ever Essex had more than one and often three - Tom Pearce and Denys Wilcox, alternating when schoolmaster and business commitments allowed, reported: *'No other county could in 1934 command the services of so many bowlers of pace as Essex and yet, paradoxically though it may seem, the fact that the bowling was less effective than in previous seasons accounted primarily for the county's drop from fourth to eighth place. It was not so much that any particular bowler fell away but because for one reason or another Essex could rarely field their best side.'*

At that time Essex undoubtedly had the best group of fast bowlers in English cricket: Nichols, not quite as fast as Farnes but more accurate and experienced, Farnes, the great white hope of English cricket and eventually the fastest of them all, and Hopper Read, who certainly up to 1936 was the fastest of the Essex trio. He had a run up that caused great merriment among those who saw him for the first time, until he actually dispatched the ball and then the laughter stopped. The captains reported:

'The Test matches took away Nichols and Farnes, the former as twelfth man. Nichols too for most of the summer was far from fit, probably the result of touring India with the MCC team, and although Read accomplished really splendid work in several matches Essex did not breach their full strength in attack until after the middle of July.

'From July 13 they went through to the end of the season unbeaten. Farnes, who up to that point had appeared only in the match at Trent Bridge in May, took part in all the last six matches and of those Essex won two and gained first innings points from three.

'The value of Farnes to the side was again very considerable, more especially as Nichols was unable to do himself justice. Farnes in all took 37 wickets and the cost was much the same as in the preceding summer.'

Those 36 wickets in August came in a great flourish after a tame start against Worcestershire at Worcester where he managed just two. Against Somerset, further west, he had their first three batsmen for six in the first innings and ended with seven wickets.

By then his heel was better and at Northampton he claimed six of their men for four apiece in the first innings, five bowled and only Bakewell caught, in a rain affected match. His bowling was deadly and they just did not know how to play him as the ball thundered towards their stumps.

84

Essex, with a fine century by O'Connor, were always the better team but the rain prevented a result. For good measure, Farnes had two more in the second innings and then took five of Lancashire's first innings wickets at his favourite Southend ground by the sea, with another when they batted again in a tightly fought match with Nichols taking five to match his partner.

Yorkshire (without Sutcliffe and Leyland) came under the lash even more heavily on the same ground when Farnes took 4 for 72 and then 7 for 59 as Essex beat them for the first time since 1911. Wisden said that Farnes bowled in *'irresistible style'* as he hit the stumps of Barber, Turner, Robinson and Macaulay and had Hutton and Davidson caught as they tumbled to 112 after Essex had scored 441 for eight with Wilcox 109. The last eight Yorkshire wickets went down for 37 after Farnes had removed Hutton and Davidson.

His final game was against Gloucestershire at Gloucester and he took two wickets to bring his county tally to 37 at a cost of 16.40.

He played in two more games, at Scarborough, first for the Gentlemen against the Players, where he took six wickets, three in each innings including Sutcliffe, Leyland and Hendren - and actually managed double figures with the bat - 18 not out!

The other was against the Australians, who were coming to the end of a long and tiring tour. It was their 33rd match out of 34 but it was true festival stuff in front of a huge crowd and played in that spirit. Bradman and McCabe made centuries and Ponsford 92 as they knocked up 442 for five in 280 minutes. Farnes had his old regulars - McCabe (for the fourth time) and Chipperfield - as well as Brown, Ebeling and O'Reilly to notch up five wickets in an innings for the fifth time in the season. He would have had Bradman as well if Wyatt had held a chance in the gully,

Jack Hobbs was there and said: *'Bradman was in his finest vein, hitting hard in all directions and this in spite of really excellent bowling by Farnes.'*

That ended a year in which he played in only 13 matches but had the excellent figures of 62 wickets at an average of 21.50. He was closing the gap on Larwood and Verity - 17.25 and 17.63 - and the reward for his fine bowling was a trip to the West Indies. It cost him 100 pounds in salary for the time he was away but he thought an England tour was well worth it, and the MCC gave him 25 pounds in compensation.

11.

WEST INDIES 1934/35

FARNES was very much a new boy among seasoned veterans like Wyatt, the captain, Hammond, Hendren, Ames, Leyland and Iddon when the party of fourteen left Avonmouth in the small liner Cavina for Barbados in December.

It soon proved that he was not much of a sailor, suffering sea sickness in the choppy Bristol Channel and the north Atlantic before getting his sea legs and settling down to enjoy his first tour.

Christmas was celebrated on board and the Cavina Cavorters played the Cavina Rollers at deck cricket, which ended in a draw with 93 runs each, the highlight of the voyage.

The ship anchored off Bridgetown, Barbados on December 27 and from their boats the local men recognised the players from newspaper photographs. One called to Leyland: *'you Mr Leyland? I bat left handed too.'* Farnes was also spotted. *'You fast bowler? We know all about you. You won't trouble us.'* And the man was right.

Those back in London who picked the team thought fourteen players was enough, but because of injury they were wrong. A strained neck kept Farnes out of two representative games and reduced his pace so that the MCC did not really have a fast bowler. At the same time the batting against the first batch of West Indies fast bowling attacks - Constantine, Martindale and Hylton - came unstuck. Wyatt described their attack as the best of its kind in the world - and how often have we heard the same description of their successors over the years?

They managed to take all but 17 of the 64 wickets that fell to bowlers in the series of four games, which resulted in England losing to the West Indies for the first time - two wins for the home side, one for the MCC and one drawn.

For Farnes it was a bitter blow. He had looked forward to reproducing his England and Essex form on the hard wickets but it never happened. The team had only one proper net practice before their first match of twelve, against Barbados, in which MCC came very close to defeat. Only solid batting by Patsy Hendren and Wyatt saving them. Farnes took a wicket in each innings and made 22 runs with the bat.

There was a huge crowd for his first experience of this kind of cricket where the crowd knows everyone and chatters away all day, so much so that one spectator, annoyed by a man who kept walking up and down in front of him, shouted in exasperation, *'keep yo'self still, man. Don't humbug my brain.'*

Farnes said after the game, in which he bowled 37 overs, *'I have never been so stiff in my life as I was after that first day's hard play before the muscles had had time to get used to the work. It was owing to this that I pulled a neck muscle so badly that the injury persisted throughout the tour and needed a specialist's attention when I got home.'*

It certainly ruined the tour for him. He did not play in the next match when Hammond made 281 and big 6' 4" 19 stone fast bowler Jim Smith 83, incredibly last man in and making 50 while Hammond made three.

Farnes went on trips and excursions to view the island and to visit any art gallery, which, as a painter himself, was something he did at every place on this and subsequent tours Before the first Test, he went to a garden party. He recorded:

'Eight hundred guests strolled about the extensive grounds where mahogany-trees, flamboyants, frangipani and shack-shacks provided plentiful shade. About a six o'clock when the crickets and frogs had begun their night-long tremulous chirruping, the brilliant crescent of the moon in an unaccustomed recumbent position gleamed in the deepening sky and in the sky opposite we noticed a great bank of cloud that glowed with the pink hue of the sunset. We were not to know then that this cloud was to help produce a very remarkable game of cricket beginning on the morrow.'

Forget the poetic style, but he was right. Rain fell in the night and having already seen how wickets behaved after rain Wyatt won the toss and sent the West Indies in to bat. By then the strip had been rolled and then rained on again and *'it was a real pig of a wicket'* said Farnes *'suited especially to fast bowlers. Occasionally the ball skidded through but more often than not it reared up, making it necessary to bowl half volleys to force the batsmen to play at the ball. The key fielding position was close in square leg and gully too was important.'*

He claimed he had a certain amount of luck in taking 4 for 40 - he made the ball rise awkwardly - as they had West Indies at 31 for 5 at one point before they recovered to 102 all out. It was to be his best analysis of the tour.

England, thanks to Hammond's 43, got to 81 for 5. Rain fell heavily during the night and play on the second day did not start until tea, when Wyatt called for a light roller. Farnes wrote: *'There is nothing more boring than waiting on the weather at a cricket match and the crowd began to voice their impatience outside while we cursed among ourselves within the pavilion.'*

Once play did resume Hammond, protecting his left ear, was caught and Errol Holmes was out first ball. The wicket was impossible so Wyatt declared even though 21 runs behind.

Within minutes Jim Smith had Grant, the West Indies captain, Martindale and Achong out for four and then Farnes got Headley, the danger man, for a duck, caught off his thumb, and the bowler's only wicket as the home side declared at 51 for 6.

The lead was only 72 but the wicket was now at its worst and the ball was stopping and kicking. So - astonishingly - Wyatt sent Farnes and Smith out to open! His reasoning was that they were the tallest, Farnes two inches higher than the Middlesex man at 6'4", and their heads would be out of reach if the ball kicked. Farnes wrote:

'Martindale opened the bowling from the pavilion end - the end from which nearly all the wickets had fallen - and Jim made mighty swings without connecting with a single ball as each one swung away. Hylton from the other end bowled too short. In the next over Jim continued his tactics and eventually got a touch.

'Christiani behind the stumps took the catch. Holmes came in. When I got out the third victim in the match to a full toss (for five - and very sick about it) I found the whole side ready with pads on as the order of batting was decided by the condition of the match.

'Errol had told me to advise Bob to send Patsy in as it was now possible to play the hook shot of which of course Patsy was the master. And before very long he had hit a six off Hylton square on the leg side and the total began to look better. With an hour left for play we needed 50 to win.'

Holmes and Leyland were quickly out (Leyland claimed that two was a good score on that wicket) and four wickets were down for 29 *'and the game was in the tensest state imaginable. Hammond, the hope of the side, walked to the middle. The crowd was in a frenzy of excitement. As we watched we willed success to our batsmen and urged the ball to reach the boundary as if it were a live thing.*

'Hendren's innings was a masterly one, the soundest in execution and technique in the match. He batted standing well away to the leg side to be in a better position to avoid the ball that lifted or popped and to prevent himself from being forced to play at such a ball pitched on the leg stump and giving a catch to short square leg. He made 20 excellent, invaluable runs. Then Martindale, bowling with wonderful speed, stamina and accuracy, bowled him one that seemed to be just over a half volley and he was gone. Hammond, considering rightly that on such a wicket defence was useless, launched a fierce attack on the bowlers and using all his power smote the ball all over the field. It was an extraordinary innings for a Test match - but then the match itself was extraordinary - and all decorum might go to the winds. The readiest were the most successful methods. With powerful cross-bat swings he kept on driving the ball over mid off's head, forcing the fielders to go deeper and deeper.'

Paine went quickly and when Wyatt went out to bat the score was 48 for 6 with 24 runs still needed. It was still a fast bowler's wicket and Wyatt joined the lashing, missing but staying in. With the score at 69 Martindale, fast as ever, bowled another over to Hammond, but the third ball was not like the others and Hammond lifted it clean over the long off boundary for six and victory. Martindale had taken 5 for 22 - *'as fine a piece of bowling as you could ever wish to see'* - but Hammond had made 29 and MCC were home by four wickets.

Farnes loved Barbados – and Trinidad too. At the island's Savannah cricket ground at Port of Spain he found matting wicket laid on fine grained mud that set like concrete. He went round the beauty spots before the first match and came across a cricket match between women. It was held in front of a largish crowd and he was surprised to see one player stop a mighty smite to cover on the nose, tossing the ball back without a *'quiver or any sign that she considered the incident the least bit untoward',* and a promising slim Indian girl who would have made quite a good score if her partner, a huge black woman, had not been too ponderous to run.

He also leapt overboard from a launch that was taking them out for a jaunt when Yorkshire batsman Bill Harbord jumped aboard causing the launch to lurch violently. If Farnes had not jumped he would have gone overboard anyway because of the slope which sent several into the water. Farnes wrote:

'When I came to the surface and scrambled on to the jetty a scene of considerable confusion met my gaze. As I looked Hammond came to the surface still wearing his hat. This he proceeded to doff and bade everyone good morning. Leslie Ames was paddling about exercising his newly acquired ability to swim. Team manager Carlton Levick was splashing after his panama that was being carried away by the wavelets and Maurice Leyland, refusing to be disturbed by the incident, was swimming around nonchantly fully clad, trying to make it appear that he had intended to bathe anyway. Wyatt and Holmes and the rest in the launch were laughing themselves silly.'

His neck strain was giving him much trouble and he missed the first match but played in the second, taking two wickets in each innings, having Learie Constantine's brother caught in the first and Learie in the second.

But the neck ruled him out of the second Test and Wisden said: *'England were undoubtedly handicapped by the inability of Farnes, owing to a strained neck muscle, to turn out; having regard to the success achieved by the West Indies pace bowlers the absence of the Essex man probably represented a greater loss than most people realised.'* The home side won by 217 runs, 302 and 280 for 6 declared, to MCC's 258 and 107, Hammond having a miserable game with 1 and 0 and no wickets.

The neck was better by the time the English party reached British Guyana after more sightseeing, and he took two wickets in a drawn game at Georgetown, notable for 148 from Hendren's ever-productive bat. Farnes wrote:

'The cricket ground is pretty with a good grass outfield and wicket and trees most of the way round which gave it a not unEnglish atmosphere. One stumpy tree on the side opposite the pavilion was more or less permanently reserved for Daddy Bell who rang his handbell whenever our opposition did anything good in batting or fielding or whenever he considered it was time for them to do so. From him came the only piece of discourtesy we suffered. He cast obeah on our skipper - obeah being a kind of black magic. Slung over a branch of his tree was a small coffin in which, surrounded by flowers, reposed a newspaper photograph of Wyatt!

'Bob certainly had bad luck there. On our first afternoon, at net practice, I bowled a short ball that he tried to hook. It was much slower than he thought and came off the dead turf more slowly. His stroke was therefore too soon and when he

had finished it the ball struck him in the rib, the muscles of which were stretched at that moment.

> *'It knocked all the breath out of his body and for some time afterwards he used to get sharp twinges in the spot where he had been hit in spite of ray treatment. He was even X-rayed but no crack or trouble of any sort was located. In addition he was mildly unwell in British Guiana. Daddy Bell's obeah seemed to have worked!'*

Farnes found the cricket there remarkably dull and reckoned if he had bowled well on the rain affected pitch they would have had the opposition out for less than their 102. Then the turf dried out and was dead and when a draw became inevitable Hendren was put on to bowl to put some life in the proceedings. He marked out an enormous run with huge strides and then tripped up lightly to the crease and bowled off the wrong foot giving away 11 runs in his only over. The crowd loved it.

In the next match Farnes's neck was playing up badly and although he bowled he did not get a wicket and missed the third Test which ended in a low scoring draw. Farnes thought it was a rather dull affair from his seat as a spectator, the highlight being Big Jim Smith's six off Constantine, which he clouted not only with Herculean power but timed it perfectly as well so that it seemed to be still rising as it skimmed over the right sightscreen into the trees, causing numerous black 'Scotsmen' to tumble from their perches with a great clamour and the sound of cracking branches. Hammond, who knew all about big hitting, said it was the best hit he had ever seen.

Farnes admired Learie Constantine. He described how he bowled fast *'with that lithe easy action of his which gives him the appearance of bowling in gym shoes.'*

The tour went on and on and Farnes kept seeing the sights and tasting every opportunity offered him, including a ride up a mountain on a donkey. He wrote: *'I was now a trifle apprehensive. "Not frightened" as a batsman once said when asked if he was scared of a certain fast bowler "just a trifle apprehensive."'* But the mules were docile in the extreme and there was no need to worry.

He enjoyed Jamaica but then he enjoyed everywhere he went with his keen, enquiring mind and his ability to see things through an artist and writer's eye so that could record what he saw and his feelings about everything (except cricket most of the time) afterwards.

The neck was better and in his first game for almost a month he was revving up to get at the batsmen, which he did with extreme hostility, taking the first four wickets for 16 runs on the Melbourne Park ground in Kingston. Then Barrow and Moody stopped the rot and he finished with 4 for 68 off 26 overs and did not get another wicket in a drawn match. He was rested for the second game in Kingston, making sure he would be fit for the final and vital Test, and saw George Headley and Barlow limbering up with centuries in another drawn game.

But by now the injuries were causing severe problems in the team. In the game in which Farnes played - troubled by his neck injury - Eric Hollies was off the field with a leg strain, Farrimond of Lancashire was hit on the head while fielding, ending of his tour, Hammond and Iddon both tore muscles in their legs and all the members of the team came out one by one to field as subs except Ames, who had not been expected to be needed and had gone off for the day. So MCC had to borrow one of the Jamaicans and he was the man who held a brilliant catch to dismiss Headley. Luckily, when the next match began after a day's rest Trevor Arnott, who used to play for Glamorgan and happened to be in Kingston, was available and was delighted to play. He took three wickets. Farnes went off to see a blind osteopath who had been recommended by a former skipper of the West Indies, RK Nunes. Farnes recalled:

'He pulled my neck about a good deal, made it crack, told me I had two vertebrae out of place and began to haul me up on a sort of noose arrangement so that I felt I was on a gibbet.

'Another misfortune occurred to us that evening. Leyland was fraternising with the Navy and was entertaining them with his large repertoire of yarns. One exceptionally hearty sailor slapped him on the back and sent him off his chair. In falling he damaged his spine so badly that he was not able to move for days. This meant that one of our most dour players was out of the coming Test. It also meant that I had to field on the boundary, which incidentally I enjoyed very much, and I added to my physical woes by weakening an ankle, though not sufficiently to prevent me playing. With only a strained neck and ankle and a thrown out arm I was among the fitter members.'

The team of crocks realised that their prospects were not good. The series stood one apiece and although Hammond, Hollies and Iddon were on the mend they had not practised. Leyland was out of the game and Headley was in his best form playing on his home ground. On top of that West Indies picked their four fast bowlers, the usual trio plus Fuller. *'He was a big Jamaican with a slinging action who was a useful batsmen as well for he made a century against us in the previous match;'* Farnes wrote. *'It is seldom good tactics to have so many bowlers of a similar type'* - if only he had had a crystal ball and a bookmaker had offered him odds.... - *'but on this occasion the selection was justified though Fuller, as things turned out, was only required for an over or two to rest the others.'*

The home side won the toss and Farnes bowled Barrow very early on. It was his only success as the MCC toiled away with Headley, dropped at 70, making an undefeated 270 out of 535 for 7 declared. MCC scored 271 (Ames with 126 the only batsman to get going) and 103 with their bad luck staying with them. In their first innings a rising ball from Martindale broke Wyatt's jaw in four places when he had scored a single. The ball, says Farnes, went with the speed of light and before Wyatt had time to make any defensive shot the ball lifted and hit him full on the side of the jaw. The crack could be heard all over the ground. If you believe in such things the obeah was still with him.

It was a miserable end to the tour. However it did not dampen Farnes' lyrical view of it all. He took six Test wickets and was second of the regular bowlers in the Test averages (Hollies was top), although only playing in two matches. None of the bowlers did really well with GE Paine of Warwickshire taking the most wickets. In the other matches he had 18 wickets at around 30 runs a time and his batting average was pathetic.

But he still wrote as the ship Carare sailed from Port Antonio home: *'Looking back we saw the rugged silhouette of the Blue Mountains against the crimson glow of the sunset with the bonfire of banana leaves on the quayside making a miniature sunset that diminished rapidly as we moved slowly into the beckoning moon path across the homeward sea.'*

Ten days later they were back in the Bristol Channel to dock in Avonmouth. It was the end of March and the winter was almost over and another season was about to begin. He wrote: *'I looked back to the far sea horizon. Beyond, somewhere beyond, lay those islands - 'islands in blue of summer, floating on'. '*

He may have dreamt of a wonderful summer stretching ahead. He certainly would have done because he was still England's premier fast bowler. But it was not to be.

12.

OTHERS

THERE IS always one difficulty when writing about someone who is dead and whose career ended 60 years ago. Few of his contemporaries are alive and for those who are, memory is not always as good as it was. So to actually discover what kind of man Kenneth Farnes was and what his ability was, one has to rely on what was written at the time, aided by memories that are still vivid in the minds of those who knew him or played with him. In this I have also been helped by journalist Lionel King who sent out a question-naire to all the Essex playing contemporaries of Farnes who were alive in the mid 1980s, asking about his temperament and attitude to the game and his bowling. He received several replies and these are incorporated with those to whom I have spoken or corresponded. Their views differ greatly, some suggesting he could be temperamental (but who isn't on occasions? And in fact he wrote about his attitude in his diary that showed he could be like everyone else), others that he needed a good push to get him going, but all agreeing he was fast and furious on the field and a nice man off it.

Bradman once said that he found it more difficult in handling Farnes than Larwood, who, though not as fast, moved the ball off the wicket and delivered it from a much greater height. And Joe Hardstaff, weaned on fast bowlers, rated him ninth out of all fast bowlers he faced in a career that spanned either side of World War Two.

But to start at the beginning in his first season, Sir Pelham 'Plum' Warner was lunching at Lord's during the Middlesex v Kent match when one of the players, HTW Hardinge, went over to him and said: *'Mr Warner, I have seen an England bowler.'*

Plum wrote: *'He then went on to talk enthusiastically of the way in which a boy of 19 called Farnes had bowled, how tall he was and how finely built. Since that day Farnes has fully borne out his judgement.*

'Some of the best fast bowling I have ever seen was by him, GO Allen and Captain JWA Stephenson in the Gentlemen v Players match at Lord's in 1936, Farnes in particular bowling at the pace of a CJ Kortright, another Essex man, and sent the bails flying and the stumps somersaulting. It was tremendous in its speed and devil.

'With his great height, splendid physique and figure Farnes is not only a fine bowler but an impressive one to watch. His arm seems to come down from the sky and his deliveries hit the ground uncommon hard.

'That must have been a rare piece of bowling of his in the fifth Test at Melbourne in 1937 and other outstanding performances of his were 10 wickets in a Test match at Trent Bridge (his first) in 1934 and 11 wickets for the Gentlemen v Players at Lord's in 1938.'

Two points arise from that. His great height also allowed him to catch balls that lesser tall mortals could not reach and he was a fine fielder anyway. In his career he held 84 catches, mainly near the bat.

And his speed is illustrated by two examples of non-first class matches. Dicky Vere Hodge remembers playing against him for Essex Club and Ground and being caught off the end of his thumb on the boundary by third man. And one of his pupils, Dr Tony Ferguson, recalls in a match between masters and school at Worksop College that a ball clipped one of the bails which flew through the air and landed against the scorebox, a distance of some 60 or 70 yards. EW Swanton, that great judge of the game, told me:

'At his best he was a high class bowler. I saw some of the fastest bowling I have ever seen in this country in the Gentlemen v Players match of 1938. I do not think I have ever seen faster bowling, not by an Englishman in this country. He was a little miffed because they had dropped him from the third Test and he was showing them at Lord's.

'He was a charming chap and off the field a bit sleepy, relaxed and laid back but not at all when bowling. He took things as they came and was a great eater but none were so hearty an eater as Paul Gibb, the biggest I have ever seen - phenomenal.

'He was a very pleasant personality and a great favourite with the girls because he was very good looking. The South African ladies (Jim was covering the tour) had a very warm regard for him, buzzing around cricketers on tour as they always did. He enjoyed the birds fluttering around him.

'He had a good action with his arm right at the top. One thing about him *in that tour: he would bowl well at sea level but like others the height of Jo'berg did him. It is not unusual at 6000 ft. The altitude affects bowlers like athletes in the discharge of their efforts.*

'He bowled well all round. Nearly all fast bowlers have their days when everything clicks, other days they try just as hard and the machinery does not quite go. When he was fired up he was as fast as anyone in his day.'

Trevor Bailey of Essex and England and the BBC commentary team only saw him as a teenage schoolboy but he recalls:

'He was a fine bowler with a sensible short run and he achieved considerable lift as a result of his height and high action.

'I am pretty sure that Farnes and Nichols opened the Essex attack against Gloucestershire and Hopper Read came on first change. Wally Hammond reckoned he was just about the fastest first change he had faced as he was quicker than either of the opening pair though not as good a bowler.'

Vere Hodge also recalls:

'I have the most pleasant memories of him. He was extremely fit and used to show his special abdominal exercises and his ability to contract one half of his abdominal muscles at a time.

'He was rather serious minded but I got to know him quite well because he had a small sports car - an MG - which he drove rather fast and some were not keen on travelling with him between matches. However I became a passenger for most of the matches we played together and got to know him quite well. I enjoyed his company as we looked at life from different angles - a school master and a medical student.

'From memory I think he had his ups and downs and was a bit of a worrier at times. He used his considerable height to lift off the pitch for a good length ball and was very fast but not intimidatory. He thought about his bowling and bowled tightly to a plan and the setting of his field. He was not merely a speed merchant.

'I remember one incident which illustrates his sense of fun. We played at Ilkeston against Derbyshire who were leading the championship up to that time. Ken was bowling very well on a fast dry wicket.

'He had placed me to field at forward short leg almost in line with the stumps and very close to the batsman. Derbyshire were finding runs difficult and had not lost a wicket for a some time so I thought that I might be able to help soften up the batsman. So I said to Ken 'do you know what the batsman said to me just now'. This was pure fiction on my part and I knew that Ken would take it as a great insult

and was what was needed by Essex at the time. 'No' said Ken. I said that the batsman had said that he thought Mr Farnes was meant to be a fast bowler not a twiddly merchant. Ken considered this and said to me that he would show him something faster. I saw Ken re-roll his sleeves and hitch up his trousers. The next ball must have been as fast as any ball bowled anywhere at any time. The batsman backed away as it passed his chest and went very white and was obviously nervous. Another similar ball followed. The batsman started muttering. The third ball bowled him, smashing his stumps to his evident relief as he passed me on his way back to the pavilion. I thought it unnecessary to tell Ken of the exchange or comment.(The match was in 1937 and Farnes took 7 for 41 and 2 for 104 and made 41 no).

'It was a great honour to play for Essex with Ken. The county had two excellent captains. The professionals were welcoming to the amateurs who did not always behave as well as the professionals, though having to earn your living with some of the luck which goes with cricket can be hard to bear.'

Not all professionals were welcoming to the amateurs in some counties, particularly when the flood of teachers and students came eager and ready to play mid-July. Some professionals were kept out of the side because of it and some did resent it. But (although it is difficult after all these years to make an expert judgement because many are sadly not here now) many did not. The good ones like Nichols, O'Connor, Smith and Wade at Essex were in no danger. Those that were might even have been glad of a break for county cricket then was hard work, not just on the field but in long tedious journeys from ground to ground and players were nothing like as fit as they are today. There were a few puffing billies on the field of play and one great Essex batsman, Peter Perrin, undoubtedly lost any chance of playing for England because of his portly gait and lack of ability in the field.

One of his captains, Colin Bray, a cricket correspondent on several papers, who did not get all that much time to play but did well when he did and wrote a good book about the history of the county, said: 'I played frequently with him in his early matches for the county and found him more than promising. He was a fast bowler who could bowl exceedingly fast from a great height with excellent control. I was thankful not to have to bat against him. His heart was always in cricket as his short but brilliant career showed. His death during the war was the greatest loss to English cricket.'

Hopper Read recalled a few years back: 'He was a man of super physique, strong and tall, and this helped him to get lift from the pitch. Batsmen always *complained that instead of playing the ball in the middle of the bat, it was always hitting the spine! He had a fine economical action and run up and used the crease well, though most of the time he bowled from close to the stumps. He had a late swing and was always doing a little off the seam. He was a great bowler and his action is a model for would be fast bowlers.'*

Tom Pearce, who shared the captaincy with Denys Wilcox, said: *'He was one of the most delightful of men and regarded by us all as a gentle giant. We often thought we ought to kick him in the shins as we went out on the field to get him a little angry.*

'He was a really fast bowler of some 6 ft 7 ins in height, who could certainly move the ball and vary its pace as well as make it rise sharply.

'He loved the game and nothing pleased him more than making a few runs, in fact I can recall his delight at making 50 on one occasion.

'I can also remember the Gents v Players match when he had half an hour's bowling at the Players and I have never seen anyone bowl so fast as he did then and really scare the batsmen. Altogether a most delightful man and a great loss to the game.' (The three scared batsmen were Walter Hammond, Joe Hardstaff and Harold Gimblett!)

Max Raison, then 85 (he played 17 times for Essex around 1930, once took 5 for 104 including Hammond v Gloucestershire and was founder of the Farmer's Weekly and New Scientist among other magazines), said: *'He came after me but I have watched him play and was much impressed with what I saw. He bowled from the top of his considerable height and made the ball rise very sharply off the pitch. As far as I can remember he moved the ball either way. Some said at the time that he would have been an even better bowler if he could get angry occasionally but his temperament was very equable and he was a nice person. His death in the war was a great loss to English cricket.'*

The career of Nigel Wykes, another schoolmaster (a house master at Eton), who only played in the summer holidays, overlapped with Farnes. He wrote: *'We all knew him well as a fine fast bowler and a most popular personality. I remember him as a quiet unassuming man, immensely impressive for his great height and massive strength.*

'He took a relatively short run up (about 15 paces I should say) and there was none of the appalling tedium of waiting for the modern fast bowler to walk very slowly back 25 yards while the close fieldsmen in turn give the ball a polish and eventually hand the ball to the bowler so that an over takes up to five minutes.

Farnes' actual delivery was remarkable for his very high arm which could bring the ball down and often give that extra bit of bounce which made batting difficult, though I can remember seeing him bowl what is now called a bouncer but he would certainly not have agreed to any form of intimidatory bodyline bowling.'

His description of his bowling is more precise than many: '*His action was curiously jerky and had not the same aesthetic appeal as we used to admire in the Australian Ted Macdonald or our own Maurice Tate. But he undoubtedly bowled fast by any standard and with his enormous hand could whip the ball in to the batsman with what was virtually a very fast and unplayable off break.*

'*Also with his great strength and stamina he could bowl for long periods and I never saw him show any sign of faint-heartedness. Off the field he was a modest and most agreeable companion and it was a great tragedy that he should have been cut off in his prime.'*

Tom Smith, a banking-amateur who once had Bradman dropped second ball and had a reputation as a stump-smasher, wrote: '*I first met him in a match before he played for Essex. He was more of an all-round player. Mr Perrin, the England selector and an old Essex player, asked me what I thought of him and I said I thought he was a better bowler than a batsman and Mr Perrin said 'so do I.' He was a fast bowler who made the ball lift off the pitch, more of a pace specialist than movement in the air. He was somewhat temperamental. In one game against Lancashire he took most of the first five wickets and when Duckworth (England wicket-keeper up into the 30's) reached top score he was most disappointed that he had got the batsmen out and been hit by the tailenders. This upset him and his bowling in the second innings was very disappointing.'*

Amateur John Dennis, a solicitor-batsman, thought the opposite. He wrote: '*He was a very pleasant person and had a placid temperament. He was a quiet, very modest man whose demeanour gave no indication of the ferocity of his bowling.*

'*His run up was rather square and he bowled from a great height. This meant that he often got more lift than a shorter man. He could use the outswinger as well as cutting the ball from the off.'*

Another schoolmaster, Brian Belle, agreed. He said: '*I have vivid memories of my few years playing holiday cricket for Essex and Ken Farnes figures largely in those memories. He was a big man in every sense. Kind and humorous off the field his personality was quite different from the terrifying one he must have presented to opposing batsmen as he tore majestically up to the wicket to bowl.*

'To meet him off the field you would call him a gentle giant. He was a *fitness fanatic and could sometimes be persuaded with a lot of cajoling to flex his muscles and give an exhibition of muscle control which was quite extraordinary in the changing room after a match. Some of the exercises he performed made him look like Mr Universe. Certainly a magnificent figure of a man. I had no idea such muscles existed, especially in the stomach.'*

Geoff Chapman was also astonished by his friend's muscles. *'He was a fitness fanatic but it was typical of him that he did not push his interest on you. I think he must have taken a body building course like the Mr Universe ones that said 'you can have a body like mine'. Once when I went to stay with his family I saw him with his pyjama jacket open and he braced his body in some way, causing a great muscle at the front of his abdomen to stick out like a lamp post! I was astounded at his muscular control. He had a very fine body.'*

Farnes's niece Joan (who twice played for Essex Ladies) told me that his strength was amazing. When she was a little girl of five or six he would carry her up to bed, not with a piggy back but by holding out a little finger which she would grasp and he would lift her off the ground and with her holding onto the finger carry her up the stairs to bed.

Brian Belle said*: 'At one party given by the wives of the professionals he was the life and soul of it. I remember that he and I were finalists in a competition for the best pair of men's legs. We had to pull up our trousers to the knees, take off our shoes and socks and parade behind a curtain so that the ladies did not know the owners of the legs on view. He enjoyed it all as much as anyone but I won the final inspection when the line was reduced to five and was presented with a pair of sock suspenders!*

'He was always most kind to me as a new boy (he played in 26 matches between 1935 and 1937 and after World War Two for Suffolk), but put a ball in his hand he was quite a different person. He was a very aggressive, very fast bowler and must have enjoyed bowling to timid batsmen.

'As a bowler I would rate him as inferior to Nichols. He was much faster and from his great height could fairly thump it in to the discomfort of the batsman. I had to field at very short leg to him several times and one could see the whites of their eyes and then tension on their faces as they prepared to receive!

'But Nichols could use the new ball much more effectively and in the opinion of the older pros should always have been given the choice of ends. Farnes got most of his wickets from sheer pace and lift rather than skilful use of the new ball.

His style of run-up was classic and upright bringing the ball down from his great height. I imagine facing a cavalry charge would be something like the ordeal of opening batsmen facing Ken.

   'I always felt it was a pity he batted at 10 or 11 as most fast bowlers seem fated to do, both then and now. He demonstrated with his 97 not out at Taunton in 1936 that he would have been a very useful hard hitting no 7 or 8.'

   Norman Borrett, who played three matches for Essex pre-war, said: *'He was a great hearted bowler, always making an effort to get a wicket. I remember him going through Worcestershire one day at Clacton on a roughish wicket. He had all the batsmen except the captain back pedalling.*

   'He had one party piece he used to do in the changing room, when asked he made his stomach muscle stand right out. He was an extremely good natured person and a fine bowler.'

   Seed merchant George Unwin was another who played little because of business but remembers one game against Farnes when he was playing for Cambridge: *'He was certainly a very formidable sight when coming to bowl against you, arms and legs flying in all directions.'*

   Amateur Ian Lavers, who played both sides of World War Two, remembers Farnes as extremely fast and also an amiable character who loved a bit of fun, once turning up for a match while still wearing his dinner jacket.

   All-rounder Frank Vigar (11 centuries, 236 wickets) said: *'I was a rookie in 1939 and the only match I can remember playing with him was against Notts at Clacton. I remember it for two reasons: firstly I found myself fielding in the slips with Ken bowling and praying like hell no one would get an edge and unfortunately or fortunately someone did and I stuck out my left hand and there it was and so my position for quite a while was in the slips. The other was seeing him break Walter Keeton's finger. He bowled a fairly short delivery that Keeton attempted to pull but was late on it and hit the middle finger of his left hand and made quite a mess of it. He got most of his wickets by sheer speed and, of course, considerable bounce off the wicket as he did come down from quite a height so tall.*

   'Regarding his temperament and attitude to the game, as a fast bowler I felt he could have been much more aggressive and he did seem to take the game in an enjoyable manner.'

   Shortly after that Peter Perrin discovered him and George Hockey, an amateur who played 19 matches around 1930, was there on the ground staff for that match, Essex Club and Ground v Gidea Park, Farnes's club:

Ken Farnes

'It was the only time Mr Perrin took a Club and Ground side anywhere during my four years and I think it is obvious that he meant to have a look at Farnes who was I would say about 19.

'I have quite a vivid memory of that match possibly because when Farnes reached the top and his name was mentioned I could say 'I played in the match when he was discovered, and of course I scored several fours off him - two were off the outside edge through the slips and another off the inside edge between my legs and the wicket!' This was in fact true. I remember him as a tall youngster coming up to bowl with his arm very straight and from the fours I scored off him I am perfectly certain that he must have been moving it either way off the seam.

'My feeling about him is that with his arm so high he must have moved it either way and I think he was an intelligent cricketer and would have realised that he could not overcome the batsmen by sheer speed unless it was phenomenal.'

And sometimes it was.

13.

1935-36

1935 WAS THE YEAR that never existed. Farnes did not bowl a ball in anger. Just why was no mystery, just bad luck. Whether it was his giant frame that sometimes let him down because of the force and power he put into his bowling it is impossible to tell all these years down the road.

What is certain is that he was a physical fitness fanatic. In these days he might have been able to make money showing off his prowess although I am sure he would not have done so. What he achieved was for his personal satisfaction and only among friends and team mates in the dressing room did he ever demonstrate his incredible muscular control ability. He could, for example, hold one half of his stomach flat while performing amazing acts of contortion on the other. His control was fantastic and famous in cricketing circles.

When he appeared at the Essex nets for pre-season practice in late April 1936, two months back from the sun, colleague Bill Reeves, a man who always spoke his mind, greeted him with: *'Well, you've had more rests than matches in the West Indies.'*

It was something that Farnes realised only too well. He wrote: *'He was not quite accurate but there was a good deal of justice in his remark. I was very painfully aware of my lack of success on the tour and extremely dissatisfied with my performance.'*

Farnes was a realist when it came to his own performances. He accepted that sometimes things did not go the way of the bowler (or the batsman) and you had to take it and just get on with the job, regarding it rather like a golfer who has had a terrible hole. Nothing is going to change what has happened so forget it.

His great hope was of showing that it was one of those lapses by getting among the wickets against that season's tourists, South Africa (who won the series by one match, the rest drawn). He did not get the chance.

'Any hopes I had of getting into better form were very soon to be dashed because I smashed a cartilage in my left knee. Towards the end of the summer I was able to hobble about and bowl leg spinners, which I enjoyed as much as the batsmen who took toll of them.'

It was nothing to do with cricket. He was out walking with his father, came to a fence with a tallish tree stump as the means of getting over and, putting the full weight of his left leg onto the stump for leverage, smashed the knee.

He could not walk and it took the operation to rebuild the knee into pristine condition. In those days it was not a quick affair. It was long, laborious and painful and meant being in bed for a long time with the leg supported and then hobbling around on a stick until full mobility was back. It was a success because he became better and stronger until the end of his career.

But that year the only first class cricket he saw was the match in which Essex beat the South Africans at Southend, and a day afterwards at the Oval, in the first Test he saw Captain JWA Stephenson (known as Stan after Stan Laurel because of the way his hair laid) for the first time and was impressed. In the second Test he was equally impressed by Hopper Read. He was bowling pretty fast and took for 5 for 125, a useful performance Farnes considered on that 'dreadful' Oval wicket and in his first Test.

Farnes did not like the ground and said: 'I also renewed acquaintance with the discomfort that besets the spectators at that arid and gasometer-ridden ground. Only once have I played there (in Hutton's 364 match v the Australians in 1938) and the experience confirmed my melancholy view that it is a pity for a ground with such associations (Hobbs in particular) to be so sordid and to have the sort of wicket that kills cricket.'

By the autumn his knee was better and he practised throughout the winter at Worksop, building up his accuracy, his speed and strength so that once more he would be able to bowl up to 40 overs in a match, a high rate for a fast bowler who always gave his all.

He wrote: 'I had heard early on that I stood a chance of going on the Australian tour in the coming winter. This was the Mecca of my cricket dreams and I set out to get fit in real earnest. It was announced that GO Allen would be the captain of the MCC side. He had an encouraging record from the previous tour in which he supported Larwood in both his bowling from the other end and in *making many fine catches at the key short leg position.* (Although Allen definitely did not support Jardine's tactics of using his fast bowlers to win theAshes).

'*The chief trial match was really the Gentlemen v Players match at Lord's in July. This was chiefly remarkable for Stephenson's bowling in the first innings. He took nine wickets. He was so fired by the occasion that he bowled probably better than he had ever done, making the ball nip off the pitch at an amazing pace. When he bowled Leyland he was shaking hands with Howard Levett, the wicket-keeper, almost before the stump had stopped spinning. It was rather like the Walt Disney film in which the hare, to show his pace, played tennis with himself during the race with the tortoise.*'

Many were greatly impressed by Stephenson that day, not least Wally Hammond, still a professional but two years later to turn amateur and become England captain against the Australians in 1938.

Hammond wrote: '*Anyone who has ever played against him can never forget his gyrations on the field. When he first started playing big cricket people thought he was playing to the gallery but it was soon realised that his animal spirits refused to be bottled up and he has brightened many a cricket field for us who play the game and for tens of thousands of spectators too. In this match when our turn came to bat Stephenson was put on to bowl and found a spot. The game was at Lord's and it was well known in those days that such spots existed; any bowler who was put on there diligently searched for one. The stumps in those days were pitched in any place where the grass was good; and on this occasion, just where a length would pitch, there was a pronounced hummock where the heavy roller had stopped during a previous game. When the Gentlemen were batting none of us had noticed this ridge but Stephenson had eyes like a hawk and he started putting the ball on it.*

'*The result was funny. One after another of the most famous batsmen in England simply had not the slightest idea where the ball would go after it touched the ground. We tried to run out to it, and we tried to play back, but Stephenson, getting more hilarious and excitable with every ball, kept taking his short run-up and swinging his arm over - and that was the end of someone. Even without any assistance from the wicket he made the ball come off the grass almost as sharply as Maurice Tate and he could use the seam devastatingly; on this occasion he was simply unplayable and I have never seen anyone enjoy a situation so much. Towards the end some of us simply could not bat for laughing. Stephenson took 9 for 45 in about 16 overs and when Farnes and Allan began to bowl in our second innings we were so shaken we could not resist them either.'*

The Players made 194 in reply to the Gentlemen's 130 and when they batted a second time they made 195 for 8 declared, leaving the Players 132 to win. In a great finish they were 63 for 5, thanks to the thunderbolt bowling of Farnes, and although I do not like to contradict a man of Hammond's stature I would make two points: there was a long gap between the hilarity caused by Stan's bowling in the first innings during which Hammond made 72 and the second innings and no one saw Hammond, Gimblett and Hardstaff falling over themselves with laughter as their stumps were uprooted and sent 12 yards head high cartwheeling through the air, one after the other in quick succession, as they went for 1, 7 and 4, in five overs! Sheer speed overcame masterly batting ability.

The bowling was described in The Cricketer thus: *'Farnes bowled magnificently, the best fast bowling seen since Lockwood was in his prime (some 40 years before). He has a beautiful action which brings the ball down from the sky and hits the ground hard. He bowled in the grand manner and sent the stumps flying. The ball that beat Joe Hardstaff pitched on the middle and leg stump and hit the top of the off stump.'*

Farnes wrote: *'I managed to get three wickets in the short time that the Players had to bat before the end of the match in their second innings. It was this, I believe, that brought me the invitation that I so much desired; I doubt if I have ever bowled faster. Certainly the stumps flew further than I have sent them on any other occasion.'*

For once Farnes is not hiding his light beneath a bushel. His bowling was superb. One after the other three leading English batsmen, Harold Gimblett of Somerset, Wally Hammond of Gloucestershire and Joe Hardstaff of Notts, were walking back to the pavilion after Farnes had sent a stump head high at great speed to land at the feet of wicket-keeper Levett. Farnes had a point to make after a year away when others were pressing for his place on the tour - and he made it.

Wisden exclaimed excitedly: *'GO Allen, who led the Gentlemen, declared his innings closed at five o'clock on the third day when eight wickets were down for 195 runs and set the Players 132 to get in roughly 75 minutes including the extra half hour. Extraordinary cricket followed. By six o'clock the Players had four men out for 33.*

'This breakthrough was caused by Kenneth Farnes, the Essex fast bowler,

who, taking a little longer run than usual and making the fullest use of his height, sent the ball down at a pace unequalled at Headquarters since the days of CJ Kortright. When Farnes bowled Gimblett, Hammond and Hardstaff he sent a stump on each case catapulting head high to drop at the feet of Levett who stood back more than a dozen yards. It is extremely possible that by this wonderful bowling Farnes won his place in the team for Australia.'

CJ Kortright, a predecessor at Essex, was considered by many judges as the fastest bowler who ever lived. His speed was that of legends and his performances were amazing. He was a contemporary of two other great fast bowlers, Richardson and Lockwood, who captured 88 and 43 Test wickets in the late 19th century, and because of them - and illness when the chance came - Kortright never played for England. But his speed in the Gentlemen v Players match when he took 7 for 73 at the turn of the century and when he bowled out Surrey - he took 6 for 4 in 15 balls including Tom Hayward at one stage - and Yorkshire in their championship years was something talked about for years afterwards.

The county report said at the end of the season: *'It was in this match that Farnes finally convinced the selectors after a season out of the game through knee trouble. He fully compensated for the inability of Read to spare time for county cricket and like that player was able, when he chose, to send down a faster ball than anyone else. Bringing the ball down from a good height he made it lift awkwardly but if exception was taken in some quarters to his bowling there were never grounds for suspicion that he was anything but a fast bowler.'*

Farnes season began early so that he could make his mark. He knew that he would not be able to play against the visiting Indians (England won the series by winning two matches) because of school commitments but he needed to be ready for the Gentlemen v Players match.

So he came back in May, playing at Brentwood, another Essex outpost ground, where he took the first four Surrey wickets in 18 sharp overs, ending with 4 for 92, not a bad first outing after his long break.

He was back at school, practising as hard as ever in his limited free time, before his next game against Somerset at Colchester in early July where he grabbed a couple of wickets, but in his next game, against Middlesex on the same ground, he showed he was getting back to his best rapidly. He clean bowled six of their batsmen, including Patsy Hendren, the young Denis Compton and his old friend Jim Smith, and had Peebles lbw. In the second innings he claimed both openers cheaply and ended up with 7 for 84 and 2 for 37 off 45 overs, showing there was nothing wrong with any department of his bowling, including stamina.

The Lord's display of fireworks followed and then it was back to school for the last two weeks of term and then back to help his county who were doing about as well as the year before, which was not good news to the Essex supporters. They were to finish ninth again, this time behind Derbyshire not Yorkshire. Not that names meant anything to Farnes because it was against Derbyshire that he started his run of eight games with the county throughout August, taking five wickets for 20 in the first innings in an inspired spell.

The Essex fast bowlers, Farnes, Nichols and Stephenson, carried everything before them as they blasted the championship leaders (and winners) out for 80 at Chelmsford and then, in a strange match, made 219 to which Derbyshire replied with 240 and bowled Essex out for 81 to win by 20 runs.

This was followed by four wickets in an innings against Worcestershire on the same ground and six in the second innings against Kent, back at his favourite sea air in Southend. Wisden said: *'Woolley was one of the few who showed any ability to play Farnes, his 53 in the second innings being a superb effort because Farnes, bowling very fast, made the ball fly about on a fiery pitch.'* But they did not tell the half of Farnes's fast and ever faster bowling, mainly off a good length, which caused havoc.

RC Robertson-Glasgow in his report was scathing: *'The Kent batting all day was a trifle thin, at times evanescent. Such a failure cannot wholly be excused. The pitch endured some unpleasant comments from those who scrutinised it with a close and knowing look but it was never the villain that the more romantic would have us believe. Indeed apart from some odd drops of petrol from the motor roller it sustained no serious damage. Indeed Kent were ruined by that old enemy, fast bowling.*

'It seems that some batsmen have no stomach for a good fight, while others lack the skill. Farnes, from the pavilion end, once again showed that he is one of the few bowlers now playing cricket who can make the ball fly from a good length, who can suggest even by his run up that the batsman would do well to stay firm.'

Kent were bowled out for 98 for an innings win for Essex. But that was by no means the end of it. No one said much after the game as the players went their separate ways but a few days later in the Kent paper for which he was a columnist, Tich Freeman let rip.

The Kent wonder spinner, who could always do it in county matches (6 for 92 in this one) but never quite for England had a real whinge. He wrote under headlines of Kent being glad to say goodbye to Southend and short pitched deliveries that were *'definitely unfair'* and *'Why the Essex Game lasted only two days'*, reminiscent of Bodyline days in the Australian press, and even having a dateline Dover showing he was writing in Kent: *'It is not often professional cricketers complain. The boot is nearly always on the other foot so that the comments passed by several Kent players on the bowling of a certain amateur in our game last week at Southend comes with especial emphasis. The bowling in our opinion was definitely unfair.'*

The amateurs in the Essex side were Leonard Crawley, Denys Wilcox, Nicky Vere Hodge, Stan Stephenson and Ken Farnes. Only Stephenson and Farnes were bowlers and Stephenson was not as fast as Farnes, although very good indeed, but no one had commented that there was anything difficult in his bowling to bring this attack.

Freeman, filing his story from the Dover dateline as if it was war, continued: *'Both Watt and Fagg were hit and others could have been had they not taken the only alternative and quickly terminated their innings.*

'Kent players made no secret of their feelings. Neither were their opinions limited to the Kent eleven for more than one Essex player holds similar views.'

From these many years after the game, and with almost everyone involved dead or unable to recollect, it is difficult to imagine who the Essex player could have conceivably been. The professionals were Nichols, O'Connor, Taylor, Smith, Eastman and Wade, the wicket keeper. It is well known that professionals in county sides, who were dropped when the amateurs who were schoolmasters came out to play at the end of summer terms, and did not - and quite understandably did not - like it, although they tended to keep their counsel even if they did feel that way for obvious reasons.

But none of these came into that category and all of them were extremely experienced, very good (some Test players) and hard playing cricketers who wanted to win. So let us dismiss the whingeing Essex man as a ghost.

Tich was not however finished: *'Five balls out of the normal six bowled by the player in question pitched less than halfway down the pitch. The light, too, was bad and the general opinion was that the sooner we said goodbye to Southend under these conditions the better. So the game lasted only two days, much to*

Ken Farnes

Nichols's disappointment for it was his benefit match - but the fault lay with his county.'

Fagg made 6 and 1 and was out both times to Stephenson. He, like Woolley and Valentine (out to Smith and Farnes), were England players. Watt was not and made 10 and 20, falling to Farnes twice, and Freeman himself bagged a not out pair.

Still he was not finished. He wrote: 'After this one views the coming trip to Australia with a little apprehension. A leading Essex amateur has been out of the side for two years because of his intense dislike of this kind of bowling. County cricketers are not squeamish but there is a limit and altogether they put up a lot before they turn.'

Many years later Leslie Todd (who was out to Nichols and Stephenson) told a friend that Farnes's bowling was terrifying and that - and he said it with an incredulous note in his voice - 'Frank (Woolley) was hit!' He considered Farnes bowled as fast as Joel Garner.

That great left hander remembered the game always and when a friend, Norman Lenton, congratulated him on his 80th birthday (Woolley was 80 in 1967, died in 1978, made 58,969 runs and 145 centuries) and mentioned the match Woolley wrote back:

'I remember the Essex match at Southend when Farnes lost his temper. The Kent team at the best of times never liked fast bowling but Farnes was bowling very fast on a nasty fiery wicket, the ball going over my head at times. He hit most of us. Yes, he hit me on the shoulder twice and when it came to our last three batsmen (no names, no pack drill) they retreated so far they were treading on the umpire's toes.'

Why Farnes lost his temper we will never know, if indeed he did. As we know he was extremely placid and needed a good shaking to get his adrenalin and aggression going. But losing his temper? Only once have I heard anyone accuse him of that and that was only in passing as if he might have been in a mood. Everything else known about him says just the opposite.

Orthopaedic surgeon Nicky Vere-Hodge was playing in his first game for Essex and but for obeying his captain, Denys Wilcox, to get a move on might have made a maiden hundred. As it was he chased a ball very wide of the off stump and was caught at extra cover on the boundary for 77. Freeman had been bowling wider and wider and the newcomer was playing so late that on one occasion he brushed the ball and the fingers of Frank Woolley at close-in first slip at the same time. So he remembers the match and as far as he is concerned there was nothing wrong with Farnes's bowling nor his attitude.

He said: *'I knew they complained but personally I thought it was legitimate. When Ken bowled, Arthur Fagg turned his back and closed his eyes on him and the ball hit him the back, in the kidney. If you do that at that standard of cricket what do you expect? I have had much worse bowling at me by Bill Copson of Derbyshire, that really was at one's head. I know Frank Woolley grumbled but he was past his best. Ken was fast and the ball was getting up a bit, that's all.'*

Mr Vere-Hodge's memory of that match shows two examples of how much the game has changed. Leonard Crawley, who was an exciting batsman as well as a top golfer and writer on the subject, told his captain that he should win the toss as he had to leave for London by 12.30 that Saturday morning. Wilcox duly did and the pair opened.

Crawley hit the first ball from Todd so hard it hit a new concrete stand and bounced back towards the wicket, scarring the ball so much that after inspecting it the umpires decided that it was out of shape and gave Todd another new ball to use for the second ball of the match. Crawley then proceeded to knock the bowlers all over the place and made 63 before being bowled by Jack Davies (he who had Bradman for his first English duck in 1934) with Wilcox not in double figures.

Crawley had ordered a pint of beer before he went into bat and sat on the railings in full view of everyone and drank it before going to London, wiping his moustache with a silk handkerchief and saying he would see his colleagues again on Monday morning, which he duly did. Nichols and O'Connor both made hundreds, Vere-Hodge kept things ticking over and he was not needed in the field until then.

The other big change was in the attitude of the Director of the Medical School where he was studying. He told his student that he had read in The Times how he was spending his time and that was all right with him because he could take his finals at any time, but he would only be able to play cricket once and that was at the age he was at. It even applied when he went on a tour of Egypt and when he did his finals and came to the oral examination it was just after he had scored his first century at his first visit to Lord's - *'I lost my way from the dressing room to the wicket and nearly ran out of time'* - and one of the examiners had been there. Vere-Hodge said: *'He said he much enjoyed my batting and asked me what I would like to talk about! It's all different now.'*

111

Cricket went on in its own sweet way and throughout the season the names of those to go to Australia were announced, and all the time Farnes was making sure his was in Gubby Allen's mind. Farnes wrote: *'Gradually the personnel of the team were announced. Robins, after much thought, agreed to go. Hammond, Verity and Leyland were early certainties. ERT Holmes was unable to accept. Ames and Duckworth were obvious choices as wicket-keepers. For the rest the form of Hardstaff, Fishlock, Worthington (who made 128 and 87 in two Test matches against the Indian touring team), Fagg, Barnett, Voce, Copson and Sims warranted their inclusion.'* Copson and Voce were his rivals for the fast bowling places.

'The final place was given to Wyatt after a good deal of speculation as to whether he or Paynter, who had made such a gallant effort at Brisbane when he was ill on the previous tour, or Gimblett who had sprung into the limelight that season by some forceful batting as an opener for Somerset, should be chosen.'

Typically - and how I wish he had been more open - he said nothing of his chances as the names trickled out. They were all expected and not even worth a bet.

But he did not do well against Hampshire at Southend, taking just one wicket in 35 overs as his friend and captain Wilcox and the ever-consistent Nichols put on 221 for the second wicket in Essex's 503 (Nichols 205, Wilcox 133).

He took five wickets in the match against Somerset at Taunton, notable for his batting which could only be described as incredible. For once all his practice in the nets, all the tutoring by his colleagues to try and make him score runs with his great strength, clicked and he scored 97 not out. He and wicket-keeper Tommy Wade put on 149 in 90 minutes and if Wade had not been out it is more than likely that Farnes would have made his maiden century. He certainly never scored so many runs in an innings again and he had only done better once before, but that was in a club match for Gidea Park years before.

Wisden said: *'Farnes surprised everybody'* - an understatement if I have ever read one - *'with the quality of his batting. He gave a chance in the deep field at 64 but he timed his drives accurately and making the highest score of his career put together in two hours hit a six and ten fours.'*

Against Notts at Clacton he came down to earth with a bang with 7 and 5. For good measure Larwood bowled Farnes, who took six wickets in

Notts' first innings, five of them bowled, and finishing with innings figures of 6 for 73. He was bowling bursts at such a speed that he was often almost unplayable, another clear hint to the selectors.

He had six wickets against Gloucestershire at Clacton, but not the great Hammond (who had him caught for two). His partners, Nichols and Stephenson did that for moderate scores, 43 and 51. His final game for Essex brought four more wickets and a season's haul of 61 for 1145 and an average of 18.77 for the county and a much better batting average - 19.50, his first time in double figures and making far more runs than wickets, a total of 234.

He picked up three wickets (including Hendren) in the Levenson Gower XI v MCC Australian X1 (for he was now one of them) at the Scarborough Festival. His national average, way behind Larwood and Verity - 12.97 and 13.18 - but ahead of Voce was 67 wickets at 19.32 each.

And so a very happy young man started to pack for Australia.

14.

AUSTRALIA & NEW ZEALAND
1936/7

The season was barely over before the MCC team, plus several press men like
Neville Cardus, CB Fry and Jack Hobbs, set sail in the Orion from
Southampton, the only flurry at departure being that Farnes had left his
spare trousers behind. Manager Rupert Howard sent an SOS to Fergie
(William Ferguson), the eternal baggage man, to collect them from Essex
and bring them overland to Toulon where he was picking up the boat.

He did so and the voyage went on with all the normal ship games,
quoits, a form of cricket, tennis and even golf round The Old Course at St
Andrews, each shot registered on a dial many, many years before the arrival
of computer games. The ship arrived after an extremely pleasant journey at
Perth on October 13.

The team that Gubby Allen led was a young one and only seven out
of a party of seventeen had been on the bodyline tour four years before.

The Telegraph, assessing the chances, said of the Essex bowler,
amongst the last to be named: *'It was at Trent Bridge (1934) that he took five
wickets in each innings in his first Test match, bowling really fast. We all then
thought that Larwood's successor had been found. And his blinding speed in the
Players' second innings at Lord's last July showed that he had not rusted through
lack of first class practise. The Selectors have taken a chance on him as being the
only bowler we possess capable of getting the Australians rattled by sheer speed.'*

In the pre-tour publicity he was described as an unmarried, almost
teetotal, non-smoker, good-looking, *'talks very little but thinks a great deal!'*

Until the last few weeks of the long exhausting tour of eight ball
overs, it looked as though the gamble was not to pay off because Farnes did
not seem able to reach full steam, but then he clicked and performed

114

extremely well. It was a purple patch that was to last through until the end of cricket in 1939.

Farnes wrote: *'In a sense the tour was more of a diplomatic mission than such tours usually are, as any bad feeling that might still remain in Australia had to be removed in order that the implications of the word cricket might persist. For the publicity given to these contests between England and Australia makes them of considerable importance. No better skipper than Allen could have been appointed. He was full of zeal on the field and off it and wore himself out in his tremendous and successful effort to re-establish the usual friendly nature of the cricket between the two countries. During the tour he made over fifty speeches, the strain of which on top of the cricket - particularly as his fast bowling and batsmanship combined made his work on the field heavier than anyone else - was too great for any man to stand without showing signs of it towards the end.'*

One sad job Allen had to do was to tell Farnes that his mother Florence had been killed in a car crash early in 1937. Her death hit Farnes very hard indeed, but typically he kept his feelings and grief to himself although his friend Geoff realised by the tone of the bowler's letter to him, telling him of what had happened half the world away when he could not get back. *'It was one of the saddest letters I have ever had. It indicated that it had affected him very deeply. It hit him very hard. He did not talk about it. He was someone who would keep it to himself, but what a terrible thing to get that awful news when on a cricket tour. Ken was very close to his mother and a lot like her. She was a very kind lady.'*

Allen nearly succeeded in getting the Ashes back in a very hard fought series with England winning the first two Tests and Australia the last three to retain them with - accepting that sometimes the English batting failed at a crucial point - the real difference between the two teams being Bradman. He was that good. He scored 300 runs more than any other player in the series and had an average of 90.

Allen, Voce, Copson and Farnes were the fast bowlers and the Essex man had high hopes of being a regular choice. But it did not work out that way and he was not given his chance - much to the surprise of some of the Australian experts - until the last two Tests, and then only because of injury to Voce, and when he did get it he seized it. In fact, he only played in 16 of the games out of 32 in the long tour which did not end until the end of April.

Before the 17 left for the cementing of relations tour, the MCC issued a statement telling how both Larwood and Voce had been approached in the summer of 1935 about their attitude towards playing in representative cricket and had been told by both men that they only wanted to play in county cricket. The MCC kept this quiet and did not consider them but when Voce changed his mind and was picked, the MCC made the facts public.

To Farnes Australia was a wonderful revelation. To Allen and team manager Rupert Howard it became a nightmare of injuries from the start - Robins had the top of the second finger of his right hand broken, ruining his spin bowling; Wyatt fractured a bone in his left arm and missed much of the tour; wicket-keeper Ames fell ill early on and the other wicket-keeper, Duckworth, dislocated a finger, but luckily Tom Wade, Farnes's Essex team mate, was out there and filled the gap; Fishlock broke a finger, Copson strained a muscle, and then so did Voce and those were only the main injuries. Farnes for once was not injured and finally got his chance because of the casualty list.

Even so the team gave the Australians a very good run for their money but, as Wisden acknowledged, it was not quite good enough, adding that it was the batting not the bowling that let them down. Without commenting the writer said: *'Farnes bowled with great heart when he received his chances in the Tests.'*

Before the first match of the tour - against Western Australia which in those days did not play in the Sheffield Shield because of the distances involved in travelling; Perth is over 2000 miles from its nearest neighbour, Adelaide - the team watched the wicket at the WACCA being rolled and rolled until it became so hard and shiny that it looked like glass. The great advantage of the hardness of the ground, Farnes found, was that however long a match lasted the bowlers never dug deep holes where their feet pound down, whereas in England footholds became very dangerous. The worst he had ever seen were at the Oval in 1938 in Hutton's match when O'Reilly and Fleetwood-Smith dug pits six to eight inches deep, and it was through one of those that Bradman damaged his ankle, which put him out of the rest of the tour. *'The thought that you might easily break your ankle if your foot comes down in one of those holes is enough to prevent any bowler from bowling with fire and accuracy,'* he wrote.

He played in the first match, taking three wickets in the first innings and two in the second and unfortunately breaking Duckworth's finger as he stopped a ball. Soon after Les Ames had terrible back trouble, and the Essex wicket-keeper Tommy Wade took over. The Evening News man wrote: *'Farnes seemed to bowl at half his usual speed and was quite harmless until shortly before lunch. He will bowl a great deal faster later on when he has loosened his muscles.'*

And after having a good lunch he was a different bowler. The News man commented: *'His speeding up made him begin to look like the quick bowler those in England know him to be.'*

Wyatt and Hammond made centuries and Hardstaff 87 not out in 469 for four and the tourists won by an innings and 180 runs. It was a marvelous start but unfortunately a false dawn in the end. He did not play in the second match in which Grimmett was hit for 137 for his one wicket by Hammond, Fishlock and Worthington - Farnes thought that that punishment kept the spinner out of the Tests - and Copson, his rival, had 4 for 82.

From Perth the team went across the desert in the Indian Pacific train and Farnes saw kangaroos by the score (there are 25 million of them on the Continent) and noted: *'The amazing enthusiasm for cricket in Australia was demonstrated to us scores of times in out of the way places at which our train stopped at any hour of the day and night, by invasions of the younger inhabitants with autograph books and bulging eyes. At Kalgoorlie (the gold rush town in the middle of the desert) I felt like a zoo inmate when we dismounted on the platform to change onto the broad gauge line that runs across the desert.'*

He loved Adelaide (and everything he saw in the country to such an extent that one agency report suggested that he might stay there and teach in Victoria but it never came to anything) which he found charming and the immortal CB Fry (scholar, cricketer, world long jump record holder, writer and once offered the crown of Albania) thought the cricket ground the finest in the world. Unfortunately Farnes was 12th man again and was saved from having to bowl on the easy paced wicket which was then known as the fast bowler's graveyard.

Fry misbehaved in Adelaide, falling asleep and leaving his wash basin tap on. In the early hours the chap below was woken by a heavy downpour and when he and the night porter went upstairs they were almost

washed off their feet by the gush as they opened Fry's door. After forcing
their way in they found him snoring happily surrounded by swirling water
that was tossing his boxes and trunks around in the current.

On his way to Melbourne Farnes saw his first koala and the laughing
jackass. He also had his first game for a fortnight and had three wickets for
56 against Victoria and saw McCormick, the new Australian fast bowler, in
action for the first time.

He commented: *'I got into a spot of trouble for bowling too much down
the leg side, a failing which besets me mostly when I am tired or out of practice.
My analysis was probably not as bad as it should have been.'*

Sydney was next stop and he had his first sight of the Hill. There
was little barracking (the name comes from the soldiers who used to be
housed in army barracks near the ground and came to the matches and yelled
and shouted as they watched and drank) although after the unique hushed
atmosphere when playing cricket at Lord's it was quite something even
though much less than he expected.

He said: *'I believe that there is not a great deal of difference in cricket
crowds the world over. Certainly there was little worse in Australia than the
barracking at Nottingham in 1938 when a section of the crowd watched
Bradman and Fingleton saving the Test match by splendid defensive play. The
play then was dull to watch but a true understanding of the game should have
been sufficient to curb undue dissatisfaction. Home crowds anywhere are inclined
to gloat when their team is winning and the gloating at Melbourne when
Australia was winning the last and final Test was only more sickening than usual
by the vastness of the crowd (over 80,000).*

*'Probably the worst features of the crowd's behaviour were at Melbourne
when Hammond's dismissal was gloated over most ungallantly, the crowing being
quite distinct from acclamation at the fall of an important wicket; and when in
the same match the umpires were cheered off the field when they justly upheld an
appeal against light when Australia were batting on an extremely difficult
wicket.'*

Farnes played and despite what he called *'some incredibly bad
umpiring'* the MCC were completely outplayed by an Australian X1 which
included Bradman (he was the third of Sydney's pride – *'our bridge, our
harbour and our Bradman'* although now as he lives in Adelaide he will have
been replaced by the Opera House) who had a quiet game with only 63 but

118

when he was out hundreds left the ground even with an hour's play to go.

New boy Badcock did the real damage with 182 until Farnes caught him off Verity, and his two victims were WA Brown and Robinson. He learnt a good lesson there from Fingleton, an expert on when to leave the ball alone and that was vital when the shine was on the ball. For Farnes discovered that the shine did not last long and with the dryness and lightness of the air made it difficult to swing the ball after the first three overs. He wrote: *'The uniform pace and texture of Australian wickets makes the bowler's art more exacting for on most English county wickets you can rely on the ball doing something different now and again - either lifting a little or moving off the seam.'*

In Brisbane three days later he was the best of the fast bowlers, which was not saying much, having Rogers and Wyeth as Verity took five and Arthur Fagg, 112, and Charlie Barnett, 259, had an opening partnership of 295 which nearly, but not quite, won the match.

The first Test came at the beginning of December and before it there was an incident which is very similar to that involving Shane Warne and Mark Waugh in modern times. Farnes wrote: *'It was about this time that Allen was promised £475 if he would divulge the composition of our team for the third Test provided the donor won the first prize outright in the forecasting competition that a newspaper were running.'* There are no prizes for guessing what Gubby's reply was.

Farnes was left out of the first Test with Copson, Sims, Duckworth and Fishlock, forming in Duckworth's words the ground staff. Farnes wrote: *'It was somewhat difficult I believe to know whether Bill Voce or I should play for Bill had taken very few wickets so far, having been most unlucky. The wisdom of the selection was to be amply illustrated'*, even though Wisden commented that Voce had not produced his anticipated bowling while Farnes had shown little of his speed and fire. Just why this was we just don't know and Farnes in his self-effacing way did not elaborate in the same way that he never bothered to mention his triumphs. It may have been the journey, it may have been fear of straining muscles, although as a fitness fanatic he should not have worried. It may just be that the fire of 1936 had been dampened and it was not until the end of the tour that it began to spark and then roar again. It certainly was not homesickness because in his autobiography he relates with delight all the sights he saw and appreciated, ready to paint when he had the opportunity.

Voce, sharing the opening attack with his captain, had six in the first innings and four in the second with match figures of 10 for 57, great bowling. He had Bradman for 38 and Robinson in both innings. And after a terrible start, McCormick taking 3 for 26 in eight overs - Worthington and Hammond for a duck and Fagg for four - and then going off with lumbago, England won by 322 runs. Much of England's victory was due to an Australian collapse to 58 all out in the second innings thanks to Voce's ability to make the ball run away. The gate was down a bit on the usual numbers but that was not due to the cricket but the pending abdication of King Edward VIII, their King 12,000 miles away, who was giving up his crown for the twice-divorced American socialite Wallis Simpson.

Farnes had a game between the first and second Tests, against a Queensland Country XI, where his bowling was pathetic. He had no life and managed just one wicket so he was not surprised when he was again omitted from the team at Sydney which England won by an innings and 22 runs with Bradman and McCabe getting ducks in the first innings and 82 and 93 in the second. Voce bowled really well, taking seven wickets including McCabe twice and Bradman once.

The third Test, in front of an enormous crowd of 87,798 on the third day and a total of over 350,000 altogether, which started on New Year's Day, saw the end of the bright and confident morn as Australia won by 365 runs, even though England were not disgraced. This was because of rain during the weekend which turned the wicket into a gluepot and ruined England's chances in reply to Australia's 200 for nine declared. O'Reilly and Sievers were almost unplayable, with the ball stopping and rising sharply. Leyland and Hammond played wonderful innings, although if Hammond had been out sooner Allen would have been able to declare and get the Australians in on the evil pitch.

As it was he finally did at 76 for nine, not knowing what the weather would be on the next day and day after, Sunday and Monday. The Australians sent in O'Reilly and Fleetwood-Smith to open in the dimming evening light. After Voce had had the Tiger for a duck bad light stopped play.

There was a record gate on Monday and the wicket had dried out so much that tail-ender Ward, who had come in after the Tiger, proved hard to shift and stayed in most of the morning. Then the mask came off and Bradman top scored with 270 out of 564, setting a record 436 sixth wicket partnership with Jack Fingleton, who made 136. England were set 689 to win and although Leyland made 111 not out they only reached 323.

Farnes had a game against Tasmania and took three minor wickets, bowling DC Green twice. It did little to advance his credentials for inclusion in the fourth Test but his next game was better. There was some pace and fire and he took four for 31 off a dozen overs, including poor Grimmett who was an outcast to the home selectors. Farnes followed this with a wicket against South Australia at Adelaide, a game in which Bradman only made 18. The game was drawn because of rain.

Farnes did not know he was going to play in the next Test until a quarter of an hour before the start - in a temperature of around 100 degrees in the shade - and he was included only because there were justifiable doubts about Voce's fitness. He had strained his back and although he played, he was not the bowler he had been in previous matches.

It is interesting that the injury was due to retaining the same sort of studs he had in England. Farnes explained: *'These are apt to skid on the iron-hard Australian turf and the best sort of spikes are running spikes put in through the bottom sole of the boot. This was a piece of counsel given to me by Allen who also did for me what he did for Maurice Tate (one of the best bowlers in the twenties and early thirties) to save bruising the big left toe against the hard leather of the boot's toecap. He set to work one evening in Adelaide and, using a razor for a cobblers tool, carved a hole in the buck for the big toe. That is a very useful tip for fast bowlers who are liable to be put out of action by a bruised and blackened big toe. It was as useful a tip as one that Walter Brearley once gave me. I suffered from shin soreness and he advised me not to wind the bootlaces round my ankles - a very simple sounding tip but one that has saved a good deal of discomfort.'*

Bradman won the toss and Farnes came on first change for Voce and Allen and promptly got two wickets, those of WA Brown and new boy K Rigg, in the same over, bowling said that great observer and writer Neville Cardus, with attack, *'swinging the ball down from his upright position on a fine length. He forced both Bradman and McCabe back and the fast bowling, especially Farnes, conquered the turf with spirit and skill.'* From then on it was hard graft as he bowled the most overs of all the English bowlers, bowling Fleetwood-Smith to end the innings at 288. He did not have McCabe, that was left to Robins, who had him hooking once too often and caught by the captain.

121

Ken Farnes

England batted well and with a fine century by Barnett went ahead with 330. When Australia went in again it was unfortunately the same old story with Bradman making 212 *('the significant thing about his phenomenal skill is that he never fails when there is a half chance of his securing a win')* out of 433. Allen kept the Don's scoring to a slow pace for a long time by having Verity bowl to him just outside the leg side with the field packed there (Verity was far too slow for complaint) while the other bowlers tried to get the others out. Bradman did not like it but he persevered and eventually it was like the tide coming in and the massive score became inevitable. It left England far too many to win and they never looked like getting them, going down by 148 as the home side levelled the series. Fleetwood-Smith had 6 for 110 to halt England. Farnes had Rigg again in the Australian's second innings and his old rival O'Reilly.

Farnes then had two minor two day games at Geelong and Canberra, where he did nothing to impress anyone, and then really got going against New South Wales in Sydney where he had three and four wickets for 124 in the match and unfortunately broke Chipperfield's jaw as he hooked and missed and was out hit wicket. He had Fingleton caught behind in the first innings and had opener Beattie twice. It was this display that kept him ahead of Copson, who only took three wickets in the captain's vision.

And so came the final Test at Melbourne to decide the Ashes. Farnes wrote: *'Can you believe there were some who believe we lost the third and fourth Tests in order to have a big gate for the last. There were people, however, crass enough to think so!'* Bradman won the toss, the new stand was ready for over 92,000 people and hard as the MCC toiled it was that man again (they should have called him ITMA rather than Tommy Handley) who finished the series with 169 aided by McCabe and Badcock who both scored centuries in an awesome 604 during which both Farnes and Allen dropped a couple of catches each on the first day. As they say, pick the bones out of that. In that total were six wickets to Farnes - Fingleton, Rigg, Bradman bowled, Gregory (c Verity and all three killed in the war), Nash and Fleetwood-Smith caught. As Wisden said: *'Farnes came out with the magnificent figures of 6 for 96 in 28.5 overs.'* Voce had 3 for 123 and Verity 3 for 127.

Cardus proclaimed: *'Farnes was easily the best bowler. He bowled determinedly and deserved his fine analysis. He alone consistently made the batsmen aware of the likelihood of a perilous ball coming along off the ground.'*

122

He nearly caught and bowled Bradman but finally had him at the start of the second day *'trying a pull from a ball a little too high for the stroke and swift as light from the ground,'* said Cardus.

England's reply was poor with 180 for four at the end of third day and matters were worse after overnight rain so O'Reilly could do his damnedest. He took 5 for 61 and England were out for 239. In the second innings he claimed three more for 36 to make sure the Ashes stayed in Australia as England limped to 165 with Farnes bagging a pair.

Such was the joy in Australia that 20,000 people turned up on the final day to see Fleetwood-Smith bowl the last two balls to finish the old enemy off. It was a sad end, one that happens too often, to a series that had started with such promise and success.

Farnes was second in the Test bowling averages with his 11 wickets at 23.27 behind Voce, who had 26 excellent wickets for 21.53. His batting average was a ludicrous 7 and it was hardly worth his while walking to the crease!

The tour went on and in his last three games, one country game in Australia and two in New Zealand, he managed only three wickets to bring his three-day match average to 21.09, second to Copson at 19.81 with only 27 wickets. Farnes took 44, second only to Jack Sims.

The trip back was long and varied, by boat to Los Angeles, flying across the United States, having to decline a game in Hollywood, and then home on the Queen Mary and school.

15.

1937

FARNES HAD high hopes when he arrived back from his successful tour of Australia after his fine 6 for 96 in the last Test. He was now well known to every cricket fan in the land. There were only a few weeks between the arrival back of the party on the Queen Mary and the two trial matches at the end of May. New Zealand were the visitors and Farnes knew that his job would not allow him to play in the first two Tests but he would be available for the third which would be in school holidays.

So when the North met the South at Lord's he was ready and his bowling that day brought him high praise indeed. In the second innings he was very difficult to play, whipping the ball off the drying pitch to take three for eight in his first six overs, and five in total. His five victims were high class - Hutton and Dollery bowled, Hardstaff, Leyland and Wyatt caught.

I can imagine the look on Hardstaff's face because he was a wonderful player of fast bowling and Farnes must have been extra fast that day. I know how Hardstaff liked to play the fast stuff because he did it in the first ever county match I saw - at Trent Bridge in 1947 - when Notts played Warwickshire. My father had some business in the city and dropped me outside the ground around tea time, arriving there to see the start of the Notts innings. For Warwickshire the New Zealander Pritchard was playing, the fastest man in England. He dismissed Harris and Simpson in the first couple of overs and then in came Hardstaff, immaculate, shirt sleeves slightly rolled back. He set about Pritchard in no uncertain fashion, hitting him straight back over his head and to all other parts of the ground. He was unbeaten on 87 at the end of play and went on to 205 the next day.

When the MCC Australian XI played the Rest of England the wickets were more difficult to take but FARNES still bowled well, taking the wicket of Eddie Paynter and - inevitably - one of the Langridge brothers in the first innings and Jim Parks in the second.

There was then a gap of six weeks while he returned to teaching and the series started - England won it with victory in the only finished match at Lord's. He was back on the first class cricket scene in mid-July to give his usual polished performance in the Gentlemen v Players game. Once again he had a five wicket haul, including Hammond and Barnett, both of whom he dismissed twice.

The Players took the lead with seven wickets in hand - replying to 165 - when, said Wisden, the Gentlemen's bowling took a deadly turn. Farnes bowled some magnificent overs and the game levelled out for a while only for the Players to win comfortably in the end.

He could not play for England and Essex until the end of the month but when the time arrived what he and they hoped for did not happen because once again he was injured, this time straining his side. He longed to be able to bowl at full speed (as did everyone else) but it was not to be. He had to miss the Test and although not at full steam for his county, who improved to sixth in the championship, he still managed 35 wickets and took five in an innings four times.

He took seven of those wickets against Derbyshire at Ilkeston, including Worthington and Townsend, and ended his 7 for 41 stint by bowling his rival and friend Copson. Wisden said: *'Farnes, by sheer pace, seemed to demoralise his opponents and in the first ten overs he sent back six of them.'* Not content with that he thumped the ball all over the place for an undefeated 41, his second highest score, and claimed the wickets of Alderman and Townsend for the second time as Essex won by 10 wickets.

He managed only one Middlesex wicket for 141 at Chelmsford when the strain really affected him, but came back with a flourish on his favourite Southend wicket, taking five Hampshire crowns in the first innings and another one in the second. His speed and that of Nichols caused havoc to Hampshire who were all out for 94, Nichols taking four of the other five wickets.

Against Notts on the same ground he only managed two victims, Harris and George Gunn, but at Trent Bridge he was back to five in an innings again, Keeton and Gunn amongst them, and Nichols took four of the rest.

125

It was Nichols who took the bowling honours against Lancashire with nine wickets in the match but Farnes's injury held him back so much that he could only bowl seven overs in the second innings as Essex won by 302 runs at Clacton. The last county game of the season found Farnes near his best and he and Nichols took five each in an innings, Farnes in the second, all clean bowled. Both men at times were unplayable with their speed off the Clacton pitch and Essex finished the season with an innings and ten run victory.

Farnes had just one game left, the usual Festival fun at Scarborough, where he took four wickets for 166 in the Leveson Gower XI innings against the MCC Australian team. He was very tired. In total in 1937 he managed 35 wickets for Essex at a cost of 22.45 and 55 nationally for 21.94.

16.

1938

1938 WAS undoubtedly his best year, a year in which he was England's leading fast bowler and harvester of wickets with speed and accuracy that was unmatched almost anywhere in the world. He nearly did the hat trick twice, for England and for the Gentlemen when, in a display of lightning speed, he showed the selectors how wrong they had been not to pick him for the Old Trafford Test (typically washed out by rain). His success made him one of Wisden's Five Cricketers of the Year in the 1939 almanac (along with Denis Compton) and he was described as *essentially a natural cricketer*.

For once he had time off school to play in the Test series, the school proud of the honour and the boys hero worshipping him for what he was doing for England. At the very start of the season Evening News journalist EM Wellings named him as probably the best fast bowler in the world and there were many who agreed with him. Alf Gover of Surrey might have been faster with the new ball but all-round Farnes was the better, he wrote.

The season started for Farnes when the MCC met the Australians at Lord's in May. He took just one wicket and four more in the Test trial a fortnight later, when Wisden said *he maintained his reputation*, dismissing Yardley twice, his friend Wilcox clean bowled for a duck in the second innings and Fishlock. Wilcox was among the names being tipped in the papers (even The Times) as the man who might lead England against the Australians but Hammond, who had become an amateur, was given the job and Wilcox, sadly, was never picked for his country despite some fine batting in an era when the standard of English batting was extraordinarily high.

Farnes then had five wickets for Essex against Bradman's men, including Hassett and Chipperfield. He had already had one game for his county (who finished sixth in the championship) when he took four Glamorgan wickets at Swansea.

The first Test at Trent Bridge was a very high scoring game with England making 658 for 8 (Hutton 100, Barnett 126, Paynter 216 not out and Compton 102) and Australia 411 (McCabe 232) and 427 for 6 dec (Brown 133, Bradman 144 not out) and it was drawn. It was McCabe's match, his innings acclaimed as one of the best ever and for once Farnes did not take his wicket. He had Brown, Ward, Barnett and O'Reilly instead, although he rued the fact that the nightwatchman Ward was the one who received a real snorter from him that would have been too good for almost any batsman while McCabe was at the other end.

Farnes did not play again until the second Test at Lord's, Hammond's match, when the England captain made 70 before lunch, 70 between lunch and tea and finally 70 between tea and the close of play, adding another 30 the next morning in his wonderful 240. Even so the rain affected game was drawn with Bradman getting another century, aided partly by the inability of Farnes to bowl anywhere but on the leg stump, which to Bradman was manna from heaven.

Farnes had McCabe again, caught by Verity, and would have done the hat trick if Compton had not dropped Fleetwood-Smith in the slips next ball. Farnes had firstly dismissed O'Reilly and McCormick, but the drop may well have saved England because Fleetwood-Smith stayed with Brown, who was on his way to 206 not out, on a rain soaked wicket that would have benefited McCormick considerably if he had been able to get at the English batsmen there and then. When he did almost an hour later he dismissed Barnett and Bill Edrich quickly before close of play.

When the team for the third Test was announced Farnes was omitted. The day after that game ended Farnes showed emphatically why he should be in the side for the Leeds fourth Test. In a quite dazzling piece of bowling he made his point with 8 for 43 as the Gentlemen beat the Players for only the second time since 1914. The most impressive part of this display was his bowling on the easy paced pitch just before the close of play on the first day when he had Edrich caught by Stephenson for a duck, managing to hit a head high ball with his gloves and face, then Price next ball, caught by Hammond, by now a Gentleman after captaining the Players the year before, and then narrowly failing to claim the wicket of Paynter for his hat trick.

Farnes in full flow

The debonaire Farnes immortalised on a cigarette card

Essex County Cricket XI 1936

Cricketing friends ready to play
Earl of Lincoln's XI v Worksop College

III

Fast bowler in his prime

The 1936/37 MCC team to Australia and New Zealand

Bowling to Bradman at Melbourne 1937

Following Walter Hammond onto the field for the 1938
Lord's Test v. Australia
From the right: Hammond, Verity, Ames, Edrich,
Hutton, Farnes, Compton(concealing Wellard),
Paynter, Wright and Barnett

Bowling to Stan McCabe during his famous 232
at Trent Bridge, 1938. For once he did not get him out.

Denis Compton's middle stump sent flying

The Gentlemen of Essex v. The Players of Essex 1938

Back row: Umpire W Mead, JWA 'Stan' Stephenson, Reginald Taylor, Nicky Vere-Hodge, John Dennis, Ken Farnes, Peter Smith, Ray Smith, Frank Vigar, Tommy Wade and Umpire Bill Reeves
Seated: Nigel Wykes, Harold Palmer, Henry Franklin, Tom Pearce, Jack O'Connor, Denys Wilcox, Morris Nichols, Laurie Eastman
In front: AR Lord, Harry Daer, Alfred Avery, Alan Lavers and Stan Cray

On tour with his camera

VIII

Sunday, 13th.

The W. Province team took us round Chapman's Peak past Hout Bay — a winding road cut out of the cliff & overlooked by the bluffs called the Twelve Apostles. At the point by Chapman's Peak, beer was produced & the lads were offered the chance of trying to throw stones into the sea — an apparently easy task as the sea looked almost directly below. As far as we could see nobody reached though one or two may have done.

Past Muizenberg & its surf — Indian Ocean & so warmer than the Atlantic Sea Point side.

On the way back we stopped at the Olympic Club near Newlands for drinks & snooker. And so back to the Queen's for dinner.

Monday 14th

Rain interrupted play considerably but we passed their score after losing 6 wickets.

Went to see "Robin Hood" — extravagant, colourful & not too bad

An extract from the South African Tour Diary

IX

Immortalised on canvas

Farnes seated left in his last match, British Empire XI v. Captain
J.W.A. Stephenson's West of England XI

Trophies:
His hat-trick ball v. Nottinghamshire, 1939
and 15 wickets v. Glamorgan 1938

A. Ellis is presenting "wings" to top cadet of the course,
L.A.C. Farnes K. at the graduation ceremony

XII

Seated right with other cadets

After joining the R.A.F.

Paul Cave

**Aeron with daughter Diana
(now the wife of film critic Barry Norman)**

His grave at the Military Cemetery,
Brookwood, Surrey

Edrich recalled afterwards: *'He was seeking his place after they had dropped him from the third Test. Everyone felt that he was bowling at the top of his form. He did not like it any more than I would have done in his boots, so he made up his mind he would show everyone what was what.*

'Farnes bowled that evening faster than any bowler I have ever met. The first ball jumped off a completely dead pitch and flew outside my off-stump head high just short of a length. The next pitched on the same length and jumped like lightning straight at my eyes. I tried to play back, a defensive back stroke while turning my head and lifting my hands. The next thing I knew was that someone was saying smoothly, "have some water, there's no hurry". The whole place was spinning. The ball had gone off my glove to my forehead and into the waiting hands of Stan Stephenson.'

He went on to go through almost all the team, including Hutton, Hardstaff, Compton, Essex team mate Nichols, Smailes and Pollard in what EW Swanton described as one of the fastest pieces of bowling he had ever seen at Lord's. In the second innings he had Price and Compton again plus TPB Smith.

The Times reported: *'In the recent Test match at Lord's he was inclined to pitch the ball over much on the leg stump. This time, again bowling from the pavilion end, he kept the ball rigorously on the wicket and in fact made it run occasionally up the hill. Without striving for any great pace he maintained both fire and accuracy to provide an example of what fast bowling should be.'*

Wisden praised him too saying: *'No effective resistance was offered to Farnes who, in a series of six spells altogether, took eight for 43. This was probably the best fast bowling in this match since Arthur Fielder dismissed all the Gentlemen at a cost of 90 runs in 1906. Farnes always bowled at the stumps and fully earned his reward.'*

He was picked for the Headingley Test which Australia won by five wickets. England made 223 and Australia 242, with another century from Bradman. Farnes took four wickets, including McCabe clean bowled, before England collapsed to 123, leaving Australia just 105 to win.

They had to fight for all of them. They lost four wickets for 61 and Hammond kept Farnes and Bowes, neither of whom were doing well, on in the appalling light without a sight screen in case Wright might be too erratic and expensive. It did not work and the Australians reached their target for the loss of five wickets.

Farnes then had a spell with his county, starting at Worcester where he took 14 wickets in the match as Essex won by four wickets. Wisden used the adjective *'superb'* for his bowling and it was just that. Only the Nawab of Pataudi could play him as four sets of stumps - and finally his own – were dismantled in the first innings and three others in the second as the Essex fury bowled just over 40 overs.

This was followed in quick succession by five wickets against Notts and six against Northants. Next came Surrey on the same ground and he had four wickets in the first innings and two in the second.

Middlesex at Lord's was the next game, where he claimed just two wickets, and then on to the Oval over the river for the final Test. It was Hutton's timeless test as he made 364 in 13 hours 20 minutes and Leyland and Hardstaff also plundered the weak Australian bowling in an innings of 903 for 7 declared. Even with that score Tiger O'Reilly never gave up and for Farnes he was the best bowler since the Golden Age of Cricket, believing it was the Irish in him that made him aggressively hostile and *'if looks or even words could kill the batsman who snicks him for four he would die on the spot.'*

When the Australians finally had a chance to bat - minus Bradman, who injured his ankle so badly he did not play again on the tour - Farnes took just one wicket, that of McCabe, who must have dreaded facing the tall Essex man because he had him caught again in the second innings when he claimed four wickets.

England won by an innings and 579 runs and drew the series with Australia taking the Ashes home where they were to stay for another 15 years.

Once the Tests were out of the way it was back to Essex and lovely Clacton-on-Sea where he had triumphed so often. He was to do it again when he had his best match ever, a haul of 15 wickets as Glamorgan were overwhelmed. The wicket, which had been covered overnight, sweated and left several damp spots. It broke up when Farnes bowled flat out and the ball constantly kicked from a good length. He bowled unchanged for 22.5 overs, clean bowling four in his seven for 75. In the second innings the helpless Welshmen found him unplayable. No one could stand up to his terrific speed on a bad wicket and in nearly 12 overs he claimed eight of them for 38.

The Daily Telegraph said: *'The captain, DR Wilcox, must have been* surprised by the success of Farnes because the pitch was not suited to his type of bowling. He broke the backbone of Glamorgan's batting. He made the ball lift viciously and the batsmen, forced to make their shots too soon, never settled down.'

Essex won by an innings and 87 runs and a few days later saw off Gloucester by an innings and 65 runs, with Farnes taking four wickets, all from catches.

He ended his longest season with three matches at Scarborough. For MCC against Yorkshire he had Sutcliffe and Mitchell (a sweet revenge) amongst his four victims and then took four more wickets in the Gentlemen v Players match, including Hutton twice after the young Yorkshireman had punished him heavily, and finally four again for Leveson-Gower's XI v the Australians, mighty tired after a punishing tour. For once he did not get McCabe but he did have poor old Bill O'Reilly again amongst his three wickets as the Aussies, were defeated.

It was at this Festival that Farnes and his lifetime friend Geoff Chapman met for the last time. Geoff was teaching at nearby Middlesbrough, and went to the coast each autumn to see Farnes. They also met occasionally at each other's family homes and down in Devon where Geoff's family were based at Newton Abbot, with a small clock golf course in the garden. The only problem was putting; lining up a putt was danger-ous because around the garden were a form of Yucca bush known as needles due to their sharp pointed ends. Once when Farnes, no mean golfer on the links, was checking the line he backed into one and a large needle stuck in his backside. This caused much hilarity from Geoff but not from his much younger brother Chris (now a west country bookseller) who thought it was not right that such a famous cricketer should suffer such an indignity.

Geoff also went to Ken's brother's house at Great Warley, Essex, where he taught the children, David and Joan, to play chopsticks on the piano, which gave their parents something to listen to! Norman, six years older, steady and placid, had a room ready for his brother but he never returned from the war.

His friend remembers watching Farnes at the Festival both on and off the field. *'Two of the players were having a friendly sort of wrestling match near the pavilion and he came out and watched them, looking at them in an interested way as if looking at animals. He was interested in his fellow man in the way that he liked people, enjoyed company and the characters who were around who amused him. He would watch them as if they were characters in a play.*

'It was on that occasion that he told me a story, the kind that he told my father which made him roar with laughter: At Scarborough there was one of those tedious people who loves to rub shoulders with top sports people and has plenty of money. He insisted in the pavilion that all the lads had a drink with him, a pint of whatever they wanted. Len Hutton kept shaking his head and the man kept on insisting that he must have a pint of something. Eventually Hutton gave in and said ' all right, I'll have a pint of shrimps' and the man sent out someone to buy a pint of them from one of the dealers on the prom.'

Back to the season. Essex reported: *'Whenever he turned out for the county the attack was doubled in strength. He took only 56 wickets but at a cheaper cost than any other bowler.'* When the averages were totted up Farnes had taken 17 Test wickets at 34.17 each. For Essex, who finished sixth in the championship, he had 56 for his best ever average of 14.89 and a total of 107 first class wickets in the season for 18.84, which put him much closer to Bowes and Verity than usual - 15.23 and 15.67.

It was excellent preparation for the tour to South Africa where timeless cricket took on an entirely new meaning.

17.

SOUTH AFRICA 1938/39

THE TOUR to South Africa in the winter of 1938/9, the last anywhere before the war, was an outstanding success, a great boost to the home country. It was also a feast for any batsman and England were superlatively strong in in this department as they took the cream of all English cricket with them, the strongest team ever to go to Africa, on pitches made just for them and equally bad news for any bowler, even those on form.

And the sad truth is that Farnes, Reg Perks, Tom Goddard, Len Wilkinson and Doug Wright were not. Wisden could not explain it, suggesting *'just the vagaries of cricket and the perfect pitches that gave the batsmen the upper hand.'*

For Farnes it was almost heart-breaking. He never really got going and once again the fiery furnace that stoked him at his best, which was little short of brilliant, was out, a wet, damp smouldering memory of what might have been.

Not that it was all disaster. He did manage five wickets in a match twice and had four wickets in the ridiculous timeless match which ended after ten days only because England, who were then 654 for four, had to leave otherwise they would have missed their boat home.

Unfortunately Farnes, as ever, gives no clue, his only comment being about the wickets. He wrote: *'I suppose that in batting the South Africans were strong. If I do not appear to be very convinced of this it is because the wickets out there make batting a comparatively straightforward business. I often had the feeling that it would not be long before the batsmen had no one to serve up the bowling for them for the turf removes nearly all the sting in the attack. There is little pace in them to encourage the fast bowler to make the little extra effort that means so much; spin seldom takes on the first few days; flight remains but even this is greatly discounted when your batsmen can just go on playing down the line. If I could have*

133

a batting average of just on 20 the wickets must obviously have been much too good.'

To have some idea of how easy they were during the tour, five English batsmen averaged over 50 in the Test matches, seven in all matches, and three double centuries were scored. The bowlers toiled for awful averages in eight ball overs and only Verity averaged under 30 in the Tests, although in all matches the averages were better, with Wilkinson 18.86 (compared to his 38.71 in Tests) and Verity under 20. Goddard, Farnes and Wright were all over 25.

Whatever the state of the cricket, though, Farnes really enjoyed himself during the long tour that lasted from November to the middle of March. He went sight-seeing everywhere, meeting as many people as he could and loving every minute of it. Whether he loved the cricket or not is hard to judge. In any event it was all rather leisurely and enjoyable and Farnes played in 15 of the 18 matches and in all the Tests.

The tour began in Cape Town and in the first match the batsmen served up a taste of what was to come, with Paynter and Hammond getting hundreds and Hutton 68. Farnes took a couple of wickets and in the second game had his best figures of the tour, with 3 for 32 in the first innings against Western Province and then a fine 7 for 38 in the second, taking the last four for 16. It gave him great confidence but in his next game, at Kimberley amongst the diamond fields, he came down to earth with no wickets in the two innings and followed this with another blank against Natal in Durban, where Hammond and Hutton hit centuries, Edrich 98 and Farnes an undefeated 33.

Farnes wrote in his diary: *'The sun glare was so great that in the afternoon it was impossible to see the ball travel from the bat. The wicket was like asphalt. Any grass there may have been was rubbed off with a brick! The outer part of the outfield was loose red gravel and energetic fieldsmen threw up clouds of red dust as they fielded the ball.'*

He managed four for 93 against Transvaal, where Ames joined the century makers, Paynter and Bryan Valentine having made one apiece in the match before against North-Eastern Transvaal in which Farnes did not play.

The first Test was over Christmas in the high altitude of Johannesburg and was a high scoring draw (Paynter scoring two centuries and Paul Gibb in his first Test almost did the same, with 93 and 106) but the bowlers laboured on such an easy pitch and Farnes managed just one wicket for 104 off a total of 30 overs. Verity bowled 60.

He wrote that at the end of the first day they were 322 for 6 and *'they* stuck to their work well and did well to get six of us out. *There may be rain and the wicket is not covered in Tests and so there may be some fun before the match ends and we've got a good start in that case.'*

There was a record crowd when play continued on Boxing Day. Farnes noted: *'Bryan (Valentine) played delightfully this morning and was out just before lunch going for his hundred with Tom (Goddard) the last man in at the other end. He made 97. Bruce Mitchell and Peter van der Bijl* (he whose ribs Farnes had cracked a few times in the Varsity match in 1932) *opened and Bruce was in his thirties in no time. Wally (Hammond) put Hedley (Verity) on for Bill (Copson) and bowled himself at my end and the scoring slowed almost immediately. Peter was lbw to Hedley for four and Alan Melville (the captain) was c and b Hedley for 0. Then Nourse and Mitchell had a long partnership of over 100.*

'At tea Wally said "we must bowl tight tonight, there's some rain about." And they played into our hands and Bruce's score stood at 56 for just on an hour! The clouds rolled up and the air was close. That and the altitude made it painful for me to bowl and I gasped for breath after only one or two balls - worse than the last match. I had two spells of one over each after tea.*

'As often happens after a long period of extremely slow and cautious play, a few wickets fall quickly. Tom caught and bowled Nourse for 73 and proceeded to do the hat-trick. Gordon came in for night patrol duty and was stumped very well by Les (Ames), Billy Wade then came in and was bowled by one that turned sharply and we all dashed over to congratulate Tom' and the South Africans were 166 for 5 and needed 107 to save the follow on.'

Next day Farnes took a wicket in the second over but this was followed by a long stand between Dalton (107) and Viljoen (50). *'Both gave several chances. Unfortunately Langton was missed at deep mid-off off Hedley by Tom who didn't see the ball properly and then proceeded to make 64 not out so that they got 390 in spite of five noughts in the side and the five new caps got four of them between them. They had all the luck and Wally said 'if we'd had as much luck as they had we'd get two million.'* Yes, they had the devil's own fortune in close shaves and missed chances.

'A cool breeze blew in the morning and gradually the day grew cooler.'

Farnes read his book the next morning as Gibb and Paynter made hundreds and *'Wally made some fine shots before declaring at ten to three. They made no attempt to score the runs and Bruce (Mitchell) was painfully slow even when they were in no danger of defeat. He came in for some barracking and Wally gave him all the bowling he could as a result. He made 48 in 2 3/4 hours. Quite a restful and futile afternoon's cricket.'*

The second Test at Cape Town followed over the New Year and was another draw with the England captain Hammond, Valentine and Ames making hundreds with Nourse getting one for the home team. Verity was again top English bowler while Farnes struggled for his solitary wicket.

Again he criticised Mitchell for his slow play. He wrote in his diary: *'The game was incredibly dull as Bruce practically never tried to make a run and didn't even run some that were there. He was in for four and a quarter hours for 42 when Doug (Wright) knocked his off peg down with a real good 'un that pitched about middle and leg. It never seems policy to refuse runs even when batting defensively and at the close they had lost six wickets for 213 after Mitchell had been third out at ten past five.'*

Just before the end Balaskas hit Verity for four fours in succession but *'the wickets had begun to take spin. I bowled poorly, feeling no spring in my body and the pitch was absolutely lifeless.'*

The next day meant a whole hot day in the field. *'The heat beat up from the ground and in the afternoon so that it was not too pleasant lying down at the fall of a wicket as you got right in the warmest layer of air.'*

When the host team was out *'the wicket was easier than it was last night for the ball no longer turned as it had done and one or two of their chaps wondered if it had had a sprinkle of water.'* South Africa followed on and played out time. *'So we plodded on till six o'clock brought the match to a close. Another draw and a dull match as it was bound to be on such a dead easy wicket.'*

He did much better against Eastern province at Port Elizabeth, bagging five in their first innings, four of them clean bowled, and another two in the second and always causing the batsmen considerable trouble. Hutton joined the century makers with 202.

His form continued in the Third Test at Durban with four for 29 in South Africa's first innings and three more for 80 in the second, the dominating role in England's victory, but he makes no mention - typically - of his success. England won the match - and unknowingly the series - by an innings and 13 runs and joint credit was given to Paynter, the captain and Farnes. Hammond (120) helped Paynter (243) in a 242 stand and held five catches in the slips, including three off Farnes, who bowled fast with verve and accuracy on the easy going pitch which also allowed Bruce Mitchell to make 109 for the hosts.

He wrote of Eddie's great batting and *'some rain stopped play for a few minutes near the end of the day and after a short resumption came down again and stopped play five minutes before time. It came down heavily for a short while and looked promising for us.'*

On day two Hammond declared at 12.30 on 496 for four having made the last 21 runs of his 120 in ten minutes. *'We failed to get a wicket before lunch although there was still a bit of juice in the pitch,'* wrote Farnes. South Africa were all out for 103 and *'after tea I got three quick wickets, a grand catch at first slip by Wally to dismiss Billy Wade. The hat trick was on as Langton was out first ball but Gordon survived it. I finished up with 4 for 29 and should have made it five as I had four balls at Davies.*

'They followed on. Peter van der Bijl was plumb lbw to me and given not out - deliberate cheating in my opinion as Les agrees that there was never anything more certainly lbw.

'Wally's catching was superb.'

When play resumed on the Monday (after a day fishing and rain in the evening when *'we looked at it with suppressed joy as it may help to get the match over soon')* he wrote: *'Thank God the match ended today. Still a bit tired and stiff from Saturday. I hated the day's play. Mitchell and Rowan batted together till after lunch when Les caught Bruce off me at 165, having batted very well for 109.*

'Owing to a special Test match rule the groundsman is allowed to do what he can to improve the wicket after rain the day before and so at 06.30 the wicket was rolled for ten minutes. I believe it was rolled over Hessian which is definitely against the rules. Also it was cut which is legal on the Monday morning of a match. Seven more minutes before play began and the wicket had rolled out plumb, more easy paced than it was on Saturday, a hard day's slogging in the field. Before tea I felt I never wanted to play another day's Test cricket and thought it would be nice to go crackers and have to be shut up away from cricket.'

The wickets fell fairly frequently and *'Wally made another magnificent catch high and wide with the right hand to get rid of Viljoen off me'* and the game was over just before six o'clock.

In three minor matches in South Africa and Rhodesia Farnes picked up six wickets and managed some runs, a 16 not out and 33, before the drawn rain affected fourth Test in Johannesburg, where amazingly no one scored a century (Hutton 92) and Farnes toiled through 26 overs for two wickets for 64.

He wrote in his diary how a heavy shower made the pitch treacherous, the ball lifting a bit and turning a little so that South Africa were on top and things not helped when Melville gave *'a most difficult chance off my last ball but it was an inside edge and had Les going the wrong way. Poor Bill Edrich was cheated out this time. I was in at the time and could see the ball wouldn't have hit another three but he was given leg before. I felt Bill O'Reilly would have liked the conditions. I felt very savage about things and bowled many outside the leg stump, curse it.'*

On the Monday he said: *'A lot of rain in the night soaked the wicket and just round it and we did not start the match until 2 o'clock. In my first over Melville took two on the torso in succession. Hedley bowled from the other end and his first ball jumped and turned. They needed 66 to save the follow on. Chances of them not making seemed not too distant. After two overs Tom bowled instead of me. Instead of following on the first pair put on more than 100. Never has Hedley bowled such stuff - full tosses and long hops that Melville smote for four without fail. He played extremely well and so did Peter (van de Bijl). Tom bowled fairly at first and he played him well. And after a while he kept bowling at or outside the leg stump.'*

Everything went wrong and MCC played terribly for he wrote: *'We've been praying for a sticky wicket to get a Test over quickly and now we had a real beauty the bowlers bowled worse than they've ever done. Things certainly did not go our way and during the day we missed many chances. I dropped Peter in the gully off Wilkie who bowled no length at all but very soon after Hedley caught Alan and Tom bowled Peter. Even then we thought we'd have them and for less than 200 possibly but chances went down and the bowling was terrible.*

'Rowan stayed and gave a couple of chances and Bruce cocked one up in Tom's leg trap which Bill held but Wilkie in excitement pounced at it too and knocked it out of Bill's hands. I bowled slowly and pretty poorly but had Bruce out just before the end. At the close they were 239 for 3 - an amazing, incredible, shocking performance by us and a good one by them.'

A day was lost by rain and then: *'I was amazed that Melville didn't declare at once for although they were only 34 ahead the wicket was still damp and the ball likely to move more in the morning than at any other time. With only today to play there was no real risk of them losing but they might have got us out cheaply. As it was they didn't even force the pace. Eric Rowan made eight in the first hour.*

'Again we didn't take the chances offered. Bill dropped Nourse at second slip off me, a fairly hard high left handed catch. Hedley bowled and one or two

138

catches went down off him. Les caught Rowan on the leg side off me and it was given not out. I bowled nearly all morning. Tom only bowled one over and Wally three at the end. Bowling was pretty painful. I took it steady and walked back very slowly. The wicket was still useful and lifted a bit now and again. Langton, sent in to force the pace, did not last long but Newsom made many passes at the ball without much success till he took eight off one over of Wally's. In all I had 10 overs for 23 runs and Rowan's wicket.'

MCC played out time and *'we were a bit lucky to get away with a draw after our shocking batting and worse bowling and fielding.'*

He had three wickets in two innings for 132 on a docile wicket like a piece of carpet against Natal and arrived with the team for the farcical fifth Test at Durban.

Farnes summed it up like this: *'For most reasons I should prefer to draw a veil over this match. Since we were only one match up in the series it was to be played to a finish. After ten days no result had been reached and it had to be abandoned so that we could reach Cape Town in time to catch the Athlone Castle home. The Kingsmead wicket at Durban was nearly as good when rain put an end to the proceedings on our last possible day as it had been all through. This was, however, largely because showers had fallen and been sufficient to bind the turf together every time it showed signs of wear. Had it lasted so long without the rain of course it would have been a thorough disgrace of over-preparation. As day followed day and we trooped in and out of the pavilion the whole performance became somewhat ludicrous. It was only raised from this by our amazing last innings score. Left with 695 to score to win we were less than 50 from our goal with four wickets in hand when the rain ended the match. There was so much batting that it would be tedious to mention details but Bill Edrich's double century in our second innings more than atoned for his previous failures and bad fortune.'*

For the record the match lasted 10 days. For South Africa (530 and 481) Van der Bijl, Nourse and captain Alan Melville made hundreds. For MCC (316 and 654 for five) Gibb, Hammond and Edrich did the same.

The poor bowlers once again took stick with Farnes taking 1 for 108 off an amazing 46 overs in the sun and four for 74 in the second innings, claiming the wickets of Melville and Nourse amongst them. He also made 20 which gave him an average, his best ever in tests, of 8.33 and over 18 in all matches.

18.

TOUR DIARY

KEN FARNES left two legacies which give clues about his personality, his thinking, his ambitions and outlook on life. One, as you know, was his autobiography which really tells little about his life after leaving the bank in 1930 and starting on his cricketing career.

The other was a diary that he kept on board the Athlone Castle on the trip with the 1938/9 touring party to South Africa and then throughout the tour until the end of the Fourth Test match when, after dozens of pages, he ran out of space, and if there was a bit more to cover the timeless fifth Test it did not survive his death.

He wrote it in his own tidy hand, sometimes drawing maps as illustrations, and for once he lets down the curtain a little and reveals the kind of man he really was - deep-thinking, unsure of his future, regretting his lack of ability at music, and at the same time a fun lover, rowdy in the many, many parties the team attended over the long months touring up and down the vast Continent, looking at everything, the wonderful scenery, the mines, the way black people lived, through artist's eyes and recounting it, some in powerful descriptive language.

He wrote too of his colleagues and none more often than Bryan Valentine of Kent, who had him in stitches with his devil-may-care attitude; he wrote much of the girls he met (and as EW Swanton who was on the tour and partied with the players, told me, he was always surrounded by lovely girls, greatly attracted by this handsome man) and one in particular whom he met on the boat out but who warned him against shipboard romances; and he wrote of the books he read, the paintings he saw, the music he heard and the films he viewed with a critical air for he was looking at writing as something that he might be able to do particularly well, having a semi-contract with Boy's Own Paper (now sadly defunct) to do six articles on his return.

140

The diary is a mixture of the great fun (and late hours when not playing) that they all had, the never-ending round of parties, visits to cinemas, every town's art gallery, museums, concerts, horse and dog racing and even ice hockey, plus the beauty spots (Victoria Falls was the best) and gold and diamond mines, playing golf, regular foursomes with girls in the evening, surf bathing, mistaking porpoises for sharks. It is an account of great camaraderie and an adventure that none would forget.

Here is a sample from it, starting with his thoughts on the night Athlone Castle set sail from Southampton on October 21 (Trafalgar Day) 1938:

'That night I felt detached, partly perhaps a reaction after the nervous strain of packing and labelling and storing the car.' (After the tour, one of his former pupils told me, he went back to Worksop College driving a Standard hp drop-head coupe, apparently a present in lieu of wages from some MCC benefactor. Farnes always liked a fast car and drove several models during the tour.)

'I settled down after dinner and jotted down some aims I had fairly clear in my mind having felt somewhat disgruntled with myself. While I am away I am determined to:

1. Try to judge the effect of external things and remain conscious of my inner, natural, more realized self instead of being overcome or swamped by successive and accumulative environments experienced on tour; in other words to attempt to get closer to realizing 'my' self.

2. Overcome my shyness which is the result of an unmoulded or unrealized self.

3. See and probe things by observing them as far as possible as complete in themselves and not just by the way they affect me: I know I have only understood the small fraction of things, people and events that have affected me instead of the events as they are inter-related to themselves.

I then thought I could see some value in changes of mood since they show up other aspects of things. Having felt depressed before leaving England prompted me in this for I have seen with a shock some children whose appearance in the East End (of London) seemed a horrible reflection on the state of civilisation or education. They were monstrous in their lack of realization.

4. Concentrate; since only by intense and continued concentration the subjugation of self to the required metaphysical state is awareness possible.

5. Refuse to be put off from the attainment of my aims and ideals by the

141

attitude of others to my ideas.

In this detached mood, not keyed up by the thought of the tour to which I had felt strongly indifferent, I picked up Dunne's The New Immortality and become absorbed and thrilled, glimpsing a new world. (Not what you expect to find in what was possibly a basis for a novel he started later on the tour or the normal cricketing autobiography, certainly of that era. But Farnes was not a normal cricketer. Later we will see how he was totally fed up with the game, certainly on the tour.)

On the journey he met a girl called Peggy to whom he was greatly attracted: *'conversations with Peggy made me want her company as much as possible and I liked everything about her and disliked nothing at all. She reminded me that the atmosphere of a voyage must be taken into account but I knew that here it was not just that'* and they continued to correspond, some of her letters cheering him greatly when depressed, but those seemed to peter out by February.

Nov 7 in Cape Town and out for an evening drive with their hosts: *'We were taken along the coast below high grey crags as far as the road went round to a point. It was a brilliant night and a superb sight as the moon's shafts came over the hills and fell on the rocks and foam below where a small river entered the sea. When we got back to the hotel the shadow of the earth had begun to creep across the moon and before I went to bed the eclipse was almost complete. During the ride some phrases had occurred to me and I tried to write some poetry, going out now and again on to the bedroom balcony to see how the moon was getting on.'*

Nov 15: match v Western province and a rare mention of his prowess: *'I got 7 for 38 - things just going my way and bagging the tail-enders too.'*

Nov 17: *'played solo with Reg Perks, Len Hutton and Hedley Verity after reading the introduction from Tagore's Gitanjale'* which Verity had lent him.

Nov 18 and visit to Kimberley diamond mine; it was the conditions of the black workers that interested him as much as anything else: *'Before leaving we went over the native compound. Here the blackmen live and are not allowed out until their terms of service is up. They sign up for a term of eight months and may sign up again for as long as they like. One boy had been there for 13 years without going out, one for ten and several for five. Before leaving they have to have three days detention while they are given castor oil etc. Every precaution is taken to prevent them from getting away with any diamonds. Their pay is 2/6d per day minimum.'*

Nov 22: discovered the effect of the heat while fielding: *'The maximum shade temperature today was 97 degrees and this with a stiff breeze and blowing dust* has made the morning pretty unpleasant. If there is any grit about it seems to make straight for my eye. The dryness of the air dries the sweat on you immediately and you don't seem to perspire while you are in the open.'

Nov 26 and on the train to Durban he has a talk with Hutton. The contrast could not be greater - the dour cricket fanatic from the grim north country Yorkshire and the part time amateur schoolmaster from semi-Metropolitan Essex: *'I shared a compartment with Len Hutton and we had a bit of a discussion. He has decided that I appear to have no ambition and my attitude to cricket and golf is different from his. He has noticed that when I beat the bat and shave the wicket I don't throw my arms up in the air at so nearly getting a wicket as Bill Bowes or Nichols do. I tried to explain something about myself but found it difficult. I had no concrete ambition, I said, for any particular job though I should like a good deal of money. The aim of getting a headmastership didn't appeal to me, firstly because the actual job itself had no great appeal though I should like the salary. My ambitions concerned myself and its realization etc. His future is clear before him and he has been well advised financially.'*

It is a shame that there is not more. On one side there was the dedicated batsman, on the other what appeared to be the dilettante bowler, broad acres apart in outlook and practice. Farnes, the amiable giant (and officially he was a giant at 6 ft 6 inches and more) who wandered round the art galleries and attracted girls like bees to the honeypot, and the determined Yorkshireman who wanted to be the best batsman in the world and who spent his leisure time playing golf - he had a level par 72 one day - who thought the amateur should show more fire. He was not alone in this because many other top cricketers thought a good kick up the backside to motivate him was just what was needed. One other point: the idea of throwing your arms up in despair or disgust when not getting a wicket does not appear to have been greatly in vogue in those days judging by the newsreels and other cricket books. It is interesting therefore that Hutton, whose own reaction to his 364 was to raise his bat half-heartedly, should expect it. That is the stuff of the kissing footballers from the age of five upwards and the modern bowlers for whom every missed ball is an appeal and every miss of the stumps an occasion for hysteria.

Nov 27 and the next day in Durban the mood must have stayed with him: *'On the way down* (from the train) *I felt in need of some good music and lo! opposite the hotel is the City Hall and a concert by the Municipal Orchestra starting*

Ken Farnes

20.30. They were good too and they played some delightful stuff and I enjoyed most Elgar's Three Bavarian Dances.

I also felt in some despair that I couldn't play or sing or perform or compose any artistic work sufficiently well and knew that somewhere in this direction lies my true bent in life - now too late to start (he was then 27). *How I wish music had been a matter of course for me and that the right sort of encouragement and force if necessary (not necessary with the right sort of encouragement) had been used as I definitely had an ear for it and - obviously - when I was a kid I was told I should never practice which is discouraging from the start and probably the reason why I howled so after my three violin lessons.'*

Again it is a pity that he does not comment further on this subject. He does write about art and he shows that he wants to write as a livelihood but whether it is to earn lots of money by combining the two jobs, writing and teaching, he just does not say.

Dec 3 and match against Natal: he had been having trouble with a strain in his neck and he thought it might reoccur but *'I was very pleased with my neck and I bowled quite well for no wickets and 14 runs in 13 overs. I was a bit untidy as they played at many without getting a tickle. I enjoyed it.'*

Dec 4 at a lunch party: *'After tea a judge and his son came along and I took a good view of the former with his cheerful conversation, grey ruffled hair, his keen face and the quite different shapes of his eyes and I also approved of him because he remarked how unlucky I was not to take any wickets yesterday.'*

Dec 5 and more of the cricket: *'I got more and more furious and disgruntled. Having played at dozens and not getting a tickle one eventually got a touch - Eric Dalton actually - Les (Ames) caught it and a great appeal went up. The umpire, curse him, gave him not out. And after lunch a plumb lbw was given not out also. Still I bowled quite quick and my neck is OK.'*

Dec 6 and party time after the game: *'Bryan (his fairly regular special companion) impetuously ordered champagne at dinner in his gusto manner. Afterwards we went to Cosmos, Durban's night club, dim red lights etc. We soon got pretty damp with sweat and pretty soon after midnight I was quite ready to depart feeling tired and satiated with dancing, the band, the majority of the people and the dim red light. Eventually we had some scrambled eggs, heard Eddie Paynter sing On Ilkley Moor through the microphone (which he can't remember) and emerged into the cool moonlit night.'*

Dec 9: at a reception he met General Smuts (South African Prime

144

Minister and great supporter of the British in both world wars) *'who looked fit and cheerful and talked with some of the lads, telling them about the Boer War and the present political situation.'* (This had now reached the stage when Hitler was beginning to invade parts of Europe and the year in which he duped Neville Chamberlain, the British Prime Minister, into believing that there would be peace in our time. War started less than ten months later when Germany invaded Poland).

Dec 10: Farnes wasn't playing in the match against NE Transvaal and while browsing in a bookshop found The Intimate Journals of Paul Gauguin which he took with him to the pretty tree-lined ground. Norman Yardley (later England captain) was standing in for the skipper Wally Hammond who was in hospital for two days with sunburn and Farnes was lying down reading his book: *'I watched intermittently but was far more interested in Gauguin though I caused some amusement in trying to get comfortable on the hard stand seats - lying down flat and looking over the edge of the seat to the book on the floor. Les, who is twelfth man, asked if I was comfortable and then I had to move as my length took up too much room.'* And later *'Saturday night drinking began and Cardinal Puff (a drinking game) came into his own.'*

Thus Dec 11: *'Bryan said he didn't feel so good this morning but he was still laughing and jumping about. He never flags. He is irrepressible and this morning before ten he came to see me and to tell me how he spoke to the band last night when they didn't play God Save the King and how he dealt with the porter when he went into Tom Goddard's room where they had foregathered at 03.00 to tell them to make less noise. Bryan, like a flash, was at him. 'First you refuse to sell us a drink at this time of night (3 am mark you!) and then you tell us to keep quiet. GET OUT!' The porter flew for his life.'*

Dec 12; *'Started my book this morning and the title might be South African Cricket Interlude but fear that those who want to read cricket will find too little; those who don't will find too much. Anyhow I don't like the beginning much, it's too precious. Mr Carew, my fictious character (the only one) may not be a good idea but I can't see that a straightforward cricket book would be any good.'* Later that day he was bored with drinking with the others after golf and wanted to get back to his book but stayed when someone told the story of a man who applied for the post of stock inspector in the Transvaal but his letter was misread and he stayed school inspector for 30 years.

Dec 15: He felt his neck during a net and then had a massage and later at the hotel met a fellow athlete from his Cambridge University athletics days and remembered him as *'one of those uncertain chaps who talk glibly with you one day and cut you the next. He asked me to go to dinner with him and I felt bound to accept I'm afraid.'*

He felt disgruntled after tea, read some Gauguin and then saw Lust for Life with illustrations of Van Gogh's paintings in colour, tone and black and white. *'I was sorely tempted but it was 24s which is rather a lot but would be a good Xmas present for myself. To Ken from Ken Jo'burg Xmas 1938'* so he bought it.

Dec 17: Hutton was knocked out by the third ball of the innings in the Transvaal match *'and was out for quarter of an hour. He seems to be OK though he is in hospital waiting to be X-rayed.'* Later went to a party with a partner one of the South African cricketers had found for him: *'It is definitely the last time I shall ever let anyone get me a partner. A lousy evening at the dance.'*

Dec 19: *'I only had five overs and felt my neck which depressed me very much.'* Later a crowd of the players went to a cocktail party *'and the house looked over a steep scarp to the surrounding country, an excellent view and rather better than I expected of Jo'bur (6000 ft above sea level) which I'm inclined to regard as a rather nasty excrescence on the countryside with its haphazard growth of tall buildings of cement and the yellow mine dumps beyond.'*

Dec 20: *'At tea time Fergie (the baggage man) said: "This Paul Gibb, he's everywhere: cricket, tennis squash, croquet all in one day. And you go into his room and it's like wild bulls have been chasing one another about in it."'*

Dec 21: *'I persuaded Doug (Kent spinner Wright) and Wilkie (Lancashire bowler Wilkinson) to walk by way of the Carlton and go in to see an exhibition of pictures by AE Mason who had some fresh painting of South African scenery and one of a cafe in the Cape which was in The Academy (in London). He came and talked for the rest of the morning to us and I should say he was a fairly slick craftsman with a good eye and a facile technique. But not a master as I think he lacked the mind of one.'*

Dec 22: At the West Rand Consolidated mine: *'In front of the office were five bars of gold weighing between them 344 pounds and £33,723 in value. I had heard that if you could lift one bar with one hand they'd give it to you. However I managed to lift one but my claim didn't meet with any response. Nobody else lifted one but Tom Goddard was late arriving and he would probably have done so.'*

Dec 24: after the first day's play in the first Test the players had a fairly riotous dinner. *'This afternoon Wilkie made a good remark. Les (Ames) had played forward at a leg spinner from Bruce Mitchell which left him sharply. I remarked to Wilkie that it looked a good un and he said 'yes, a good thrutchin length. Tonight at dinner he gave us the clue by the following rhyme:*

> *"If you want to shit with ease,*
> *Place your hands upon your knees*
> *Give a thrutch and then a squeeze*
> *And out it comes like lemon cheese."*

Then he and Doug Wright went into Jo'burg to find thousands of people in paper hats were rollicking about in the streets *'kicking tins and boxes and flipping everybody in the face with paper streamers fixed on the end of sticks and blowing toy trumpets...moderately drunken but good humoured, the streets were full of people like a Saturday night crowd in Worksop gone crazy.'*

Jan 2: in reflective mood went to watch the sunset *'and the silhouetted promontories of the peninsula and the loom of the Lion's Head. And when the sunset glow died the moon glistened on the lazy surf as the tide came in.*

'I was enjoying it immensely and indescribably and had come to the definite conclusion that God isn't interested in man's affairs in the slightest and Hitler's disturbances won't be altered by any amount of prayer. The old wonder was back at the meaning of things, this unbending beauty of the lonely world. When a fellow came up for the second time since I'd been up there on the rocks and probed me - where I came from, whether there were restrictions on the team (he guessed I was in it after a bit), whether we met many women on the boat etc... I strongly suspected him and was reminded of Eric Muspratt in Venice in Wild Oats and so moved off back to the hotel.'

Jan 7: for once happy about his bowling: *'I took five wickets. They weren't very much good but I enjoyed bowling and fielding and the game was more or less a picnic.'*

Jan 13: He got 4 for 34 but preferred a small collection from the National and Tate in the City Hall.

Jan 17: in Durban all the team gave one pound ten shillings each to a fund for Bakewell of Northants (and England, an opening batsman) *'who was down and out as a result of a motor accident in which Northway was killed. He hasn't played for two seasons but may be able to next season.'*

Reginald Northway was a Northants opener too. Bakewell's arm was badly injured and he did not play again. He scored 31 centuries.

Jan 23: the pressures and travel of the tour had got to him. It was the third Test and he wrote: *'thank God the match ended today... before tea I felt it would be nice to go crackers and have to be shut up away from cricket.'*

Jan 27: he felt the same about the match against Combined Transvaal writing *'another horrible day's cricket'* and feeling fed up.

Feb 2: but at the Victoria Falls he livened up and felt he had found the real Africa in the Falls and the area surrounding it.

Feb 9: having been given a lion skin he took it to be cured and listened to Hedley Verity on his favourite subject - Air Raid Precautions.

Feb 11: Much happier in Rhodesia. *'The evening turned out to be an excellent one, everyone in good form at the hotel. Soon after dinner I was supporting Reg Perks (of Worcestershire) on my shoulders while he tried to read some escaped balloons. Castle Lager shares must have gone up.'* That night he made three dates with three different girls.

Feb 12: he met some Irish chaps and there was much joshing about Ireland beating England at rugby. Farnes replied: *'I asked if they knew anything about the bomb outrages by the IRA at home. They were most pleasant, friendly and hospitable.'*

And then he stopped. Why we will never know because there were a dozen or so pages left.

19.

1939

HIS LAST season was short and extremely successful, taking five wickets in an innings four times in just eight matches.

Because of the long tour of South Africa, during which he missed two terms at school, he was not available to play cricket for either Essex nor England until the end of July.

He kept in trim after his disappointing - to him - display on the easy batting wickets in South Africa and practiced continuously in the nets in his spare time at school and also by playing occasionally in the Yorkshire League for Doncaster.

He had just one game in the national arena, his favourite Gentlemen v Players at Lord's, the match in which he always shone and seemed to find an extra bit of pace and fury. He was able to get leave from school because the School and Higher School certificate (pre O and A levels) were over.

He showed that he had lost none of his fire and skill with a devastating spell in the Players' first innings, taking 5 for 78, bowling Gimblett, Hardstaff and Copson with Doug Wright hitting his wicket and Dollery caught by Chalk, who was killed in World War Two. Wisden (who had chosen him as one of the Five Cricketers of the Year) commented: *'Farnes, making his first appearance of the season, was allowed only short spells and he finished the Players' first innings by dismissing three men in one over.'*

His Essex colleague, Captain JWA Stephenson, had a great match, taking six wickets before being hurt and having to retire, missing - like former England captain Bob Wyatt, also injured - the second innings.

And then came August, a glorious August, seven matches for his county (who equalled their 1933 fourth place in the championship, their best since 1897) during which he took 33 wickets including five in an innings three times and his first ever hat-trick in first-class cricket.

His first county match was against Kent at Clacton, a washed out affair followed by an equally soggy game at Old Trafford. Back in Essex at Southend by the sea, where the sun shone and the holiday-making crowd cheered, he swept through Derbyshire in the second innings with 5 for 52 including three bowled - Nicholson, Worthington and Pope. Essex had the visitors out for 70 and 79 and won by an innings and 31 runs.

He took six wickets against Middlesex on the same ground - whipping out the stumps of Roberston and Bill Edrich in the second innings. But Nichols was the hero of the day, becoming the first man to do the double - 100 wickets, 1000 runs - five seasons in succession. He took six wickets and scored 58.

Up north at Sheffield Farnes had Sutcliffe, Barber and England captain-to-be Norman Yardley in a spell which brought 3 for 55. He was bowled by Verity for a duck. But back in the bracing south coast sea air at Clacton he finished off as he began with the county nine years before by bowling extremely well against Notts. He was faster, moved the ball in the air and gave the batsmen a very nasty time with his height and bounce and speed.

He started his spell by accidentally breaking Keeton's finger very early on as Hardstaff got hold of the bowling in that casual way he had, looking as unruffled as ever, for 117 as his side made 271 and Farnes took three wickets including Harris. In the second innings he achieved his hat-trick. First he dismissed Harris with Notts on 29 without loss, and in the next over he had Hearne, Hardstaff and Gunn (the only one bowled) in successive deliveries and later added Wheat to finish with 5 for 30 as Notts were all out for 74.

And then there was Northamptonshire on the same ground. Essex won by 210 runs in a month when England was on the very brink of war and the sun never stopped shining, as if making sure that no one would forget it as the carnage came.

The men of Essex and Northamptonshire in their whites and the large crowd with their flasks and sandwiches and deck chairs assembled almost sure that this would be the last time they would be together, but for how long would it be before they met again? It was a moment to enjoy and relish and retain memories for all those long years without cricket that were to come.

Wisden said: '*Impending war did not prevent the players of giving of their best and the cricket was always interesting.*' Essex won the toss and made 206, with Farnes scoring two. He took two wickets in Northants' first innings with Nichols finishing with 6 for 38. Not to be outdone by his senior Farnes did the same in the second innings, ripping through the Midlanders with 6 for 47 (Nichols took another 3 - for 26), three bowled, three caught. Wisden commented: '*Nichols bowled with extreme accuracy and Farnes demonstrated his ability in the second innings.*'

And that was it. The England fast bowler walked off the field and went back to Worksop for a year and then, with many of his colleagues, left at the end of the 1940 summer term because they could not bear not to be fighting the Germans who were by then threatening our existence.

He had some splendid memories to take with him, two of which he recounted. One involved the first time he saw Hopper Read. He took a very long run and as he strode back from the wicket to mark it out the crowd began to hoot when he had gone ten yards, laugh when he reached fifteen, and at twenty yards there was pandemonium which annoyed him a great deal. Farnes could barely see him run because his eyes were full of tears but the crowd saw him - thundering along, his knees scraping his chin - and they roared with laughter and booed. Not when he took a wicket however, which he often did. Farnes admired him for his batting. He got more ducks than he!

And the other: '*I was once the scapegoat in a scene of more sustained mirth than I have ever known in a cricket match before or since - my batting against Derbyshire at Chelmsford. I was determined to hit the ball but every time I did so it went vertically up in the air. My first ball was from Bill Copson. Tommy Mitchell came in so close in the gully that I could have tweaked his nose. The ball hit the shoulder of my bat and bounced up gently over Tommy's head and landed about a foot behind him. The next over I faced Alf Pope (medium fast). Each time I struck the ball it was another balloon. Each time a fielder circled underneath it, waiting, it went down again. Brian Castor, counting the gate money or something in his tent, became alarmed at the huge gusts of laughter from the Bank holiday crowd and was just in time to see me caught at the seventh attempt and everybody doubled up with mirth except Tommy Mitchell whose face was black having dropped me twice. We ran two each time the ball was in the air so, plus a nick for two also, my score was 14!*'

151

There was another which he did not mention but showed the kind of man he was. A little boy of seven finally plucked up the courage to ask this towering hero in flannels for his autograph. He was given more than just that. Farnes invited the boy to have a drink with him and they shared some lemonade. The boy grew up to captain England and Derbyshire and eventually to become secretary of the Test and County Cricket Board, Donald Carr.

His last season produced great figures. For Essex he took 33 wickets at a cost of 18.57. Nationally he had 38 for 726, averaging 19.10, behind his colleague Nichols who had 111 wickets, and a bit more behind Verity who headed the averages with 191 wickets for 13.13.

Farnes and Verity would never play again.

20.

1940

CRICKET like everything else came to a halt at the end of 1939, and as the battle to save the island intensified there was little inclination to play the game. But as people became more used to war their thoughts turned to recreation and as the evacuation of Dunkirk went on there was cricket at Lord's.

On June 1 the British Empire XI played at the home of cricket for the first time. The XI were to play throughout the war and some of the great names in the game were able to turn out when on leave or if they were in the London Fire Service or Civil Defence. Matches started again in the towns and villages too and - typically British - they were fought with the intensity that was otherwise reserved for the Germans, Italians and Japanese. The government approved of it because they considered it involved *'the healthy distraction of a keen game.'*

Farnes played his last games of cricket for the British Empire XI, not being able to play as usual until the end of term, his last term at Worksop College. Like other masters who were above the conscription age he could not stand aside while the war went on. The invasion of France and the low countries and most of the rest of Europe by the Germans was too much. He volunteered for the RAF Volunteer Reserve and before he went for pilot and navigator training in Canada played some cricket.

His first match was on August 15 against the Public Schools, where he showed his customary skill for he was 'quick and fiery' as he took seven wickets for 25 in the first innings and three in the second.

Crowds were getting larger and there was always a collection for the Red Cross or similar organisations, all of which raised a lot of money

Over 8,000 saw 540 runs scored in less than seven hours when Sir Pelham Warner's XI met the Club Cricket Conference in a fine match, with a young club cricketer called Parslow playing England's top fast bowler, who was a little out of practice, with skill, leaving Farnes with 1 for 50 in 14 overs with his old colleague Captain JWA 'Stan' Stepehnson top wicket taker with four. Sgt Denis Compton headed the batsmen with 101 in seventy minutes.

Farnes was also in Warner's team to play the West Indies on August 22, a mid-week fixture attended by 7,000, and had the fast bowler Clarke caught by his old skipper Gubby Allen. Top scorer in the game was Sgt Denis Compton (73), Sgt Instructor Len Hutton made 44 and others playing included Farnes's old friend Cadet Bryan Valentine, Lt Freddie Brown, Flt Lt RWV Robins, Captain SC Griffith (later Secretary of the MCC), Leslie Compton (brother of Denis and an England soccer international like his brother) and Learie Constantine.

It was the Essex man's last appearance at Lord's but he did play in two more matches before he joined up. The first was for the British Empire against the RAF at Mill Hill where he took two wickets for 42 (one of them Alec Bedser). The second was his last game - again with the British Empire team - against Stan Stephenson's XI at Cheltenham. Farnes took three wickets, including bowling Stan, which was the last wicket he ever took, and that of England opener Charlie Barnett. And then - just for once - he came good with the bat, giving his team an air of respectability as he top scored with 25 not out!

Off he went to war and never came back. His was the first household name from cricket to die. He was well known, not just to cricket fans but to a far wider field because his face had been on cigarette cards (like Hedley Verity to die in action two years later), and his picture was regularly in the papers. He was someone boys looked up to as they did to a greater extent with Hammond, Hutton and Compton, but he was also one of the stars of his day.

His death was not only tragic but it left a great gap in English fast bowling which was not really filled until Freddie Trueman, Brian Statham and Frank Tyson appeared in the 1950s.

21.

LOVE AND DEATH

FARNES found love near the end of his short life, and it was love at first sight. He always had a girl friend or girl friends. He was tall and handsome and girls liked to be with him; they liked his sense of fun and his rather shy, diffident manner and good manners. He attracted them in a way that some men can. You either have that magnetic pull or you do not. He also liked them and he was often seen roaring round the lanes of Nottinghamshire and Essex and many places abroad in his sports car with one in the passenger seat.

But when he met Catherine Aeron Franklin (known as Aeron after the river in Wales) in a services canteen in Torquay on December 16, 1940 he fell really in love.

The Devon seaside town was full of airmen at that period of the war and Aeron had been sent there by her husband, Arthur Narracott, Aeronautical correspondent on The Times who became a press liaison officer with the RAF with an honorary commission. He wanted his wife and little daughter, Diana, their only child, away from the Blitz.

Aeron had spent her teen years in the town where her father was chief engineer at the Imperial Hotel, which, at that time, was perhaps the best and biggest provincial hotel in the country. She trained as a nurse and met Arthur, a reporter on a local paper, when she nursed him in the local hospital where he was recovering from appendicitis. They moved to London when Arthur got a job with the Press Association and then The Times. But by the time she and Pilot Officer Farnes met her marriage was breaking up, as so many did during the war, because of long separations and the rush to be happy in case death came in the next moment.

Aeron first stayed with her parents and then, with a girl friend, found a home on the headland in the suburb of St Marychurch where they

Ken Farnes

set up a War Nursery for the babies of women going into munitions work (it was the brainchild of her father's uncle, the Minister of Health in Churchill's coalition Cabinet, the Rt Hon Ernest Brown). The house was always full of cots and babies and later in the war it was bombed, but luckily no one was hurt. Aeron did other voluntary work, using her nursing experience particularly when a hotel got a direct hit and a lot of RAF people were killed and wounded.

In the evenings she worked in the canteen and it was there that she met Ken Farnes. He was easy to notice and so must she have been with her attractive face and smile. She had a great sense of humour and fun, was a great mimic and had a wonderful sparkling personality. Whatever the chemistry of love is that attracts people to each other it certainly worked in this case.

Within a few days the two were inseparable when he had leave of any kind. They would go for walks - to her little daughter, a toddler at the time *'it was like going for a walk with a tower block'* - and they would talk and laugh as all young lovers do.

He was a great James Elroy Flecker fan and he would quote from the early 20th century poet's love song Hassan:

> *'And some to Mecca turn to pray,*
> *But I, towards thy bed, Yasmin'*

and sadly:

> *'But one night or the other night*
> *Will come the gardener in white*
> *And gathered flowers are dead, Yasmin.'*

He gave her a copy of Hassan as well as his autobiography, which she kept until she died aged 86 in 1994. He wooed her with love letters, the writings of a man who had found true happiness.

From the Bath Hotel at West Worthing he wrote, careful not to give away why he was there because of war secrecy, dating it New Year's Day 1941:

> *'My darling, my darling,*
> *It's an entirely lovely day but that don't matter. After a splendidly late breakfast (yes, toast and marmalade an' all!) I've been sitting in an armchair and*

156

*hoping I should be able to write a letter that would please you and now at last I've
embarked. I can see I shall become intolerably Voyage-minded.*

*In the train I thought of you - or rather you were in my mind entirely
which is really a very different thing. And I expected that by the time I wrote I
should have destroyed the envelope that was in The Voyage* (by Charles Morgan)
and so should be able to tell you that I had done so since you wish it' - a reference
to a letter she had written him, I guess - *'and then I should be able to say that
the joy of finding the words there at a comparatively dim time made my heart leap.
You being in it ought by rights to have felt the effects of altitude - eg, popping of
the ears due to disturbance of anvil, hammer and stirrup, possibly a trace of
frostbite and a tendency to vomit. However I haven't destroyed it yet but shall do
so today as I have the courage to believe the spirit remains behind the smoke.*

'But perhaps that paragraph is like a Sunday afternoon Cockington-way
(near Torquay) *and you with blue tabs and tolerance.*

(He quotes from his book The Voyage*) 'Everything is changed when
one is happy, everything except the knowledge that to be happy is a kind of
madness, that sanity will return as clouds return, that the instant is a gleam - you
stretch out your hands to feel the sun on them and you say: There is the sun, I feel
it. I am happy. I am alive.*

*'Well, you wild Welsh river (you extroverted sensation type!) you who are
the Music and the Flowers, the summer day that holds together the seas far below
and the high cliffs that know their murmur, you that are the wind in the trees or
what the wind in the trees must love, I love the sunshine and the sun shines from
your eyes. I stretch out my hands to feel the sun on them and I say....*

'The form here (the hotel) *flashes like the glint from a smoke-blackened
kettle bottom. Mr Smith reminds me of you. He has a large mauve wart on his
forehead. Mrs Jackson is too nervous to play singles at ping-pong but enjoys a four.
There is a warm and friendly atmosphere and two rain-smelling dogs. And I'm a
little perturbed because you may think I should try to put into words a dream that
I had a night or two ago.*

*I shall emerge at the station on Friday, your old husk, your decrepit old
broken-down flower, your slave that dares to send you his love. Written by the hand
of one who now kisses yours this first day of January that is not June. Ken'*

Another letter came from somewhere in Scotland where he was
learning to fly in a Tiger Moth:

'Most beloved,

'Real summer day except there is no green on the trees yet. Matt, Davies and I have been lying in the grass sheltered from the wind at the edge of a golf course, sleeping and doing a spot of work. Came along after 11.30 breakfast and a trace of shopping and the old and bold.

'About 30 out of 75 have been turned off the course - don't think I told you, did I, including the Unwashable whom I intercepted last night on his way back from a bath! Poor lad, I don't know what's wrong but he was unwell a short time ago and when I asked him last night why he hadn't been in flying kit earlier in the day he said it was a long story but he didn't think he would ever fly again. As soon as I saw him in Room 23 at Templestone I thought he looked like a consumptive but he seemed to be able to stand the PT and runs as well as any of us.

'Gad, we could have used this day darling! Double sunshine, thought of it on the way to the bus at Scone this morning and felt pretty wistful.

'Don't suppose we shall do much this evening - perhaps the odd shot and an early return to polish and maybe do a little more work. This sun - first time it's been warm since Torquay, warmth OK at Crewe, stap me!

'Move now indicated, God what a fearful note - thought I'd nip one in though as there's no post from Scone on a Sunday.

'Flying time is now 20 1/2 hours see - so it's nipping up a bit better.

'   Aeron, my love, I adore you, Kenneth.

'PS. On coming into Perth we hear a monstrous rumour that this coming week we are to fly till 7 every night as they want us out by Saturday - presumably to go straight in to SFTS (more training but at a higher level). Don't know the full truth of this darling but there must be something in it. What about leave is what I want to know. What do you think about it sweetheart? My love, my love.'

After 30 hours of flying the lovesick pilot wrote:

'Oh darling, I'm a bit fed up today, you know getting worse now as the days go on increasing our time away from each other. The time and the distance grow. Two nights ago some good but melancholy music on the Unwashable's wireless as I was going to bed brought home the separation and I'm slumping more and more. When, when can we be together again, my wart-ridden, most darling one, eh? I desperately want to be with you, see!

'A ground instructor told us today that we each cost £3 a minute to Air Co. while we're in the air. Having had nearly 30 hours now I've cost about £5000 so far. Do you think I'm worth it, sweetheart? No rude remarks now.

'Matt, Davies and Emery have been told today that the local powers are *recommending them to instructors' courses. Matt doesn't fancy it but has been told by the Flight Commander that he (the FC) wants to recommend him and that he must improve his flying which has been a bit off the last day or two probably because of his slight mishap a few days ago.*

'*The flying is not unpleasant at all, a bit cold the last two days and the old Moths are a trifle small after an hour or two and my last trip this morning in an old machine whose straps only just meet, made my bum damned cramped. I was strapped in like a foot in one of those torture boots.*

'*Last night they got through to Torquay an hour before I eventually got in touch with you but I was in the Writing room and Allen, the caretaker, was not there. Did they actually ring?*

'*Gad, I'm looking forward to hearing you tomorrow lunchtime. Apart from the odd trace getting your letters, writing to you and hearing you are my total pleasures and when we can't be together there is nothing else to count, nothing to be thought of.*

'*Sweetheart, Aeron, darling, I love you, want you, cry out for you. What can be done about it?*'

On the six months anniversary of their meeting in June he sent her a telegram from Scotland which simply said: '*Six months today and this had hoped celebrate together love Polycarp*'.

He was going on leave prior to going operational after a training flight on the night of October 20, 1941 at Chipping Warden. He had only been there four weeks, having come back from Canada where he received his wings as top of his group at Medicine Hat, Alberta and had volunteered for night flying when Britain was desperately short of pilots who could fly at night. Farnes was too big to fit into any fighter, which he dearly longed to fly. He wanted to be a flyer, not a gunner or the man who pressed the button to release the bombs because he told his family he could not do that, not drop a bomb on someone hundreds of feet below whom he did not know nor could see. So he went flying at night.

But tragically on his first unsupervised night training flight in a Wellington bomber (and under some pressure from the Officer Commanding Flying) he was trying to overshoot and crash landed in the village. He managed to avoid most of the houses, hitting the ground in a tennis court and coming to rest in a garden at Hogg End. He was killed immediately and his co-pilot died later in hospital. The crash set the roofs of some thatched houses on fire but no villager, incredibly, was killed.

It was appalling for the woman he loved because she was waiting at the airfield for him. She was there when he crashed and was killed. Within minutes of the disaster she knew.

Her daughter, now Diana Norman, wife of cricket fan, TV presenter, film critic and author Barry Norman, said: *'I do know he sent her a cable or telegram asking her to meet him at the airfield where he failed to arrive on that last flight and that she was there waiting for him.*

'Young as I was, I could tell he was a lovely and joyous man. As far as I can tell it was love at first sight. I know he quoted lots of James Elroy Flecker at her. I strongly got the impression that they would have married if he had lived.

'But she came of a generation that was reticent about personal matters and kept its grief to itself so I can't tell you much more about their relationship.'

For the lady who would have been Mrs Farnes, life had to go on. Her daughter said: *'She was an amazing woman, very charming and attractive to the end of her life, very funny and a good mimic. From moderately humble beginnings she was able to act as hostess for my great uncle Ernest when he was a Cabinet Minister (she and my father lived with him and his wife for a while just before the war). After the divorce (from Diana's father) we were pretty poor and she had to work all hours as a chemist's assistant to keep the family going. She coped with all these fluctuations with the same unfailing grace.*

'After I was married and her parents died she came to our village and lived just along the lane from us, helping to bring up our daughters, Samantha and Emma, while I was working. I don't think a grandmother ever meant more to her grand-daughters than she did, or they to her.

'She and Barry were very fond of each other, always talking cricket, which she adored (I think my father played for Devon). She'd watch Tests with the television sound turned down and the radio commentary on. One of her happiest days was when Barry and my son-in-law took her to Lord's.

'She found great pleasure in working for the church and old people in our village and when she died aged 86, the church was packed.'

Nothing can replace fact but it is reasonable to suggest that if Farnes had lived and they had married they would have had a wonderful marriage, two very nice people, greatly in love, being happy.

Aeron never forgot. With her belongings when she died were the books and the obituary in The Times, published a few days after his death.

APPENDIX ONE

FARNES ended his autobiography with a chapter called *Some Thoughts on First-Class Cricket To-Day*. He was not to know that his thoughts were the definitive words from a Test player and that it would be over six years before anyone would be able to write similar thoughts based on a season's play. It is one of cricket's tragedies that he was not there to be able to repeat what he thought after 1946, a year when he was sorely missed.

Some of the great men of 1939 were still around, particularly Hammond, Hutton, Compton, Bill Edrich, Hardstaff, Washbrook and Doug Wright. But not Farnes and not Verity, the two fast and slow spearheads.

He wrote (and much of it is as true today as it was then): *'It is rather surprising to find that very few first-class cricketers have much knowledge of the cricketers of the past. They are familiar with the great names but do not revere them or look back to their skill for inspiration. They get as far as making a cynical remark such as 'Ranji would have made a packet on this!' when they find themselves on a sticky dog of a wicket. But that is about all. They seem (this is a very general statement) to be satisfied that the skill of the past masters is more myth than truth, and that what they themselves can do to-day was not bettered in the Golden Era. There is no boastfulness in their attitude which is due, I believe, to two things - a certain lack of ability to appreciate something which they have not seen with their own eyes, and a materialistic attitude towards their art. This, being a general statement on first-class cricket in England. refers particularly to the professionals who form the main element.*

'Cricket is an art - a game first if you like but a game in which skill becomes an art. Today the business side of it has rather swamped the artistic side. In the Golden Era professionals were, if not in the minority, certainly a much smaller element in the game; their attitude to cricket as a game, and, even unconsciously, as an art, was bound to be absorbed by the professionals playing with them. This is not to decry the intelligence, enthusiasm and pleasant nature of most professionals playing today. I make this statement only in the endeavour to explain the difference between the game of to-day and of yesterday. Few men engaged in business careers look back with reverence to the tradition of their predecessors. They carry on with a comparably dull

161

efficiency the job in hand. And I believe that cricket today is more generally efficient than it was in the days of WG - less scintillating, less zestful but more efficient, taking the first-class game as a whole.

'*There is an often repeated moan about the lack of personalities in the game today. The same reasons for this lack obtain as those that explain the changed aspect of the modern game. Where the general standard of efficiency is high the giants do not appear. Just as in literature there will never be another Shakespeare so in cricket we shall not see another WG Grace. If you say 'what about Bradman ?' I reply that he is not a giant in the sense that WG was a giant. His technical efficiency is astounding, as a box-office attraction he is supreme but as a personality I do not believe there is any comparison. Bradman is the symbol of modern efficiency, Grace of latter-day genius.*

'*Not long ago I had a conversation with DJ Knight who after a lapse of a dozen years came back to play for Surrey for a season or two. He found himself playing an entirely different game. The chief difference he noted were firstly in the placing of the field and secondly in the character of the bowling. Before the Great War and for a few years after it, off-driving and late-cutting were favourite strokes. The old school that look on from the pavilion at Lord's nowadays bemoan the absence of the cover-drive. The fact is that it is not possible to drive in-swingers through the covers; and in-swingers, for better or worse, form an integral part of modern bowling. Though it is not possible to place an exact date to the change it is significant that Fred Root (Worcestershire and England), with his leg-side field and in-swingers completely upset the apple-cart of the Australians when he bowled against them in 1926. DJ Knight remembers that as a boy he was taken to the Oval and saw George Hirst make a ball swerve in the air. This was then regarded as an astonishing thing. Today it is, possibly too much, a commonplace.*

'*In cricket, firstly bowling prevails over batting and secondly the batsmen evolve a technique to counteract the particular methods of attack in vogue. Then for a time batting triumphs until the bowlers find new means of dislodging the batsmen. And so the pendulum goes on swinging from side to side. The fast bowlers of the time of Richardson and Lockwood relied on making the ball come back from the off - a body-break largely - on their speed, length, yorker, etc,. It is astonishing that they did not seem to have made the ball swerve in the air. They must have done so occasionally but if so, it was done unconsciously, and people cannot have believed their eyes. Nowadays swing is so commonplace and the new ball consequently so important that no county opens the attack, except in exceptional circumstances, without two bowlers who can on most days make the ball move a bit in the air.*

'*The field, so DJ Knight said, is much more significantly set than it used to be and this, together with the dangers and difficulty of off-driving and cutting, helps to explain the generally less flashing, less beautiful nature of the game today. Off-spin bowling that was so successful against the one-eyed stance and the cover-drive become much less useful when the batsman used his head and the old lbw rule to think of obstructing his wicket with his legs when the ball was pitched outside the off-stump, or on the wicket if the bowler bowled over the wicket, knowing that it was almost impossible to be out leg before unless the ball were pitched right up to him. On turning wickets the bowler could counteract this by going round the wicket, pitching the ball in line with the wickets and straightening it to keep that line. But the two-eyed stance has come to stay. The ugliness of this kind of batting has brought the new lbw rule to prevent excessive use of the legs in defence and to endeavour to encourage the forward play - the use of the left leg in defence and driving.*

'*Probably it is already successful. A number of very good batsmen were upset by it for a few seasons, those going in for excessive pad play that is. And it does seem to synchronise with a definite revival of attacking batsmanship, a decrease in the number of drawn matches and a big crop of wickets taken by off-spin bowlers.*'

Then a theme that is as constant now as it was then: '*About eight years ago cricket in England was in rather a poor way. Hobbs and Sutcliffe were at the end of the splendid period as England's opening pair. Hammond was certainly brilliant but a number of well-known batsmen were beginning to fade. Frank Woolley and Jack Hearne were getting old. Patsy Hendren too, though as good as ever, was not as young as his ability and speed made him appear. Leyland remained as dour and splendid in a crisis as ever. But there was a dearth of coming young men. (When did* we last hear that?). *Maurice Tate was just past his best and had begun to lose a little of his fire and amazing nip off the pitch. Voce, of course, was a fine bowler and his Nottinghamshire partner - well what can I say of Larwood who remains for me a hero? Certainly he's one of the world's great bowlers. What a wonderful action, what accuracy and stamina! I can see him now as I write - a demon of destruction to batsmen with all the concentrated antagonism that a fast bowler should have.*'

He adds with inside knowledge that would have done him credit now: '*But there was a dearth of fast bowlers and there still is.*

'*Old George Geary was still good - one of the old school. Tich Freeman continues to take an incredible number of wickets in county but not in international cricket. Among the fast men Nobby Clark should have been as good as any but was prone to strains. Nichols* (his senior county club colleague) *is as good now as he ever*

163

was - a fine trier with an amazing ability to move the ball off the seam from leg on a wicket that is still green. GO Allen proved himself in his two tours in Australia. Verity was alone among the slow left-handers for Rhodes and JC White had practically finished and Charlie Parker was getting old and somehow missed the boat in international cricket.

'This survey is not meant to be exhaustive and probably I have done injustice to many by not recalling them at the moment, but the fact remains that young bowlers were not appearing as they might have been expected to. Perhaps the chief lack is of some first-class medium-paced bowlers with an ability to spin the ball and vary their pace without loss of control. I can think of none today. Perhaps Hammond might have filled the bill if he had not been chiefly occupied in run getting. It may be that the reason is partly in the nature of the wickets which became more and more lifeless. Part of the trouble is probably due to the increasingly businesslike nature of the cricket. Cricket on six days a week throughout a long season is bound to sap enthusiasm and energy to a very considerable extent and lust for the game degenerates into a smooth, dull level of proficiency.

'Of the slow leg-spinner-cum-googly type of bowler, several men have not quite lived up to their promise. Ian Peebles has never been able to bowl so well since he got a common complaint of bowlers of this sort - a damaged shoulder muscle. I doubt if Walter Robins has bowled as well as he did since Aubrey Faulkner died (a wonderful South African all rounder, master of the googly and superb batsman who ran a famous coaching school in Fulham, London, until his death in 1930) *or perhaps since he had a protracted spell of inferior cricket with only sporadic appearances in the first-class game. Freddie Brown, so fine a bowler at Cambridge in 1931 and for Surrey in the following year, was possibly more disheartened by the Australian tour than he would like to admit* (but did lead England in Australia 1950/1 where England gained their first victory over Australia after the war). *Tommy Mitchell has been mostly on the fringe of international cricket. Today the most promising are Doug Wright of Kent and Len Wilkinson of Lancashire. Both bowl rather faster than most men of their type. Wright especially bangs the ball in at a rare pace sometimes and yet spins the ball a great deal. Wilkinson had a bad spell in 1939 after his South Africa trip but was probably no more than a spell out of form that comes to every one.*

'Wright will be unplayable at times. On the tail of these is Peter Smith who is very consistent in county cricket.

'Of the off-spinners our best are not young. Tom Goddard is nearly forty,

John Clay seems practically to have stopped playing. Reg Sinfield has been playing for many years.'

But there is hope: *'The most encouraging thing about cricket today is the arrival of a number of young batsmen of real distinction. Hutton is as sound as Yorkshire can make and his range of strokes and growth of power have increased remarkably in the last two seasons; at last another great opener for England. Next is Denis Compton with a southerner's outlook distinguishing him from northern dourness, and a greater range of strokes than almost anyone playing. Still young, bred on Hendren, he is not the least disturbed by the greatness of an occasion. Edrich may yet be as good as many thought he would be but has had a thin time in Test matches so far except for an excellent double century in South Africa. A third in the Middlesex side who may become the partner we require for Hutton is Robertson; he showed much promise last season. Middlesex are amazingly lucky to have players to fill so soon the places of Hendren and Hearne. There are other young batsmen of considerable powers. Dollery (Warwickshire) for example and Avery (Essex). There are others like Joe Hardstaff who are by now well established.*

'The bowling outlook may not be too good (and it is a pity that his modesty was overwhelming in not discussing fast bowling and who would partner him and what his prospects were) *but in batting we seem to have an array of talent that should confound the Australians when the war permits us to come to grips with them again.*

'As for the wickets, a move in the right direction was made at the beginning of last season when the MCC issued a command that county groundsmen were not to over-prepare their wickets. The doping of wickets, aiming at the protraction of matches to get the full three days gate money, was a false economy, for cricket good to watch and good to play cannot take place on wickets that are too lifeless even for batsmen to make strokes on, let alone the poor bowler to attack on. The greater number of matches finished last year than for a long time is a good sign.'

And for once the journalists came in for a good word: *'The Press has exerted an increasing influence on the game in recent years. Not a great number of years ago a century by Grace was recorded in two or three lines of small type. Nowadays a Test match has as sensational a notice as a war. The Press produces the crowds as much or more than cricket and publicity is of enormous importance in the financial success of the first-class counties. Much good has been done in the last few years by newspaper agitation for more interesting, brighter cricket, pointing out that individuals and counties must produce more entertaining play if they are to survive.'*

165

(It's the same cry now. Nothing changes, just goes round in circles!)

But as true as it is now, *'Cricket journalists are not for the most part very popular with the players for very few have both knowledge of the game and ability to write well about it. Some are unkind in their criticisms; others, even with some real experience of the first-class game, occasionally write complete rubbish and betray to those in touch with the technique of modern methods an infuriating ignorance. However the more responsible newspapers have correspondents whose articles are a pleasure to read for both players and fan alike. It is the sensation-mongers who are the real menace.'*

The words come trundling down the years and are as valid in the eyes of many today as they were then when this young Pilot Officer sat down and wrote them. Circles seem faster and faster and the passing years have not changed the outlook of many fans. It shows that whatever people say about how the British have changed as a nation their cricketers and cricket lovers have not. Their minds are fixed as they were in 1939/40 and that is nothing but a force for good.

'In spite of the sophistication of the modern game and the encroachment of business into the art, county cricket in England is in a fairly flourishing state. Some counties certainly are poorly supported but I believe that the first-class game as a whole is in a better condition today than it has been for a long time - I am speaking, of course, without taking the war into consideration.'

What a terrible shame that he was not able to continue after the consideration of the war.

APPENDIX TWO

Boy's Own Paper August 1939

One of the articles commissioned by the now defunct magazine (1879 to 1967) while Farnes was in South Africa on the 1938/9 tour.

Bowling to Bradman and others
specially written for the BOP by Kenneth Farnes, the famous Essex and England Fast Bowler

'I played my first county match in 1930 - against Gloucester. They bowled Essex out pretty cheaply and by the middle of the afternoon we were in the field. Nichols and Peter Smith opened for us with the new ball and I went on as first change. It was a strange experience as I had hardly dared believe that I was up to first-class standard and soon found that bowling to experienced first-class batsmen was very different from bowling in club cricket in which one occasionally comes up against quite a good player. For in the first-class game a loose bowl frequently gets what it deserves, and so, far greater concentration on length and direction is required; also, a first-class batsman's defence usually has fewer loopholes in it than that of a Saturday afternoon player. Ability and experience combine to form an efficient technique.

'The first match hammered home to me, more than ever before, the essential quality of length. Dacre was the chief batsman to teach me that day. He was a punishing player and hooked my short ones and drove the over-pitched deliveries through the covers or over mid-off's head unmercifully. I took no wickets for sixty runs in the first innings and only had an over or two in the second. Feeling pretty disturbed about my poor form I said to the skipper 'I'm going home and I'm going to practise and practise bowling a length.'

'A few months later I was given another chance for Essex and this time things went well for me as, in the first innings, I took five wickets. But more important for me was that amongst those I had Frank Woolley caught by Jack Russell in the slips. As you know Woolley has just retired from first-class cricket at the age of 52. The two most striking things about his batsmanship were the superb gracefulness of his strokes and

167

the astonishing power behind them.

'He never appeared to hit the ball and yet from an apparently languid stroke the ball would be rebounding from a boundary post before a fieldsman had time to move and save it from going for four. He was a great player of fast bowling. Against Gregory and Macdonald at Lords in 1921 (v Australia) he made over ninety in each innings and several years later he played one of his greatest innings at the Folkestone Festival against the West Indies. Constantine and Martindale, both really fast and on this day bowling their fastest, had frightened one or two players by short, bumping deliveries. Woolley came in (and remember in those days batsmen wore no protective clothing apart from a box to cover their groin) *and proceeded to score a century before lunch, hooking and driving with the greatest of ease. He was a natural rather than a made player - in fact, a genius.*

'Having achieved a certain amount of success in this match against Kent, I was assured of more first-class cricket and have gone on playing consistently since then. During the next few years I came up against most of the prominent batsmen in the country and also against touring sides from India and the West Indies.'

My First Test Match

'In 1934 the Australians came to England again. They were captained by Woodfull, known at one time as the unbowlable, and in the side were Bradman, already holder of the world's record score of 452 not out, Ponsford, previous holder of the world's highest first-class score, and McCabe, always one of the most delightful free-scoring batsmen. England was rather short of fast bowlers at this time.Larwood had injured his foot beyond repair on the hard Australian grounds; Voce was out of international cricket for a while until an amicable settlement of the bodyline controversy was reached; GO Allen was not available at first and Bowes was not quite fit. In the Test trial at Lord's I bowled quite well and most unfortunately broke Wyatt's thumb (the England captain), Clark of Northants, a really magnificent fast bowler when he was fit, strained himself in the match and Tiger Smith, then umpiring, bet me a penny I should play in the first Test match. It doesn't sound as if he was risking too much but in the end, on the morning of the match, I was given preference over my club friend, Nichols.

Woodfull and Ponsford both got out and in came Bradman. Here he comes, small and lithe, with legs a little long in proportion to his body, walking slowly to the wicket with a broad grin on his face as he passes me on his way to the crease. He takes guard and I bowl my first ball to the Don. He makes a tremendous swish, misses the ball completely and the ball misses the leg stump by the smallest margin. There is only a short time until lunch but he takes all sorts of risk instead of getting a sight of the ball first and playing quietly until lunch time as most players would do.

'*This was my first experience of bowling to Bradman. Earlier in the season he had slashed and carved a lightning, audacious century at Lord's against the MCC and for a few matches he appeared to try and do the same thing every time. He found it wouldn't work every time and after a few matches we had the real Bradman again, pulling up scores of over 200 without giving a chance. He made low scores in each innings of the first Test. At the second at Lord's I bowled when he came in. In the first over I bowled three long-hops. Have you ever seen him hook? The power he puts into that shot is amazing and he hits the ball down along the ground just wide of mid on. It travels like a shot out of a gun and those three long hops crashed along the boundary fence by the Tavern. The spectators there must have begun to think they'd be safer at home. Fortunately for us the Australians hadn't scored enough runs by the close of play on Saturday night to save the follow on. Rain came over the weekend and Verity, in his element, bowled them all out twice on the Monday. Bradman looked like staying in the second innings but he was again inclined to take risks and on such a wicket these tactics proved fatal.*

'*In inter-state matches in Australia the wickets are covered and rain therefore has no effect on the pitch. Bradman was brought up on wickets that were of a uniform condition and although they were probably responsible for his wonderful array of strokes they were also responsible for limiting his ability on wickets which rain made tricky. Again on our 1936/7 tour of Australia he failed, like everyone else, on the sticky wickets at Brisbane and Melbourne. Hammond was a far better player on these. Now Bradman has had more experience and even on a sticky wicket he is still hard to get out.*

'*In Australia he was an even greater proposition, I think, as he seems to produce even more strokes. For example, when I bowled to him there I found that if I bowled a ball of reasonable length on or just outside the off stump he hit it back past mid off or where mid off would usually stand, like a shot out of a gun. I had to concentrate on trying to bowl a good length, preferably a shade overpitched on the middle and leg stumps, and very often he would score a single off such a ball to a place fairly wide and deep at mid on. I was then able to have a shot at the other batsmen. A good recipe for bowling to Bradman - it sounds a bit Irish - would be: 'Bowl at the other chap all the time if you can.'*

169

Other Famous Australians

'In international cricket the players are so often playing against each other that they form pretty shrewd conclusions about each other's capabilities. The weaknesses, if any, are fairly soon known and the right sort of bowlers are brought on and peg away as hard as possible against the batsmen's weak spots. Such tactics may or may not come off but they are worth persevering with for some time.

'Bradman probably is less fallable than any other batsman today but there is a chance of getting him out with the new ball if you can get it to swing away late. As you know, the new ball usually swerves in the air more than the old one and anyone is liable to get out to such a ball as I have described. Perhaps Bradman is more likely to get out more to fast bowling than to any other type, but it has got to be extremely fast to be effective. Even against Larwood at his fastest in 1932/3 he averaged 56 runs an innings in the Test.

'Fingleton is a very good player against the new ball and fast bowling and is very hard to shift, but he is not sound against really good spin bowling. Brown, his Test match opening partner, is a very sound player and is hard to bowl to. I have found that he is an excellent judge of the ball to leave alone on the off side and has a most annoying ability to play anything straight round to leg.

'Badcock, who had such a bad time in the Test matches in 1938, is a very fine player when he has settled down and has a fine array of powerful strokes all round the wicket. Don't bowl him anything short or he'll take full toll of it and above all try to keep them well up to him when he first goes in. He is short, thicket and strong and he hits the ball terribly had.

'One of the finest players in the world to watch and one of the most difficult to bowl to, is Stan McCabe. He has a wide range of strokes and is especially strong on the leg side. The result is that if you bowl about the middle and leg he is able to turn it round between mid on and square leg. I think it is one of his most impressive strokes. His timing is so perfect that with little apparent effort he makes the ball fly to the boundary. In the Nottingham Test match last year he hit me for six in that direction without appearing to hit the ball at all hard. He is one of the few players who goes on playing his natural game whatever the circumstance so that even in timeless Test matches you well

never find him dull to watch. As he is going for the ball all the time you may get him nibbling at a ball outside the off stump and a catch in the slips may be possible. The finest innings I have seen him play was this same match at Nottingham in which he scored over 200 and saved Australia from what looked like almost certain defeat as with the last man in, Fleetwood-Smith, he monopolised nearly all the bowling and hit every bowler so that no one knew how or where to bowl to him to stop him from scoring or from taking a run of he last ball of each over.

'I have had comparatively little experience of bowling to South African batsmen but I have learnt how hard they are to get out on their own wickets. One of their best stroke players is Eric Dalton who, like McCabe, gets on with the game. Mitchell has a remarkably efficient defence and is a very polished player. Rowan and van der Bijl are also very solid and Nourse is an excellent player, particularly when he has settled down.

'Always, it seems to me, the bowler must have a little luck to be successful for without he may never get a wicket at all. I've seen Nichols of Essex bowl magnificently and yet finish up with an analysis of 0 for 80. There are many ways of getting a batsman out but if things are just going against you, nothing seems to happen as the bowler wishes. Needless to say the luck usually evens out in the end.

'Well, bowling to the best batsmen is sometimes a very laborious task and you occasionally feel that you are just serving up the fodder for their guns. Nevertheless the compensation and the satisfaction comes when you take a valuable wicket and merely to make things difficult for the Bradmans and the Hammonds is part of the joy of the game.'

APPENDIX THREE

Obituary from The Times, 24 October 1941:

'Pilot Officer Kenneth Farnes, RAFVR, was a fast bowler in the true sense in which the adjective is applied to Kortright, Lockwood and Richardson and to no other Englishman of his generation except Larwood. He was, perhaps, a bowler of moods - either destructively hostile or complacently amicable - but in his full fighting feathers he was a danger to any batsman in the world.

'An easy and economical run up to the wicket was the prelude to a controlled delivery from a great height and he had the pace to make the ball rise sharply and to excuse what in the case of others might have been regarded as a shortness of length. EA McDonald (Australia and Lancashire), that prince of modern fast bowlers, once remarked that when batsmen edged away from the wicket the ball was liable to follow them. Woe betide those, too, who ran away from Kenneth Farnes.

'Son of Mr Sidney H Farnes and the late Mrs Farnes he was educated at the Royal Liberty School, Romford, and went to Pembroke College, Cambridge, in 1931 to gain his place in the University Xl as a Freshman, having already had some experience of county cricket in the Essex Xl. He again played in the University match in the following two years and he had by then established himself as an outstanding bowler. In 1934 he played in two Test matches in this country against Australia and in 1938 was a regular member of England's team.

'He went out to Australia in GO Allen's side in the season 1936/7 and took part in each of the Test matches in South Africa under WR Hammond's captaincy in 1938/9. One of his most notable successes was in the Gentlemen v Players match of 1936 when he spread havoc among the professional batsmen. It would have required a George Gunn on that day to have tamed him.

'His progress in the cricket field was interrupted when he became a schoolmaster at Worksop College but he left a memory of a young man of a charming modesty and a gentleness of manner who did much to lend distinction to amateur cricket when talent was not easy to find.'

172

His Headmaster (the Rev BC Molony) wrote in The Times:

'The news of his death has come as a great shock to all who knew him at Worksop. To the majority of his countrymen the news has come of the loss of one of the greatest fast bowlers; to masters and boys at this school it means the loss of a valued friend and counsellor. Farnes was an energetic and untiring teacher of history and geography and an able and much-loved housemaster. To this latter position he was appointed at an unusually young age and his success therein was largely due to the quite natural modesty of the man which made him as willing to learn from boys as they were to learn from him.

'A giant in stature, he had the gentleness of voice and manner which so often accompanies great size and strength and though on the cricket field he would rouse himself to devastating action, he never let his strength run away with him in his dealing with boys.'

In the school magazine the headmaster wrote:

'It is with great personal loss that we record his death.

'He went up to Cambridge in 1930 and besides gaining Blues for cricket and athletics - putting the weight - he took sound Honours in the Historical and Geographical Triposes. He was appointed to Worksop College as an assistant master in 1933 by the distinguished headmaster, Dr FJ Shirley (subsequently Headmaster of The King's School, Canterbury) and joined the very talented young staff which Shirley had gathered around him.

'He was appointed Housemaster of Pelham House in 1934 and served in this capacity until 1940 when he joined the RAF - with eight of his colleagues joining the Forces at the same time. In 1941 he won his pilot's wings in Canda, passing out top of his group. He had been back in England only a few weeks when his tragic death occurred.

'His cricketing career is too well known to need more than a brief recapitulation here. He stood easily in the forefront of the fast bowlers of his generation, not only because of his magnificent natural gifts but because of his determination. It was this determination that transformed him from the loose-limbed promising youngster we knew at Fenner's to the mature man with the classically perfect action we saw at Trent Bridge; which raised his fielding from

mediocrirty to excellence and which changed him from being a mere slogger into an able, hard-hitting batsman who made plenty of runs in the best of company.

'Despite his well-deserved success and popularity he never became swollen-headed; his innate modesty - almost shyness - prevented him from the usual fault of the outstanding athlete. Even in his own book on cricket, Tours and Test, he tells us little of himself, nothing of the varied interests of his mind.

'And yet that mind was well stocked with varied interests; he painted and sketched with more than ordinary talent, his knowledge and appreciation of Art were sound and keen, his reading was wide and his literary enthusiams unusual, his chief love being the stylists, among whom he reverenced above all George Moore.

'Yet more striking perhaps than any other characteristic about him was his love of life, his enjoyment of fun, his quickness of response, his gusto. His house, the school and most of all the Common Room will be eternally poorer for the loss of him.'

The Royal Liberty Magazine, journal of his old school, said in a tribute signed simply H, who was headmaster and cricket coach, SB Hartley:

'A grievous blow came to all connected with the school and others when in October it was announced that Ken Farnes had been killed in a flying accident. He was the idol of many of our boys and Old Boys and by cricket enthusiasts was recognised as one of the world's best fast bowlers and by some even the best.

'Among other achievements at the game he had been in the Cambridge team for three successive years, for a considerable period a leading member of the Essex county team, in his first Test match against Australia he obtained 10 wickets for 179 runs. In 1939 his bowling played a great part in the victory of the Gentlemen over the Professionals; during his cricket career he obtained the wickets of most of the world's leading batsmen, and in addition to representing his country in Test matches at home had been on tour with the MCC England elevens in Australia, South Africa and the West Indies.

'On the trip to Australia in 1936 and 1937 he jointly, with another bowler, topped the list for the number of wickets taken and was beaten by only one other bowler for the cheapness of cost.

'Some of us will not easily forget how in 1938 at Lord's he would have achieved a Test match hat-trick if second slip had accepted a fairly easy chance to give the bowler the third Australian wicket.

'One could have wished that with the war finished he might have been

able to resume his development in this sport and have continued to delight thousands by his prowess.

'But besides recognising his pre-eminence in this sport some of us knew the other aspects of his life. One can remember him as a small dark-haired boy of ten and a half years in the first section of pupils to attend our school, eager to create a good impression both in work and at play; or again as a tall loose-limbed Fourth former still concentrating on his studies and then again, with a gleam in his eye as he turned out for the first X1 cricket practice. In 1928 as captain of cricket he was equally good with bat as with ball and his team was one of the strongest we have ever had.

'After he left I played side by side with him as a member of Gidea Park 1st X1 and on one occasion had the pleasure of making a partnership of about 100 with him. In the end, curiously enough, each of us had exactly 47 runs to his credit.

'Both at that age and later he was always a loyal and courteous Old Boy, modest in the highest degree and infected with a quiet humour which made him a delightful companion.

'His prowess at sport - in addition to pre-eminence at cricket he was a good high jumper and at Cambridge obtained a second Blue for putting the weight - somewhat overshadowed his other attainments and it is not always remembered that he was a good history and geography scholar and obtained a Second Class Honours Degree at Cambridge. In addition he had an excellent literary ability. His letters, especially written on his world tours, include a wealth of imaginative description of a very high order and his cricket volume, Tours and Tests, is a book of much finer literary quality than is usually associated with sport.

'Our Old Boy has left us, but it is some consolation for us to believe he has gone to a realm in which justice reigns, and in which at least the spirit of cricket with its encouragement of fair dealing, stern doggedness and mutual trust is ever alive. There, too, he will have reward not only for his major act of sacrifice on our behalf but also for

> *His little nameless unremember'd acts*
> *Of kindness and of love.*

His brother Norman and his wife, and friend Geoff Chapman, were at the funeral in the RAF part of the military cemetery at Brookwood. It was a bright sunny day with robins flitting and dark conifers, Geoff remembers, and *'it seemed to have nothing to do with the flag draped coffin and the smart bearer party though I sensed his presence in some mysterious way. I felt or had a tear with the Farnes family and Norman said to me in a bitter way 'I hope you have better luck.'*

'Perhaps I did, perhaps I didn't. These things were 50 years ago. If Ken had had better luck he would have lived to play for England again but for his death helping to end and win the war. It was the result of a tragic blunder as were so many lives.

'They shall not grow old as we that are left grow old. Age shall not weary them nor the years condemn.' Five lines we all know by heart, a comfort of a sort to we survivors but would they necessarily be so for the fallen? Ken deliberately chose to join the RAF on an active service basis, saying that he had no wish to be a penguin. He obviously knew the fearful risk involved. I made no such choice but left the decision to fate, content to know that I was making a contribution, not disappointed that I was not eventually sent to join the fray and sent overseas as so many were. I was thus enabled to complete a useful service as a school master and after 25 years I was engaged in historical research, writing three books.'

Who can know who was right.

APPENDIX FOUR

First Class Career Bowling Statistics

Year by Year Analyses:

1930

Essex v Gloucesterahire, Chelmsford	11-0-60-0 and 4-0-16-0
Essex v Kent, Southend	17-4-36-5 and 29-4-82-1
Essex v Glamorgan, Swansea	3-0-6-0
Essex v Derbyshire, Derby	18-1-39-2 and 3-0-10-0
Essex v Lancashire, Blackpool	29-10-51-4 and 12.4-1-36-1
Essex v Warwickshire Leyton	13-3-35-2 and 20.1-6-50-4

TOTAL: 159.5ovs 29mdns 421runs 19 wkts 22.15ave.

1931

Cambridge v Yorkshire, Fenner's	24-2-88-1
Cambridge v Middlesex, Fenner's	13-2-27-0
Cambridge v Warwickshire, Fenner's	19-4-36-1 and 14-5-23-2
Cambridge v Nottinghamshire, Fenner's	16-6-25-1 and 25-7-60-3
Cambridge v Leicestershire, Leicester	22.5-6-62-2 and 18-4-26-1
Cambridge v Free Foresters, Fenner's	24-7-52-4 and 9-2-14-0
Cambridge v Sussex, Brighton	23.1-7-51-5 and 17-4-33-1
Cambridge v MCC, Lord's	19-8-33-1 and 13-2-29-3
Cambridge v HDG Leveson-Gower XI, Eastbourne	15-8-32-2 and 18.1-6-36-3
Cambridge v Oxford University, Lord's	28-5-79-1 and 8-2-18-0
Essex v Sussex, Brighton	30-1-124-3
Essex v Yorkshire, Leeds	18-7-24-1 and 9-2-21-0
Essex v Lancashire, Clacton	17-1-55-0 and 20-3-57-6
Essex v Somerset, Leyton	19.5-7-45-2
Essex v Northamptonshire, Northampton	2-0-7-0 and 11-3-19-0
Essex v Worcestershire, Worcester	33-2-107-2 and 6-0-12-1
Essex v Middlesex, Leyton	10-4-23-1 and 6-1-22-0
Essex v Glamorgan, Cowbridge	3-0-34-1 and 2-0-9-0
Essex v Nottinghamshire, Southend	8-1-19-2 and 10-1-19-1

TOTAL: 525ovs 121mdns 1291runs 51wkts 25.31ave.

1932

Cambridge v Essex, Fenner's	19-6-26-2 and 24-6-62-3
Cambridge v Middlesex, Fenner's	19-7-22-5 and 24-7-41-3
Cambridge v Nottinghamshire, Fenner's	27-3-73-2
Cambridge v All India, Fenner's	20.1-5-40-3 and 12-6-19-1
Cambridge v Free Foresters, Fenner's	25-3-53-1 and 29-8-71-6
Cambridge v Sussex, Hove	29-5-80-3 and 24-5-64-2
Cambridge v HDG Leveson Gower X1, Eastbourne	13-5-22-1 and 17.5-5-43-1
Cambridge v MCC, Lord's	22-2-90-1 and 18-6-42-2
Cambridge v Oxford University, Lord's	32-2-98-5
Test Trial, Cardiff	18-5-37-0
Essex v Hampshire, Southampton	15.5-7-34-2 and 22-4-52-5
Essex v Sussex, Clacton	23.1-6-56-3
Essex v Worcestershire, Worcester	25-4-50-0 and 12-4-25-1
Essex v Notts, Leyton	27-7-37-1 and 16-3-46-1
Essex v Somerset, Weston Super Mare	25-3-90-2 and 5-1-17-0
Essex v Yorkshire, Scarborough	24-3-135-2
Essex v Gloucestershire, Cheltenham	15.1-4-46-2
Essex v Hampshire, Southend	18.1-2-52-3 and 14-3-41-1
Essex v Gloucestershire, Southend	15-6-46-5 and 7-3-17-0
Essex v Sussex, Eastbourne	21-5-53-1
Essex v Kent, Leyton	18.2-3-68-2

TOTAL: 671.4ovs 155mdns 1750runs 72wkts 24.30ave.

1933

Cambridge v Sussex, Fenner's	27-10-38-4
Cambridge v Yorkshire, Fenner's	12-0-32-0 and 8-2-18-1
Cambridge v West Indies, Fenner's	18-2-51-2
Cambridge v Middlesex, Fenner's	26-5-86-3 and 18-5-40-2
Cambridge v Nottinghamshire, Fenner's	36-14-71-3 and 9-2-18-1
Cambridge v Free Foresters, Fenner's	26-3-85-3 and 8-1-20-1
Cambridge v Sussex, Hove	20-3-56-5 and 20-6-25-1
Cambridge v Essex, Chelmsford	16-5-34-5 and 12.3-1-41-3
Cambridge v MCC, Lord's	9-1-24-0
Cambridge v Leveson Gower X1, Eastbourne	3-1-3-0
Cambridge v Oxford, Lord's	24.4-9-44-3 and 16-7-27-4
Gentlemen v Players, Lord's	25-6-53-2
Essex v Glamorgan, Clacton	17.4-4-46-3 and 14-5-43-6
Essex v Gloucestershire, Clacton	10-4-10-2 and 15.4-2-68-3
Essex v Middlesex, Clacton	16-1-40-1 and 15-4-19-3

Essex v Surrey, Southend	22-1-93-4 and 10-2-21-7
Essex v Northamptonshire, Southend	23.3-6-66-1 and 16-3-66-3
Essex v Lancashire, Liverpool	27-2-72-6 and 7-1-19-0
Essex v Somerset, Taunton	24.2-6-72-7 and 13-5-26-6
Essex v Worcestershire, Worcester	24-5-74-5 and 20-0-94-1
Essex v Hampshire, Bournemouth	35-7-114-4 and 11-1-42-3
Essex v Sussex, Leyton	23-8-60-2 and 8-1-32-0
HDG Leveson Gower v MCC Australia XI, Scarborough	23-3-119-1 and 11-0-83-0
HDG Leveson-Gower XI v West Indies, Scarborough	10-4-23-1 and 5-1-10-1

TOTAL: 735.2ovs 162mdns 2078runs 113wkts 18.38ave.

1934

Essex v Australia, Chelmsford	24-5-111-3
Essex v Nottinghamshire, Nottingham	38-9-119-1
Test Trial, Lord's	39-5-132-1
England v Australia, Trent Bridge 1st Test	40.2-10-102-5 and 25-3-77-5
England v Australia, Lord's 2nd Test	12-3-43-0 and 4-2-6-0
Essex v Worcestershire, Worcester	15-3-40-1 and 4-2-6-1
Essex v Somerset, Weston super Mare	11-4-35-4 and 15-2-37-3
Essex v Northamptonshire, Northampton	29-10-23-6 and 5-1-7-2
Essex v Lancashire, Southend	19.3-8-55-5 and 25-8-53-1
Essex v Yorkshire, Southend	25.1-2-72-4 and 23-7-59-7
Essex v Gloucestershire, Gloucester	23-4-88-2 and 4-1-13-0
Gentlemen v Players, Scarborough	36-8-99-3 and 12-5-24-3
HDG Leveson-Gower XI v Australia	31.3-4-132-5

TOTAL: 451.3ovs 101mdns 1333runs 62wkts 21.50ave.

Tour of West Indies 1934/35

MCC v Barbados	22-3-81-1 and 15-1-45-1
England v West Indies, Barbados 1st Test	15-4-40-4 and 9-2-22-1
MCC v Trinidad	16-2-47-2 and 6-0-43-2
MCC v British Guiana, Georgetown	8-1-14-2 and 24-5-76-0
MCC v Jamaica, Kingston	26-7-68-4 and 8-2-21-0
MCC v West Indies, Kingston 4th Test	24-4-72-1

TOTAL:184ovs 34mdns 550runs 18wkts 30.55ave.

1936

Essex v Surrey, Brentwood	18-1-92-4 and 4-0-20-0
Essex v Somerset, Colchester	12-3-20-1 and 3.2-0-7-1
Essex v Middlesex, Colchester	29.2-7-84-7 and 16-6-37-2
Gentlemen v Players, Lord's	16-3-43-0 and 9-3-22-3
Essex v Derbyshsire, Chelmsford	13-6-20-5 and 27-5-56-1
Essex v Worcestershire, Chelmsford	17-5-38-4 and 33-6-78-2
Essex v Kent, Southend	14-0-43-2 and 12.5-0-69-6
Essex v Hampshire, Southend	24-3-70-1 and 11-1-36-0
Essex v Somerset, Taunton	13-2-38-3 and 22-4-60-2
Essex v Nottinghamshire, Clacton	29.4-5-73-6 and 22-3-61-3
Essex v Gloucestershire, Clacton	13.1-1-37-3 and 23-2-88-3
Essex v Worcestershire, Worcester	28-5-69-1 and 18-5-49-3
HDG Leveson Gower XI v MCC Australia XI	12-2-51-2 and 14-3-35-1

TOTAL: 447.2ovs 78mdns 1296runs 67wkts 19.34ave.

Tour to Australia and New Zealand 1936/37

MCC v Western Australia, Perth	10-0-35-3 and 8-1-26-2
MCC v Victoria, Melbourne	22-2-56-3
MCC v Australian XI, Sydney	25-4-112-2
MCC v Queensland, Brisbane	19-4-45-2 and 9-1-45-3
MCC v Queensland Country XI, Ipswich	11-3-45-1 and 6-2-18-0
MCC v Tasmania, Launceston	5-0-27-2 and 10-1-30-1
MCC v Tasmania Combined XI	12-3-31-4
MCC v South Australia, Adelaide	10-1-28-1
England v Australia, Adelaide 4th Test	20.6-1-71-3 and 24-2-89-2
MCC v Victoria Country XI, Geelong	9-1-24-0
MCC v NSW Southern District, Canberra	9-0-30-2 and 6-0-27-1
MCC v NSW, Sydney	13-1-65-3 and 10-0-59-4
England v Australia, Melbourne 5th Test	28.5-5-96-6
MCC v Victoria Country XII, Benalia	3-1-14-0
MCC v Canterbury and Otago, Christchurch	13-2-37-1
MCC v Auckland, Auckland	11-1-33-1 and 7-1-13-1

TOTAL: 256ovs 30mdns 928runs 44wkts 21.09ave.

1937

North v South, Lord's	21-6-35-2 and 17-8-43-5
MCC XI v Rest of England, Lord's	20-3-54-2 and 16-4-30-1
Gentlemen v Players, Lord's	22-2-65-5 and 7-0-28-1
Essex v Yorkshire, Huddersfield	37-11-92-2 and 8-2-33-0
Essex v Derbyshire, Ilkeston	14-1-41-7 and 26-2-104-2
Essex v Middlesex, Chelmsford	19-3-78-1 and 11-0-53-0
Essex v Hampshire, Southend	22-8-45-5 and 20-1-45-1
Essex v Nottinghamshire, Southend	25-4-65-2 and 3-0-10-0
Essex v Nottinghamshire, Nottingham	37.1-8-90-5
Essex v Lancashire, Clacton	20-5-28-2 and 7-1-23-0
Essex v Worcestershire, Clacton	9.5-1-38-3 and 22.1-6-41-5
HDG Leveson Gower XI v MCC Australian XI	26-2-107-3 and 10-1-59-1

TOTAL: 420.1ovs 80mdns 1207runs 55wkts 21.94ave.

1938

Essex v Glamorgan, Swansea	19-4-28-4
Test Trial, Lord's	23.2-7-51-3 and 9-2-19-2
MCC v Australia, Lord's	32-3-88-1
England v Australia, Southend	21-7-43-4 and 13-5-24-1
England v Australia, Trent Bridge 1st Test	37-11-106-4 and 23-1-78-0
England v Australia, Lord's 2nd Test	43-6-135-3 and 13-3-51-0
Gentlemen v Players, Lord's	21.3-6-43-8 and 24-6-60-3
England v Australia, Leeds 4th Test	26-2-77-4 and 11.3-4-17-1
Essex v Worcestershire, Worcester	16.1-2-43-6 and 24.1-5-76-8
Essex v Nottinghamshire, Chelmsford	20-3-58-3 and 14-4-23-2
Essex v Northamptonshire, Westcliff	25.2-7-69-2 and 22-5-56-4
Essex v Surrey, Westcliff	14.5-3-58-4 and 31-5-92-2
Essex v Middlesex, Lord's	23-2-79-2 and 3-0-8-0
England v Australia, The Oval 5th Test	13-2-54-1 and 12.1-1-63-4
Essex v Glamorgan, Clacton	22.5-4-75-7 and 11.5-0-38-8
Essex v Gloucestershire, Gloucester	12-1-44-1 and 27-2-90-3
MCC v Yorkshire, Scarborough	19.1-5-38-4 and 4-2-7-0
HDG Leveson-Gower XI v Australia, Scarborough 23-3-75-3 and 8-4-10-1	
Gentlemen v Players, Scarborough	32.2-7-105-3 and 5-0-38-1

TOTAL: 701.2ovs 137mdns 2016runs 107wkts 18.84ave.

Tour to South Africa 1938/39 (8-ball overs)

MCC v Western Province Country XI	7-1-30-1 and 5-0-21-1
MCC v Western Province, Cape Town	12-3-32-3 and 12.4-2-38-7
MCC v Griqualand West, Kimberley	5-1-34-0 and 9-1-29-0
MCC v Natal, Durban	26-5-59-0
MCC v Transvaal, Johannesburg	23-2-93-4 and 4-0-17-0
England v South Africa, Johannesburg 1st Test	23-1-87-1 and 7-3-17-0
England v South Africa, Cape Town 2nd Test	13-3-37-0 and 8-1-23-1
MCC v Eastern Province, Port Elizabeth	15-0-58-5 and 5-1-14-2
England v South Africa, Durban 3rd Test	13-1-29-4 and 28.2-8-80-3
MCC v Combined Transvaal XI, Johannesburg	21-0-86-2 and 4-0-21-0
MCC v Rhodesia, Bulawayo	9-0-32-1
MCC v Rhodesia. Salisbury	11-0-18-2 and 11-4-25-1
England v South Africa, Johannesburg 4th Test	26-7-64-1
MCC v Natal, Pietermaritzburg	17-2-61-0 and 13-3-71-3
England v South Africa, Durban 5th Test	46-9-108-1 and 22.1-2-74-4

TOTAL: 384.7ovs 59mdns 1207runs 44 wkts 27.43ave.

1939

Gentlemen v Players, Lord's	19.5-2-78-5 and 11-2-35-0
Essex v Kent, Clacton	7-0-24-1
Essex v Lancashire, Manchester	7-2-20-1
Essex v Derbyshire, Southend	6-0-24-0 and 10-2-52-5
Essex v Middlesex	16.5-2-62-3 and 15-3-53-3
Essex v Yorkshire, Sheffield	14-1-55-3 and 17-1-61-1
Essex v Nottinghamshire, Clacton	19-0-90-3 and 10.3-2-10-5
Essex v Northamptonshire, Clacton	17-2-79-2 and 12-0-47-6

TOTAL: 179.6ovs 18mdns 726runs 38wkts 19.10ave.

CAREER BESTS:

10 wickets in a match (seven times):

11-114 Essex v Surrey, Southend 1933
13-97   Essex v Somerset, Taunton 1933
10-179 England v Australia, Trent Bridge 1934
11-131 Essex v Yorkshire, Southend 1934
11-103 Gentlemen v Players, Lord's 1938
14-119 Essex v Worcestershire, Worcester 1938
15-113 Essex v Glamorgan, Clacton 1938

5 wickets in an innings (41 times):

5-36 Essex v Kent, Southend 1930
5-51 Cambridge v Sussex, Brighton 1931
6-57 Essex v Lancashire, Clacton 1931
5-22 Cambridge v Middlesex, Fenner's 1932
6-61 Cambridge v Free Foresters 1932
5-52 Essex v Hampshire, Southampton 1932
5-46 Essex v Gloucestershire, Southend 1932
5-56 Cambridge v Sussex, Hove 1933
5-34 Cambridge v Essex, Chelmsford 1933
7-21 Essex v Surrey, Southend 1933
6-72 Essex v Lancashire, Liverpool 1933
7-72 Essex v Somerset, Taunton 1933
6-26 Essex v Somerset, Taunton 1933
5-74 Essex v Worcester, Worcester 1933
5-102 England v Australia, Trent Bridge 1934
5-77 England v Australia, Trent Bridge 1934
6-23 Essex v Northamptonshire, Northampton 1934
5-55 Essex v Lancashire, Southend 1934
7-59 Essex v Yorkshire, Southend 1934
5-132 HDG Leveson-Gower XI v Australia, Scarborough 1934
7-84 Essex v Middlesex, Colchester 1936

5-20 Essex v Derbyshire, Chelmsford 1936
6-69 Essex v Kent, Southend 1936
6-73 Essex v Nottinghamshire, Clacton 1936
6-96 England v Australia, Melbourne 1937
5-43 North v South, Lord's 1937
5-65 Gentlemen v Players, Lord's 1937
7-41 Essex v Derbyshire, Ilkeston 1937
5-45 Essex v Hampshire, Southend 1937
5-90 Essex v Nottinghamshire, Nottingham 1937
5-41 Essex v Worcestershire, Clacton 1937
8-43 Gentlemen v Players, Lord's 1938
6-43 Essex v Worcestershire, Worcester 1938
8-76 Essex v Worcestershire, Worcester 1938
7-75 Essex v Glamorgan, Clacton 1938
8-38 Essex v Glamorgan, Clacton 1938
5-58 MCC v Eastern Province, Port Elizabeth 1939
5-78 Gentlemen v Players, Lord's 1939
5-52 Essex v Derbyshire, Southend 1939
5-30 Essex v Nottinghamshire, Clacton 1939
6-47 Essex v Northamptonshire, Clacton 1939

For Essex

Year	Ovs	Mdns	Runs	Wkts	Ave
1930	159.5	29	421	19	22.15
1931	203.5	34	567	20	28.35
1932	298.4	69	858	31	27.67
1933	352.1	85	1077	67	16.07
1934	251.4	61	718	40	17.09
1936	396.2	67	1145	60	19.08
1937	281.1	54	786	35	22.45
1938	286.1	48	834	56	14.89
1939	149	14	613	33	18.57
TOTAL	2289.5	463	7,017	362	19.11

For Cambridge

1931	321.1	87	724	31	23.35
1932	335	81	855	41	20.85
1933	309.1	77	713	41	17.39
TOTAL	**965.2**	**245**	**2,292**	**113**	**20.28**

For England

1934	81.2	18	228	10	22.80
1934/5	48	10	134	6	22.33
1936/7	73.3	8	256	11	23.27
1938	179.4	32	581	17	34.17
1938/9	186.3	35	519	16	32.43
TOTAL	**569**	**103**	**1,718**	**60**	**28.63**

Other

1932	18	5	37	0	–
1933	73	14	288	5	57.60
1934	118.3	17	387	12	32.25
1934/35	136	24	416	12	34.30
1936	51	11	151	6	25.17
1936/37	182.3	22	652	33	19.76
1937	139	26	421	20	21.05
1938	202.2	45	534	29	18. 45
1938/9	198.4	24	688	28	24.57
1939	30.5	4	113	5	22.60
TOTAL	**1,256.1**	**202**	**4,013**	**150**	**23.06**

CAREER TOTAL	**5,079.1**	**1,013**	**15,040**	**685**	**21.97**

INDEX OF PEOPLE

189

Ken Farnes

Unwin, George	101	Watt, A.E.	109
		Wellard, A.W.	20
Valentine, B.H.	19,54,109,134,135,136,	Wellings, E.M.	127
	140,145,154	Whitaker, Rev P.H.K.	
Van de Bijl, P.G.	57,135,137,138,139		8,10
Vere-Hodge, Nicholas		White, J.C.	163
	16,95,96-97,109,110-111	Wigmore, Jack	76
Verity, H.	5,19-20,52,55,59,75,80,	Wilcox, D.R.	13,49,50,56,57,58,59,64,
	83,85,112,113,119,122,		65,66-67,72,83,85,98,
	128,132,134,135-136,		109,111,112,127,130
	138,139,142,148,152,	Wilkinson, L.L.	133,134,138,146147,164
	154,161,163,169	Wodehouse, P.G.	13
Vigar, Frank	101	Wood, A.	7
Viljoen, R.G.	135,137	Woodfull, W.M.	38,79-80,81,168
Voce, W.	16,17,20,55,57,58,112,	Woolley, F.E.	3,40-41,108,109,110,
	115-116,119-120,121,		111,167-168
	122,123,163,168	Worthington, T.S.	42,112,117,120,125,150
		Wright, D.V.P.	16,20,40,129,133,134,
Wade, T.H.	15,97,109,112,116-117		146,147,149,161,164
Wade, W.W.	135,137	Wyatt, R.E.S.	20,79,81,85,86,87,88,89,
Walker, D.F.	62		90-91,93,112,116,117,
Walters, C.F.	79,82		124,149,168
Ward, F.A.	120,128	Wykes, Nigel	15,42,98-99
Warner, Sir P.F.	64-66,94-95,153-154		
Washbrook, C.	12,161	Yardley, N.W.D.	127,145,150

191